D0343377

CAN WE
SAVE THE
CATHOLIC
CHURCH?

¡HƆЯUHƆ
ƆITOHTAƆ
ƎHT ƎVAƧ
NAƆ ƎW

HANS KÜNG

CAN WE SAVE THE CATHOLIC CHURCH?

¡ ?

¡HƆЯUHƆ
ƆITOHTAƆ
ƎHT ƎVAƧ
ИAƆ ƎW
ƓИÜⱯ ƧИAH

WILLIAM COLLINS

William Collins
An imprint of HarperCollins*Publishers*
77–85 Fulham Palace Road
Hammersmith, London W6 8JB

WilliamCollinsBooks.com

First published in Great Britain by William Collins 2013

Copyright © Hans Küng 2013

Scripture quotations are taken from the New Revised Standard Version
Bible, copyright © 1989 by the Division of Christian Education of
the National Council of the Churches of Christ in the USA, and are
used by permission. All rights reserved.

Hans Küng asserts the moral right to
be identified as the author of this work

A catalogue record for this book is
available from the British Library

ISBN 978-0-00-752202-6

Printed and bound in Great Britain by
Clays Ltd, St Ives plc

All rights reserved. No part of this publication may be
reproduced, stored in a retrieval system, or transmitted,
in any form or by any means, electronic, mechanical,
photocopying, recording or otherwise, without the prior
permission of the publishers.

MIX
Paper from
responsible sources
FSC C007454

FSC™ is a non-profit international organisation established to promote
the responsible management of the world's forests. Products carrying the
FSC label are independently certified to assure consumers that they come
from forests that are managed to meet the social, economic and
ecological needs of present and future generations,
and other controlled sources.

Find out more about HarperCollins and the environment at
www.harpercollins.co.uk/green

CONTENTS

ABOUT THE AUTHOR

Hans Küng was born into a Catholic family and grew up in the small Catholic Swiss town of Sursee. He attended secondary school in the Catholic city of Lucerne.

He spent a full seven years living in Rome at the elite Collegium Germanicum et Hungaricum, where he completed his philosophical and theological studies at the Pontifical University Gregoriana. After being ordained a priest, he celebrated his first Eucharist in St Peter's Basilica and preached his first sermon to the Swiss Papal Guard.

He completed his doctorate on the Protestant theologian Karl Barth at the Institut Catholique in Paris, where he was awarded a PhD in theology. After two years' pastoral ministry in Lucerne, in 1960 he became professor for Catholic theology at Tübingen University at the age of 32.

He attended the Second Vatican Council from 1962 to 1965 as a theological advisor appointed by John XXIII, and taught theology for two decades at the Catholic theological faculty in Tübingen, where he also founded and headed the Institute for Ecumenical Research of the University of Tübingen.

In 1979 he gained first-hand experience of the Inquisition under the new pope, John Paul II, quite a different pope from his namesake. At the order of the Congregation for the Doctrine of the Faith, he was stripped of his ecclesiastical licence to teach as a Catholic theologian; but thanks to the fairness of German law and the good will of the federal state of Baden-Württemberg and the University of Tübingen, he retained his chair of theology and his institute, which was officially separated from the Catholic theological faculty, although friendly relations continued to prevail.

For three more decades his devotion to his Church has remained unshaken, although this loyalty has never been uncritical. The recipient of numerous awards and prizes, he has remained to this day a professor of ecumenical theology, although now officially retired, and he has remained a Catholic priest 'in good standing', authorized to preach and to perform all priestly offices.

He has always supported the papacy as a pastoral Petrine office within the Catholic Church, but, taking the Gospel as his yardstick, he has also assiduously called for radical reform of the papacy and especially of the Roman System which has dominated the Catholic Church for over a millennium.

Despite all his often painful and bitter experiences with this merciless Roman System, his spiritual home remains the Catholic community of faith. He has written this book to aid its recovery and to help it survive within the ecumenical Christian community.

Impressed by the decision of Pope Francis in May 2013 to appoint a committee of eight cardinals – most of them from outside the Roman Curia – to make proposals for Vatican reform, Küng resolved to send copies of this book to

all of the cardinals on the committee, as the required transla-
tions become available. On 13 May 2013, Küng wrote to the
pope personally, expressing his joy over the pope's bold decision and enclosing a copy of the Spanish edition of this book.
Pope Francis responded in a personal, handwritten note thank-
ing Küng for sending him the book and indicating his interest
in reading it. He closed the letter with the unpretentious
friendly greeting 'Fraternamente, Francisco'.

A WORD OF THANKS

This book has already been published in German, French, Italian, Spanish, Portuguese and Dutch. To my great joy the English edition is now available – and it is being published at just the right moment! During recent months it has become clear that Pope Francis is striving for serious reform within the Catholic Church, as I request in the preface of this book. The pope has already made some important steps: first of all he appointed a group of eight cardinals from all continents with the mandate to initiate the reform of the Roman Curia.

Because of this development, I felt encouraged to send this book in Spanish to Pope Francis, and I was privileged to receive a personal, fraternal handwritten letter from him, in which he promises to read this book. I also sent the book, in their respective languages, to the eight cardinals.

I am deeply grateful to Collins for publishing this English edition; many of my most important books since the early 1970s have been published by Collins. My thanks go especially to Andrew Lyon, Editorial Director, Religious Publishing, who cared for this publication with tremendous competency and energy. The *Sprachendienst* Dr Herrlinger, a translation company in Tübingen, provided the basic translation. Dr Thomas Riplinger, a theologian and native English speaker, reworked and amended the text with extraordinary diligence in close collaboration with Andrew Lyon.

My thanks also go to Ben North for his creativity in inventing the ingenious dual title for the book, and the design team at Collins for the eye-catching cover. I am grateful to everybody for their excellent cooperation and I hope very much that this book will assist the English-speaking world in supporting Pope Francis's reforms by offering a precise historic and systematic analysis and viable, practical proposals for reform.

PREFACE FOR THE ENGLISH EDITION

The Arab Spring has shaken a whole series of autocratic regimes. With the resignation of Pope Benedict XVI and the election of Pope Francis, might something like this be possible in the Catholic Church as well – a 'Vatican Spring'?

Of course, the system of the Roman Catholic Church is quite different from those prevailing in Tunisia and Egypt, to say nothing of the absolute monarchies like Saudi Arabia. In all these countries, the reforms that have taken place until now are often no more than minor concessions, and even these are often threatened by those who oppose any progressive reforms in the name of tradition. In Saudi Arabia, most of the traditions, in fact, are only two centuries old; the Catholic Church, by contrast, claims to rest on traditions that go back twenty centuries to Jesus Christ himself.

Is this claim true? In reality, throughout its first millennium, the Church got along quite well without the monarchist–absolutist papacy that we now take for granted. It was only in the eleventh century that a 'revolution from above', started by Pope Gregory VII and known as the 'Gregorian Reform', gave us the three outstanding features that mark the Roman System to this day:

- a centralist–absolutist papacy;

- clericalist juridicism; and,

- obligatory celibacy for the clergy.

Efforts to reform this system by the reforming councils in the fifteenth century, by the Protestant and Catholic reformers of the sixteenth century, by the supporters of the Enlightenment and the French Revolution in the seventeenth and eighteenth centuries and, most recently, by the champions of a progressive-liberal theology in the nineteenth and twentieth centuries, managed to achieve only partial success. Even the Second Vatican Council, from 1962 to 1965, while addressing many concerns of the reformers and modern critics, was effectively thwarted by the power of the papal Curia and managed to implement only a few of the demanded changes. To this day the Curia – in its current form a creature of the eleventh century – is the chief obstacle to any thorough-going reform of the Catholic Church, to any honest ecumenical reconciliation with the other Christian Churches and the world religions, and to any critical, constructive coming-to-terms with the modern world. To make things worse, supported by the Curia, under the previous two popes, there has been a fatal return to old absolutist attitudes and practices.

Had Jorge Mario Bergoglio asked himself why, until now, no pope had ever dared to take the name Francis? This Argentine Jesuit with Italian roots was, in any case, well aware that in choosing this name he was calling up the memory of Francis of Assisi, that famous social dropout of the thirteenth century. As a young man, Francis, the son of a wealthy silk merchant of Assisi, had led a high-spirited, worldly life like other well-situated young men of the city; then suddenly, at the age of 24, a series of experiences led him to renounce family, wealth and career. In a dramatic gesture before the judgement seat of the Bishop of Assisi, he stripped off his sumptuous clothing and deposited it at his father's feet.

It was astonishing to see how Pope Francis, from the moment of his election, clearly chose a new style quite different from that of his predecessor: no bejewelled golden mitre, no ermine-trimmed crimson shoulder-cape, no tailor-made red shoes and ermine-trimmed red cap, no pompous papal throne decorated with the triple crown, the emblem of papal political might.

Equally astonishing is the way the new pope consciously refrains from melodramatic gestures and high-blown rhetoric and speaks the language of ordinary people, just as a layperson would do, were the laity not forbidden to preach by Rome.

Lastly, it is astonishing how the new pope emphasizes his human side: he asked people to pray for him before he blessed them; like every other cardinal, he paid his own hotel bill after his election; he showed his solidarity with the cardinals by taking the same bus back to their residence and then cordially taking leave of them. On Maundy Thursday he went to a local prison to wash the feet of young convicts, including a woman – and a Muslim at that. Clearly, he is showing himself to be a man with his feet on the ground.

All of this would have pleased Francis of Assisi, and it is exactly the opposite of everything that his papal contemporary – Innocent III (1198–1216), the mightiest pope of the Middle Ages – stood for. In reality, Francis of Assisi represents the alternative to the Roman System that has dominated the Catholic Church since the beginning of the end of the first millennium. What might have happened had Innocent III and his entourage listened to Francis and rediscovered the demands of the Gospel? Without question, one need not take them as literally as Francis did; it is the spirit behind them that counts. The teachings of the Gospel represent a mighty challenge to the Roman System – that centralistic, juridicized, politicized and clericalized power structure that has dominated Christ's Church in the West since the eleventh century.

What, then, should the new pope do? The big question for him is: where does he stand on serious church reform? Will he carry out the long-overdue reforms that have become log-jammed in the past decades? Or will he allow things to go on in the way they have done under his predecessors? In either case, the outcome is clear:

- *If he embarks on a course of reform*, he will find broad support, even beyond the boundaries of the Roman Catholic Church. Many Orthodox and Protestant Christians, Jews and believers of other faiths – to say nothing of many non-believers – have long awaited these reforms, which are absolutely imperative if the Roman Catholic Church is to realize its potential to give convincing witness to the Gospel and to voice the urgent demands for peace and justice in today's world. The Church can only give such witness when it ceases to be turned in on itself, fixed on defending its institutional structures and its traditional manner of speaking.

- *If he continues the present course of retrenchment*, the call to rise up and revolt (exemplified in Stéphane Hessel's *Time for Outrage: Indignez-vous!*, [2011]) will grow ever louder in the Catholic Church and increasingly incite people to take things into their own hands, initiating reforms from below without hierarchical approval and often in the face of all attempts to thwart them. In the worst case, the Catholic Church will experience a new Ice Age instead of a new spring, and it will run the risk of shrinking down to a mere sect, still counting many members but otherwise socially and religiously irrelevant.

Nevertheless, I have well-founded hopes that the concerns expressed in this book will be taken seriously by the new pope. To use the medical analogy that serves as the leitmotif of this book, the Church's only alternative to what would amount to assisted suicide is radical cure. That means more than a new style, a new language, a new collegial tone; it means carrying out the long-overdue, radical structural reforms and the urgently needed revision of the obsolete and unfounded theology behind the many problematical dogmatic and ethical positions that his predecessors have attempted to impose upon the Church. If Pope Francis commits himself to such a radical reform, he will not only find broad support within the Church, but he will also win back many of those who, publicly or privately, have long since abandoned the Church. Such a renewed Roman Catholic Church could once again become the witness to the Gospel of Christ that it was meant to be.

Hans Küng
Tübingen, July 2013

Note on the Present English Edition

This book originally appeared in 2011 under the title *Ist die Kirche noch zu retten?* For this revised version, the first in the English language, material of interest only to the German audience has been omitted and the text has also been updated to reflect events which have occurred since 2011, especially in connection with the resignation of Pope Benedict XVI and appointment of Pope Francis earlier this year.

This English translation was generously supported by a grant from the Herbert Haag Foundation for Freedom in the Church, Lucerne, Switzerland.

INTRODUCTION: A DIAGNOSIS

Let me begin by saying that I would have preferred not to have had to write this book. But with the appointment of Pope Francis we have an unprecedented opportunity, not seen since the days of John XXIII, to fulfil the aims and promises of his Second Vatican Council, and truly bring the Church into a meaningful dialogue with the modern world.

I would have preferred not to write this book because, despite this time of great hope and promise, it will not make pleasant or comfortable reading for many Catholics. And it is not at all pleasant for me, either, to address such a critical publication to the people who make up the Church, because, despite my often painful and bitter experiences with the merciless Roman System which up to now has governed the Church, the Catholic community of faith remains my spiritual home. But it is my hope that the recommendations in this book will aid the Church's recovery from what I see, and what I will go on to describe, as a debilitating and potentially terminal illness from which the Church is presently suffering.

For decades now, with mixed success at best and with virtually no impact at all on the Church's hierarchy, I have repeatedly called attention to the serious, growing crisis within the Catholic Church, pointing out that it is primarily a crisis of the Church's leadership and not of the faithful, as many in the hierarchy would have us believe. In recent years, however, the revelations of countless cases of sexual abuse by Catholic clergymen – cases that have been occurring for decades and which have been consistently hushed up both by Rome and by bishops around the world – has made this systemic crisis clearly visible to the world at large, and calls for a well-thought-out theological response. With Pope Francis's appointment of a panel of cardinals to advise him on a reform of the Roman Curia (the machinery of power surrounding the pope in the Vatican), such a theological response is now more urgent than ever to support the voices of many people within the Church who have long been crying out for change.

A reform of the Curia presents us, at this fiftieth anniversary of the Second Vatican Council, with an opportunity to effect a paradigm shift in the Catholic Church. Under Popes Karol Wojtyla and Joseph Ratzinger, over the last three decades, a course of restoration to pre-Council times, rather than reform, was pursued relentlessly and this continues to exert an increasingly dramatic and deadly influence not just within the Catholic Church but also within the whole Christian ecumenical movement. Benedict XVI's pontificate was, for me, a pontificate of missed opportunities. None of his triumphal appearances and journeys (whether staged as 'pilgrimages' or 'state visits'), none of his brilliant encyclicals, nor his communication offensives, could hide the existence of the long-standing crisis in which the Church now finds itself. In the Federal Republic of Germany alone, in the last five years, hundreds of thousands of people have left the Church, and the population generally is becoming increasingly estranged from church institutions of any kind.

I repeat: I would have preferred not to write this book. In fact, I would not have written it, if:

- my hope that Pope Benedict would lead our Church forward in the spirit of the Second Vatican Council had not been so thoroughly destroyed. Back in 2005, in our four-hour, private and friendly conversation in Castel Gandolfo, my former Tübingen colleague seemed to hold out such a promise. Instead, however, Benedict obstinately adhered to the path of restoration pursued by his predecessor, distancing himself from the Council's spirit in important points and from the many faithful Catholics whom the Council inspired. Furthermore, Ratzinger signally failed in his handling of the sexual abuses committed by Catholic clergymen all over the world.

- the bishops had exercised their collective responsibility for the Church as a whole – a responsibility explicitly acknowledged and encouraged by the Vatican Council – and had themselves vigorously spoken out and taken effective action against the scandals in the Church. Instead, however, under Wojtyla's and Ratzinger's rule, most of them became subservient once again to the Vatican, only too eager to toe the line without attempting to voice opinions of their own or to act independently. At best, they gave only hesitant and unconvincing answers to questions raised by the modern challenges facing the Church.

- the theologians had, as in former times, strongly and publicly stood together to oppose Rome's new repressive measures and its attempts to control the selection of the next generation of teachers in university faculties and seminaries. Instead, however, most Catholic theologians, fearing censure and marginalization, now skirt around taboo topics of dogmatic or moral theology rather than face up to them in an unbiased and critical manner. Only very few, therefore, dare to support the global and grassroots Catholic reform organizations such as We are Church, Call to Action and, in Ireland, the Association of Catholic Priests.

To make matters worse, the advocates of reform in the Roman Catholic Church receive little support from Protestant theologians and church leaders, many of whom consider the reform issues to be a purely internal affair of the Catholic Church. All too often, they are content to cultivate cosy, friendly relations with the Vatican instead of exercising the freedom of a true Christian to speak out when needed. In the latest disputes about the Catholic Church and other churches, just as in other public discussions, lively theological discussion and fruitful controversy play only a minor role; thus the theologians miss their opportunity to issue a vigorous call for much-needed reform.

From many quarters, I have been urged to take a strong and clear stand on the current and future condition of the Catholic Church. And so, rather than writing individual newspaper columns and articles, I have decided to pen this compact summary to set forth and justify my carefully considered view of the crux of this crisis: namely that the Catholic Church – this great community of faith – is seriously ill, suffering under the Roman system of rule, a system which developed during the second millennium and which, despite opposition, remains in place today.

As I will show later, this Roman system of rule is characterized by a monopoly on power and truth, by legalism and clericalism, by hostility to sexuality, by misogyny and by clerical use of pressure on the laity. This system is not exclusively responsible for (though it does bear the main responsibility for) the three great divisions, or schisms, of Christianity: first, the East–West schism in the eleventh century, dividing the Western from the Eastern branches of the Church; then, the Reformation schism in the sixteenth century, dividing the Western (i.e. Roman Catholic) Church from the Protestant churches; and, finally, in the eighteenth and nineteenth century, the separation of Roman Catholicism from the enlightened modern world.

The Cause of the Illness

To begin, let me make one thing clear: I am an ecumenical theologian concerned with the Church in all its manifestations, and I am by no means fixated exclusively on the figure of the pope. In my book *Christianity: Its Essence and History* (1995), I devoted over 1,000 pages to a description and analysis of the history of Christianity as a whole. But it cannot be denied that the papacy is the central element of the Roman Catholic paradigm, and it is the papacy and its power that is primarily and urgently in need of reform.

The papacy as it took shape in the Christian Church of the first centuries, i.e. as a ministry in succession to St Peter, was and remains to this day a meaningful institution for many Christians, not just Roman Catholics. But, from the eleventh century onwards, this institution gradually morphed into the monarchical–absolutist papacy that has dominated the history of the Roman Catholic Church ever since. It is this monarchical–absolutist papacy that has been responsible for the three great schisms mentioned above. Ever since the Middle Ages, the growing power of the papacy within the Catholic Church, notwithstanding numerous political setbacks and cultural defeats, has become the crux of the Roman Catholic Church's history. Thus, Catholicism's contemporary neuralgia is not a problem of liturgy, theology, lay piety, monastic rules or art, but rather a problem linked to the very constitution of the Roman Catholic Church. In traditional histories of the Catholic Church, however, far too little critical attention has been given to the problems generated by how the papacy has developed. For this reason, I will examine these problems with special care in the present book, not least because of their explosive ecumenical significance, for their consequences are not confined to the Roman Catholic Church alone; they also affect the other Christian denominations, the dialogue with other religions and ideologies, and the relationship of the Catholic Church to the modern world as a whole.

Fifty years ago, Joseph Ratzinger and I were the two youngest official advisors to the Second Vatican Council (1962–5). That Council tried to reform important elements of the Roman system, but, unfortunately, the stubborn resistance of the Roman Curia managed by and large to hamper these efforts and to restrict their success. In the decades since the Council, Rome has gradually been turning back the clock on the proposals for reform and renewal, and this has in turn led to a renewed outbreak of an already rampant and alarming disease in the Catholic Church. The sexual abuse scandals caused by

Catholic clergymen are only the latest symptom. The objections to these scandals have become so vehement that, in any other large organization, they would have triggered an intensive investigation into the reasons behind such a tragedy. Not so, however, for the Roman Curia or the Catholic episcopate! At first, Rome and the episcopate simply denied any share in the responsibility for the systematic cover-up of these cases. And, when that strategy failed, they have, with very few exceptions, shown little interest in uncovering the deep historical and systemic reasons for such horrific aberrations.

The regrettable refusal to look at the causes of this sickness compels me to bring out into the open the historical truth about the Christian Church, starting from its origins – in the face of all the current attempts to forget, conceal and cover them up. For people with little detailed historical education, for traditional Catholic readers, and possibly even for some bishops, these facts will undoubtedly prove frightening and disillusioning. Someone who has never been seriously confronted with historical facts of this kind will certainly be dismayed to learn how things have been done over long periods of time and how all too human so many Church institutions and constitutions – particularly the core Roman Catholic institution of the papacy – are.

However, there is also a positive side to these disappointing and disillusioning facts: they show that the Church's institutions and its character – beginning with the papacy – can in fact be changed, even fundamentally reformed. The papacy need not be abolished, but it should be renewed in such a way that the Petrine ministry once again becomes the office in the succession to St Peter described in the Bible. However, what does need to be abolished is the Medieval Roman system of governance and control. My critical destruction is therefore done in the service of committed construction, of reform and renewal, in the hope that, despite all appearances to the contrary, the Catholic Church will remain viable into the third millennium.

Physician, not Judge

Many readers will be surprised that I use so many medical metaphors in this book. This is because, in terms of health and disease, similarities between the body corporate of the Catholic Church and the human organism immediately spring to mind. Moreover, using medical language in analysing the Church's condition allows me to formulate certain truths more clearly than if I were to use legal language. I do not see myself as a judge, but rather – in the broadest sense of the term – as a kind of physician.

My fundamental criticism of the Roman System is grave, and I will give my reasons for it, point by point. I will attempt, to the best of my knowledge and in all conscience, to make an honest diagnosis throughout this book and to offer effective suggestions for treatment. Doubtlessly, the medicine will often be bitter, but the Church requires such medicine if it hopes to recover. The story I tell here is a gripping one, and – as is usually the case with descriptions of progressive disease – it is hardly pleasant. But I have not described my diagnosis so explicitly simply because I testily insist on being right or because I enjoy being contentious, but only to fulfil my duty in conscience to offer this service (possibly my last?) to my Church, a Church which I have endeavoured to serve all my life.

Based on my previous experience, I expect that Rome will do everything it can, if not to condemn such an uncomfortable and inconvenient book, then at least to keep it as far as possible under wraps. I hope, however, that this book will receive support from within the church community and from the public at large, in particular from theologians and, if possible, also from those bishops who genuinely wish for change. I also hope that this book will shake up those who are ideologically hidebound, and awaken the legally and financially entrenched Roman hierarchy from its complacent slumber, so that they will at least begin to take note of the pathogenesis presented here and to give thought to my explanation of how the disease from which the Catholic Church is suffering has developed, and of the consequences of this disease, so that they will not obstruct the unpleasant but urgently necessary therapy.

What a wonderful way this would be to mark the fiftieth anniversary of the prophetic Second Vatican Council! While not everything can be healed overnight, the agenda set forth here will, I am convinced, remain on the table as an important order of business for the Catholic Church in the coming years. And if that is the case, all of my effort has been worthwhile.

CHAPTER 1

A GRAVELY, PERHAPS EVEN TERMINALLY, ILL CHURCH?

The Church Cannot Go On in This Way

'Things just can't go on like this in our Church'; 'The powers that be, those up there in Rome, are doing their best to tear the Church apart!' Complaints like these, and similarly bitter, outraged or despairing cries have frequently been heard over the past few years, in both Europe and the United States.

As Alois Glück, the clear-sighted and courageous chairman of the Central Committee of German Catholics, put it after the Second Ecumenical Church Congress in Munich back in May 2010:

> The alternatives are either resignation, accompanied by a deliberate shrinking of the Church until it consists of only a small community of 'staunch Christians' as some have little or no regrets about doing, or getting up the courage and determination to try something new.

His words expressed the concerns and hopes of many Catholics, especially the most dedicated and highly motivated members of the Church. The response of the bishops, however, was slow and reluctant; many clearly wanted to continue as before. And that explains the frustration, the anger and the despair that is particularly strong among the most loyal Catholics, who have not yet forgotten the Second Vatican Council.

The Catholic Church is in its deepest crisis of confidence since the Reformation, and nobody can overlook it. As Pope Benedict XVI, Joseph Ratzinger missed a great opportunity to make the forward-looking ideas of the Second Vatican Council the lodestone of the Catholic Church worldwide and especially within the Vatican itself. Instead of courageously pushing forward the reforms begun by the Council, he did the opposite: again and again, he qualified and weakened the statements of the Council, interpreting them retrogressively, contrary to the spirit of the Council fathers. He even expressly set his face against Vatican II, which, as an ecumenical council, represents, according to the great Catholic tradition, the highest authority within the Catholic Church. He did this by:

- accepting, without any preconditions, the illegally ordained bishops from the traditionalist Pius X Fraternity, which has separated itself from the Catholic Church and which continues to reject central elements of the Council's teaching;

- actively promoting the use of the Medieval Tridentine Mass and, on occasion, celebrating the Eucharist himself in Latin with his back to the congregation;

- creating a deep mistrust of the Protestant churches by continuing to insist that they do not constitute 'Churches' in the true sense of the word;

- failing to pursue the paths to understanding and communication with the Anglican Church as outlined in official (ARCIC) ecumenical documents, attempting instead to lure conservative married Anglican clergymen into the Roman Catholic Church by waiving their obligation to celibacy; and

- strengthening the forces opposing the Second Vatican Council within the Church by appointing men who are opposed to the Council to important administrative positions (e.g. the Secretariat of State, Congregation for Divine Worship and the Discipline of the Sacraments, and the Congregation of Bishops) and installing reactionary bishops around the world.

Benedict XVI's now-notorious *faux pas* made it clear that Pope Ratzinger was becoming increasingly distant from the great majority of churchgoers and believers in our countries, many of whom pay increasingly little attention to pronouncements from Rome. At best, these churchgoers relate to their local parish, their pastor and possibly their local bishop. Benedict's courageous decision, in February 2013, to resign his office deserves our full respect, but it was motivated explicitly for reasons of health; it is not an acknowledgement of mistakes made in the past or a call to take a different course in the future. Thus, of itself, Benedict's resignation changed nothing, and everything will depend on the course steered by his successor, Pope Francis.

In implementing his anti-Council policies, Benedict XVI, like his own predecessor, enjoyed the full support of the Roman Curia, a Curia in which those persons who support the Council have long since been isolated or eliminated. In the years that have passed since the Council, a highly efficient propaganda machine has been set up to serve the Roman cult of personality. Modern mass media (television, the internet, YouTube and now Twitter) are being used systematically, professionally and successfully to promote the vested interests of the Curia. When you watch the huge Masses at the Vatican, or the gatherings surrounding papal visits and journeys, you could be excused for believing that all is in order in the Catholic Church. But the question we must ask is: what is the substance behind this glittering façade? On the local level, things look quite different.

Decline of Church Institutions

I do not, of course, underestimate the immense amount of good work done all over the world at the local level, especially in individual parishes and in local institutions, the countless pastoral and social contributions of innumerable priests and lay people, men and, above all, women; time and again I have met these people, whose work is a true testimony to their faith. Where would the Catholic Church be today without the untiring commitment of such people? But who has thanked them? So many of them feel they are hindered rather than helped by 'those up there', by policies, theology and discipline formulated in Rome. Complaints are pouring in from all over the world about the decline of traditional church structures built up over years or even centuries.

I, too, have been affected personally. I refer to the drastic reduction in pastoral care not merely in the university city of Tübingen and in the entire diocese of Rottenburg-Stuttgart but also in my native Swiss town of Sursee near Lucerne, where I return every year in the summer and where I continue to celebrate the Eucharist. But the joy I experience in celebrating the liturgy is diminishing year on year. What I learned in August 2010 provides a saddening snapshot of the current state of affairs.

For centuries, the town parish of Sursee always had at least four ordained priests, the so-called 'Vierherren'. Now, however, it no longer enjoys the services of even a single ordained priest. Instead, it is headed by the lay theologian and deacon Markus Heil, who would make an excellent priest; however, because he is married, he cannot be ordained. And, therefore, although he and his team do an excellent job, in order to be able to celebrate the Eucharist they must fall back on the services offered by retired priests – for as long as such retired priests are still available. In Switzerland, too, celibate clergymen are a vanishing species. Nobody knows how long it will be possible to continue to offer pastoral care or regular Eucharistic services.

The Capuchin friars, important providers of pastoral care since the early seventeenth century, have had to close their monastery in Sursee and sell the site; the same has happened in many other places due to the lack of new blood. New recruits to the diocesan clergy are equally rare.

In nearby Lucerne, the theological faculty (and the kernel out of which the university developed in the last century) now fears for its survival. Because of the declining numbers of students, some politicians have proposed that it be merged with the Catholic Theological Faculty of Fribourg or with the Protestant Theological Faculty in Zurich and that the medical school should be expanded in its place. The fact is that, in Switzerland today, there are simply too few students wanting to study Catholic theology and too many centres offering theological training.

This is a typical example of the damage that can be done by a single bishop pursuing the reactionary policies of Popes John Paul II and Benedict XVI. The responsibility for this sad state of affairs lies in no small measure, in my view, with Kurt Koch, the former Bishop of Basle, who became extremely unpopular with both the clergy and the laity in his diocese because of his hard-line Roman views, his opposition to established Swiss laws on church–state relations which ensure strong lay participation in church life, and finally the way in which he handled a five-year conflict with one of the parishes of his diocese after he had arbitrarily dismissed its pastor. Thus it came as no surprise that, at the end of July 2010, Koch hastily abandoned his diocese, announcing his resignation while sojourning in Rome. In recompense, the pope soon appointed him head of the Secretariat for Christian Unity, and in connection with his ecumenical activities as a Vatican official I will have reason to come back to him later.

The situation in my home diocese is typical of many other dioceses all over the world. Not long ago, our Sursee pastor wrote to me that it is

> noticeable how many people have already emotionally and mentally written off our Church … Perhaps we too should note how a mood of resignation is taking hold within ourselves. This resignation is rooted in the feeling that, whatever we do, nothing will change.

The gradual withering away of the Church continues apace in other places of the world as well. Since the Council, tens of thousands of priests have abandoned their ministry, mainly because of the obligation to live in celibacy. Similarly, the number of people in religious orders, nuns, clerics and lay brothers, has dropped sharply, and the pool of intellectually and emotionally qualified potential candidates for both the secular priesthood and the religious life is shrinking alarmingly. Resignation and frustration are spreading among the clergy as well as among the most active lay people. Many of them feel that they have been abandoned in their difficulties, and they suffer intensely from the Church's evident incapacity for reform.

More and more places of worship, seminaries and presbyteries now stand empty. In many countries parishes are being amalgamated into large 'pastoral units' contrary to the wishes of their parishioners, simply because there are not enough priests to serve the separate parishes. The priests in these new conglomerate parishes are so completely overburdened with work that they rarely know many of their parishioners personally and have little time for real pastoral ministry. Such changes only simulate an attempt at Church reform.

Canon 515 of the Code of Canon Law gives every bishop the unlimited right to establish parishes and to abolish them again. This canonical law was recently cited by the highest court of the Roman Curia in support of bishops such as Cardinal Sean O'Malley of Boston, when ten parishes that he had abolished appealed to the Holy See – of course, to no avail! Since then, the expression doing the rounds in the United States, and elsewhere, is: 'No parish is safe.' The parish churches may be safe from robbers, but they are certainly not safe from those higher up in the Church who insist on economizing. The hierarchy prefers to deny the faithful a close-to-home celebration of the Holy Eucharist – the central element of the New Testament religious community – for the sake of maintaining the 'even holier' Medieval obligation of celibacy. This allows the Church not only to save on priests but also to save money, of course. Thus, Bishop Richard Lennon closed 27 parishes in his diocese of Cleveland, Ohio and announced plans to merge an additional 41 into only 18 new parishes. These affected parishes also appealed, but given the stubbornness of the bureaucrats in Rome it was once again merely a waste of time and effort. In many places in Germany such parish mergers are being denounced as a 'persecution of Christians from above'.

I suspect that a theologian like Joseph Ratzinger, who has lived at the Vatican court for more than three decades, is not able to understand how sore my heart is when I see only a few dozen of the faithful attending Sunday church services in my home parish where, in earlier decades, I used to see a full congregation. But this is not, as Rome repeatedly insists, merely the result of increased secularization but is also the consequence of fatal developments within the Church for which Rome must be held responsible.

Many places still have active Catholic youth groups and a functioning community life, supported by the work of brave women and men in these parishes. Yet, on the whole, the Church appears to be disappearing more and more from the consciousness of the younger generation. This younger generation does not even feel annoyed any more by the out-of-touch backwardness of the Church hierarchy in so many areas of morality and dogma. The younger generation simply is no longer interested in the Church: it has become meaningless to their lives. Little of this, however, has been noted within the

Vatican, which still proudly boasts of the high numbers of pilgrims (even though many of them are simply tourists) and considers the elaborately staged youth rallies with the pope to be representative of the youth of today.

The Failed Restoration Policies of Two Popes

It never ceases to astonish me how even secular contemporaries who do not consider themselves part of the Church and aesthetically minded intellectuals allow themselves to be dazzled by the return of Baroque splendour and impressively staged papal liturgies used by Rome to demonstrate the presence of a strong Church and the undisputed authority of the pope. All this religious magnificence, however, cannot disguise the fact that the restoration policies of John Paul II and Benedict XVI failed in the areas that count the most. All the papal appearances, journeys and teachings have not been able to change the opinions of most Catholics on controversial questions or to convince them to toe the Roman line. Even papal youth rallies, attended for the most part by conservative charismatic groups and promoted by traditionalist organizations, have failed to slow the numbers of people leaving the Church or to increase substantially the number of candidates for the priesthood. Even in the diocese of Rottenburg-Stuttgart, commonly considered to be broad-minded and appreciative of grassroots initiatives, 17,169 deeply disappointed Catholics, i.e. 0.9 per cent of the total membership, left the Church between January and mid-November 2010.

This progressive erosion of the Church, sketched above, has accelerated over the past three decades. However, despite all complaints and lamentations, the process is largely accepted as irreversible and irremediable, reflecting the will of God (or perhaps only of the pope?). Only relatively recently has the world at large been awakened by the growing numbers of abhorrent sexual scandals, in particular the abuse of thousands of children and adolescents by Catholic clergymen in the United States, Ireland, Belgium, Germany, the United Kingdom and other countries. And the revelation of how these cases of abuse have been handled by the hierarchy has resulted in an overall crisis of leadership and confidence, the like of which has never been seen before in the Church.

We cannot ignore the fact that the system devised to conceal clerical sexual misbehaviour and then set in motion all over the world was led by the Roman Congregation for the Doctrine of the Faith, headed by Cardinal Joseph Ratzinger from 1981 until 2005. Under John Paul II, reports of cases were already being collected by the Roman Congregation under the cloak of strict confidentiality. As late as 18 May 2001, Ratzinger sent a formal letter (*Epistula de delictis gravioribus*) to all bishops. According to this letter, cases of abuse were to be classed as *secretum pontificium* – a pontifical secret. Thus, those who made the abuse public – rather than the abusers themselves – were threatened with the most dire church sanctions. That letter has still not been retracted.

Many people rightly demand a personal *mea culpa* on the part of the then prefect of the Congregation for the Doctrine of the Faith, Joseph Ratzinger. But, regrettably, he missed the opportunity to do so in Holy Week of 2010. Instead, in an unprecedented and embarrassing ceremony on Easter Sunday, staged before the beginning of the solemn Easter Mass, he let Cardinal Angelo Sodano, formerly Cardinal Secretary of State and Dean of the College of Cardinals, attest to his innocence *urbi et orbi.* This scandalous ceremony was all the more shameful because Sodano himself had come under public criticism for his personal embroilment in the scandal. Although Benedict XVI has repeatedly voiced his regret about the abuse, he has remained silent about his own personal responsibility for its cover-up, just as many other bishops have remained silent about their own similar roles. Not even in his recent book *Light of the World* did Ratzinger offer any comment on his role in the affair. This is not a mere coincidence; it is part and parcel of the overall structure.

The Transition from a 'Wintry' Church to a Gravely Ill Church

In an interview given shortly before his death in 1984 and later published in *Faith in a Wintry Season: Conversations and Interviews with Karl Rahner* (1990), Karl Rahner, the great Jesuit theologian of the Council, described the desolate state the Church had fallen into as existing 'in a wintry season'; this striking image soon made the rounds as a perfect description of the Church's plight. Already in 1970, only a few years after the Council, Rahner used the opportunity afforded by his nomination as the first recipient of the Romano Guardini Prize to lash out openly against those responsible for this situation. At the award ceremony attended by Germany's leading bishops, Rahner pilloried the 'institutionalized mentality' of the episcopate, describing it as 'feudal, rude and paternalistic'. Behind this bitter outburst lay Rahner's deep personal disappointment over the German episcopate's cold-shouldered reaction to the cautiously formulated, confidential memorandum on clerical celibacy that he had drafted some months previously and sent to the German bishops with the signatures of eight other prominent German theologians. Not only did the bishops fail to respond to the theologian's appeal to rethink the matter and take appropriate action; with two exceptions, they failed even to acknowledge receipt of the document.

Despite Rahner's bitter words at the award ceremony, Cardinals Julius Döpfner and Hermann Volk and the other attending bishops showed not the slightest indication of a willingness to reconsider the prevailing position or to express even regret; instead they reacted with incomprehension, indignation and anger. From that time on, Karl Rahner became *persona non grata*, even among more progressive churchmen. Even Rahner's own former assistant Karl Lehmann, who as professor in Mainz had personally subscribed to the memorandum and who would later become the Cardinal-Bishop of Mainz, did not support the increasingly critical course of his old friend. Commenting on Lehmann's decision, Daniel Decker, his authorized biographer, wrote: 'on that day, it became clear that Lehmann's path within the Church could not be that of his theological mentor K. Rahner'.

Although in 1968, in the wake of Paul VI's encyclical squashing further discussion of the celibacy issue, Rahner, on the orders of Cardinal Döpfner, had dutifully supported the official position with his own widely publicized *Open Letter to the Clergy* and although he had painstakingly formulated his confidential memorandum two years later in a moderate, submissive tone, he was denounced in conservative Catholic circles for using provocative formulations and embarrassing exposures to foment scandals, making use of popular media in order to publicly orchestrate conflict and controversy. Since then, compulsory celibacy – despite the dwindling numbers of priests and the emergency situation of many parishes – had been a taboo topic for the German Bishops' Conference until 2010, when suddenly the breaking news of numerous hushed-up cases of clerical sexual abuse brought it to the fore. In other countries, it was the same story; the bishops, intimidated by Rome or prevented by their own dogmatic views, did their best to sit out the ongoing debates and ignore the increasingly vociferous demands for reform until they were pushed to take up the matter by public scandal and indignation.

Karl Rahner died in 1984 in wintry resignation, without having seen any harbingers of a new spring under a new pope. What would he say about the situation of his Church thirty years later? After three disappointing decades of Roman restoration under the pontificates of Wojtyla and Ratzinger, I am sure that he would agree that the advent of spring after such an icy winter will only be possible when we frankly admit that the Church is now seriously ill. It is not simply a matter of the individual, 'ecclesiogenic neuroses created by the Church', which the eminent Catholic psychotherapist Albert Görres had long ago diagnosed in the Church; the illness under which the Roman Catholic Church has long been suffering goes far beyond that: it consists in pathological, morbid structures within the Church itself. Not surprisingly, many now ask themselves: is the Church not critically, even terminally, ill?

My assessment of the prevailing condition of the Church has been confirmed by the analysis undertaken by Thomas von Mitschke-Collande, and underpinned by the results of numerous surveys. Mitschke-Collande, director emeritus of McKinsey/Germany and himself a committed Catholic, published a book in September 2010 entitled *Kirche – was nun? Die Identitätskrise der katholischen Kirche in Deutschland* (*'What's Next for the Church? The Identity Crisis of the Catholic Church in Germany'*). According to him, the problem involves five interlinked crises mutually reinforcing each other:

- a crisis of faith;

- a crisis of confidence;

- a crisis of authority;

- a crisis of leadership; and

- a crisis of dissemination.

Many people experience doubts about their belief in God for a variety of reasons, but when they find themselves in this situation they have little confidence in the ability of the Church and its representatives to help them. And that is understandable, because the authority of the Church itself is at an all-time low; the Church is suffering from a deep crisis of leadership and is virtually incapable of giving convincing witness to its official beliefs or explaining them in a way that can be understood.

Many recent events have combined to worsen the health of the Catholic Church. These events acted upon the Church like a case of chills, sending shivers down its body which – to continue with this analogy – served as warnings of repeated attacks of fever.

Attacks of Fever

The Catholic Church is suffering from an 'attack of fever', declared Archbishop André-Joseph Léonard, president of the Belgian Conference of Bishops, in September 2010 in Brussels. The conservative expert on canon law, whom the Vatican had appointed as head of the Belgian church in direct opposition to the wishes of the majority, was referring only to a single centre of disease – but one that had become alarmingly visible in Catholic Belgium – the sex scandals. In fact, in 2010 the Catholic Church experienced several fever attacks, which usually alternated with fever-free intervals, especially during the festive season.

The First Fever Attack:
Police Investigation of Bishops

In Belgium, an independent investigative committee compiled a document of around 200 pages containing reports of at least 475 cases of sexual abuse of children by clergymen and 19 suicide attempts by victims, 13 of which ended tragically. Ever since the Bishop of Bruges, Roger Vangheluwe, had to step down in April 2010 after sexually abusing his own nephew, the number of reports made to the police had increased. As the Belgian judiciary suspected an urgent risk of collusion, they ordered that three police raids be carried out on the same day. The first raid occurred during a meeting of the Belgian Conference of Bishops in Brussels: during the raid, all Belgian bishops, together with the Apostolic Nuncio, were detained for several hours and numerous documents were seized by the police; documents were also seized from the private residence of Cardinal Godfried Danneels, who had been the Primate of Belgium until the end of 2009; and in Leuven, a centre headed by the child psychiatrist Peter Adriaenssen that had been dealing with cases of sexual abuse was also searched. Peter Adriaenssen had spoken of an *affaire Dutroux* [after the Belgian serial child-abuser Marc Dutroux] within the Belgian Catholic Church'.

These were all unprecedented events in a Catholic country, and they turned up the heat on other bishoprics and, above all, on the Vatican. Subsequently, however, at the urging of the Catholic Church, the Brussels Court of Appeal declared the police operations illegal because the police had acted out of all proportion. However, there can be no question that the investigations exposed rotten areas in the Church: the sexual abuse itself, and the cover-ups initiated by the bishops.

At least Cardinal Danneels immediately apologized in several interviews (as reported by the Associated Press on 30 August 2010 and Reuters News Agency on 8 September 2010) for his 'errors of judgement' in not urging the incriminated bishop to step down immediately and in attempting to dissuade the victim, who was the bishop's own nephew, from immediately making public his charges against his uncle after having kept silent about them for so many years. At the same time, however, Bishop Guy Harpigny, who was given the responsibility of reviewing and dealing with cases of abuse, declared that Archbishop André-Joseph Léonard, the head of the Bishops' Conference, had refrained from issuing a clear statement of apology because the Church feared potential financial claims by victims for compensation.

In any case, it was clear that, even in Catholic countries, the days when the Catholic Church could demand separate jurisdiction and enforce its own laws contrary to those of the state had come to an end.

The Second Fever Attack: The Vatican Called to Account

The Supreme Court in the USA rejected an appeal by which the Vatican attempted to challenge the verdict of a court in the state of Oregon. The Oregon court had declared that the Vatican itself could be put on trial for the sexual abuse carried out by Catholic priests and that, on conviction, it could be forced to pay punitive damages. The US Supreme Court also rejected the Vatican's argument invoking its legal immunity as a sovereign state. Attorney Jeff Anderson (St Paul, Minnesota), who has been extremely successful in bringing class action suits against individual clerical perpetrators of sexual abuse and whose own daughter had herself been abused by an ex-priest, declared that this verdict meant that, after eight years of obstruction since 2002, the path was finally clear for a class action suit in which the Vatican could be held criminally accountable for its role in concealing cases of abuse. It is expected that such a suit will soon be filed against Cardinal Angelo Sodano, the former Cardinal Secretary of State and current Dean of the College of Cardinals, and against the current Cardinal Secretary of State Tarcisio Bertone. Moreover, a suit could also be filed directly against Ratzinger himself, for he was the man who, according to a detailed report by the *New York Times*, while he was prefect of the Congregation for the Doctrine of the Faith, abstained from issuing any sanctions against the priest Lawrence Murphy. Lawrence Murphy abused some 200 deaf boys in Milwaukee between 1950 and 1975.

Even if the pope as head of state enjoys immunity from prosecution, these are disastrous prospects.

The Third Fever Attack:
Exposure of Financial Scandals in the Vatican

In the recent past, the Vatican has come in for much criticism because certain companies with financial ties to the Vatican have been involved in the armaments industry or in the manufacture and distribution of birth control pills. More serious were the revelations of the shady operations of the Vatican Bank which took place under the presidency of the American Archbishop Paul Marcinkus (1971–1989), a trusted friend of Pope John Paul II, and which continued behind the back of Marcinkus's successors Angelo Caloia and Ettore Gotti Tedeschi despite their efforts to stop them. The details of these machinations were exposed in the book *Vaticano S.p.A.* by the Italian journalist Gianluigi Nuzzi, published in 2009, and on pages 279–280 of this book I will give a fuller account of them. In 2010, the Vatican was again shaken to the core when the news broke that the Italian authorities had confiscated 23 million euros lodged in an account held by the Vatican Bank at the Italian bank Credito Artigiano, and that a suit had been filed against the new president of the Vatican Bank, Ettore Gotti Tedeschi, known to have close ties to Opus Dei, and against the bank's director Paolo Cipriani. In view of the many earlier scandals, all of these separate events probably represent only the tip of the iceberg. Is the Vatican's 'national' independence now under threat, not merely from legal attacks but also financially? And is not the pope himself as the bank's sole owner legally liable? At least, the new EU guidelines on money laundering now also apply to the Vatican. I will be considering this point in more detail in Chapter 6.

The Fourth Fever Attack: Conflicts within the Top Echelons of Church Leadership

The Archbishop of Vienna, Cardinal Christoph Schönborn, a former doctoral student of Ratzinger and his protégé since the latter was a cardinal, asserted that the then Cardinal Secretary of State Angelo Sodano had been responsible for ensuring that proceedings against the child-abusing Cardinal Hans Hermann Groër, Schönborn's predecessor in Vienna, had been blocked for a long time, even though the Austrian Conference of Bishops had declared that it was 'morally certain' of Groër's guilt. Although the paedophile cardinal resigned in 1995, he was still permitted to attend Cardinal Schönborn's installation ceremony in Rome in full regalia. No condemnation of Hermann Groër occurred before his death in March 2003. But it was clear that Schönborn's public criticism of Cardinal Sodano and his moderate comments on priestly celibacy and homosexuality had provoked more ire in the Vatican than the misdeeds of Groër. At all events, Cardinal Schönborn was ordered to Rome, and, in Austria, his trip was generally interpreted as an act of self-abasement. After a private talk between the four of them (Cardinal Secretary of State Bertone had also been invited), a press statement was issued expressing no criticism of Sodano whatsoever but culminating instead in the assertion that criticizing the behaviour of cardinals was solely within the purview of the pope. Why? And since when? Clearly, 'reasons of state', or better 'reasons of the Church hierarchy', were behind this unprecedented humiliation of the Archbishop of Vienna. Whether, as the press release suggested, Benedict's 'great affection' for Austria and his invocation of the 'heavenly protection of the Virgin Mary, so highly venerated in Mariazell' would pave 'the way for a renewal of the Church community' is more than questionable. Nevertheless, the mere fact that Cardinal Schönborn had dared to voice such open criticism of one of the most powerful men within the Roman Curia was viewed positively in Austria.

The Fifth Fever Attack:
The Flurry of Excitement about Condoms

A long interview given by Benedict XVI to his favourite German reporter, Peter Seewald, and published as a book under the title *Light of the World*, caused a considerable stir. In the interview, the pope admitted, for the first time, that in the battle against AIDS the use of condoms might be permissible under certain circumstances. Of course, a pope can make his opinion known in interviews, but whether such a delicate and intimate issue should be treated in this informal manner is debatable. Initially it was unclear how authoritative such an interview was. Its prior publication in *Osservatore Romano* (even before the press release embargo date had expired!) was clearly part of a carefully directed, widespread publicity campaign, and the result was international media frenzy. A heated discussion immediately erupted as to whether this pronouncement by the pope represented a policy change or not. In reality, it was both. After Pope Benedict, during his trip to Africa, had branded the use of condoms as unconditionally immoral, he appeared, to all intents and purposes, to have changed his mind, at least with regard to male homosexuals. Nevertheless, that effectively amounted to a belated admission that it was no longer possible to uphold the previously rigid doctrine on artificial techniques of birth control. The pope knew that even some otherwise conservative Catholics, including bishops and theologians, and, even more importantly, certain Church organizations involved in providing aid to the developing world, rejected the Church's rigid prohibition of condoms, and that the irrational Vatican policy was making the Church look ridiculous all over the world. Thus, the pope's statement was mainly a tactical manoeuvre and did not represent a fundamental change. Limiting the ethical concession to male prostitutes constituted an affront to all married couples and particularly to women, who are the principal victims of the spread of AIDS in Africa.

A truly fundamental reversal of the Church's previously held position would have occurred if Benedict had not limited his casuistic response to male prostitutes but instead had given a fundamental answer to the question being asked by millions of heterosexual married couples, namely whether the Roman Magisterium no longer considers every form of 'artificial' birth control intrinsically evil. There is nothing on this topic in the Bible. In reality, the idea derives from a false understanding of natural law, assuming that every act of sexual intercourse must always be directed towards propagating the species. Clearly, the then pope intended to continue to adhere to the position set forth in Paul VI's controversial encyclical *Humanae vitae*. And so he got caught in the infallibility trap, a trap that needs to be discussed openly and honestly. The provisional result of this obfuscation was formulated by the *International Herald Tribune* in an article under the headline 'Confusion, not clarity from Pope' (23 November 2010). Paradoxically, this confusion was confirmed four weeks later by the Congregation for the Doctrine of the Faith itself in a statement that attempted to pour oil on the troubled waters stirred up by its former prefect by publishing, just before Christmas, a memorandum in six languages entitled 'On the Trivialization of Sexuality'. According to the memorandum, Benedict's comment on the permissibility of using condoms was in no way intended to be understood as implying the principle (otherwise well-established in ethics) that a lesser evil should be balanced against a greater one. What a pity.

Perhaps an end to reports of such fever attacks might indicate a drop in the severity of the illness affecting the Church; unfortunately, however, it looks as though there will be no end to such reports. How then should we react?

Seven Reactions to the Illness of the Church

Every Christian, man or woman, and, all the more, every theologian, needs to face this question. Millions of Catholics do not agree with or approve of the course charted by the Church. In all, I identify seven different reactions to the current situation, but I consider the first four of them to be out of the question:

1. One can leave the Church, as tens of thousands of people have done because of the scandalous revelations. As I mentioned previously, the figures for Germany were around 250,000, and in Austria (based on a projection by Cardinal Schönborn) the numbers were approximately 80,000.

2. One can create a schism within the Church by seceding together with a group of other people, as the reactionary former archbishop Marcel Lefebvre (excommunicated in 1988) did with his traditionalist Fraternity of St Pius X. However, it should be noted that not a single reform-minded group has done this to date.

3. One can retreat into a state of inner emigration and remain silent. Many previously reform-minded persons have done this; giving up in frustration, they remain in the Church, but cease to be involved: 'It is all to no avail, the system simply cannot be reformed!' And so, everywhere, fewer and fewer high-profile people are prepared to offer resistance.

4. One can outwardly conform but privately hold dissenting opinions. This is the path pursued by people who are willing outwardly, at least, to toe the prevailing line whatever direction it takes. In particular, it is the course taken by conformist politicians, who place great store on maintaining good relationships with the institutional Church and enjoy sitting in the first row at church conventions and papal appearances, and who flatter the church hierarchy outwardly but voice their objections to official doctrines or ethics only in private or not at all.

But three other reactions are also observable, all of which I consider to be important and helpful:

5. One can get involved in the local church community and work together with the local pastor and others, disregarding the popes and bishops. Alternatively, as

increasing numbers of men and women who want to remain involved are doing, one can take over, officially or unofficially, some of the tasks of the absent priests.

6. One can protest publicly, and vigorously demand reforms on the part of the ecclesiastical leadership. Unfortunately, the number of involved people who are willing to criticize the Church openly in this way has been dropping continually in the face of the massive resistance offered by the Roman Catholic establishment. Even the organized reform movements now suffer from a shortage of active supporters and especially from the lack of young people willing to get involved.

7. One can study the situation academically and publish the findings, hoping that these publications will inspire and guide individual church members and communities. That is what those theologians are doing who have not simply given up in despair or retreated to their comfortable academic ivory towers, but instead continue to take seriously their responsibilities as teachers (cf. 1 Corinthians 12:28 ff.). This is where I see my own special duty as a teacher of theology.

No less important, however, is the question: how have the bishops reacted to the situation?

Bishops Prepared to Enter into a Dialogue

In December 2010, a specially commissioned report on the archbishopric of Munich and Freising – a former workplace of the seminarian, priest, professor and bishop, Joseph Ratzinger

– concluded that between 1945 and 2009 at least 159 priests had committed acts of sexual or physical abuse in the archbishopric. The real number was probably 'considerably higher', according to Marion Westpfahl, the lawyer responsible for the report. However, only 26 priests were convicted of sexual offences. In the past, cases were systematically hushed up: 'We are dealing with a widespread practice of destroying documents.'

Nevertheless, the fact that the Archbishop of Munich, Cardinal Reinhard Marx, allowed the incriminating report to be published and publicly admitted that these were the 'worst months' of his life, must be acknowledged with respect. It shows that some theologically conservative bishops are beginning to understand how serious the situation within the church is. The Archbishop of Munich and the Bavarian bishops have drafted a joint prayer for forgiveness and pledged to do more in terms of prevention and to work more closely with the public prosecution authorities. At the end of 2010, Archbishop Marx once again spoke out in favour 'of a policy of openness, of looking more closely, and of transparency'. He considered the crisis and its aftermath to be far from over.

But Christian Weisner, the speaker of the reform movement We are Church, argues that to overcome the deep crisis of credibility it will be necessary to tackle the underlying problems, namely, the abuses of power, the inhibitions in dealing with sexuality, the lack of equality between men and women, celibacy … The bishops should not cherish the hope that the cases of abuse will be quickly forgotten: 'The memory of these abuse cases is not going to go away.' It is not enough to get these cases of abuse under control within the organization. Surely, all of the bishops need to recognize how serious the situation is.

To paraphrase the beginning of the famous poem of Heinrich Heine: 'Thinking of Germany's Church at night/puts all thoughts of sleep to flight.' In 2010, despite two heavily promoted and expensive campaigns launched that year – the Year of Vocations and the Year of Priests – only 150 candidates responded from all over Germany. This is the lowest number ever reported. And how many of them will change their minds before they are ordained? Moreover, how many priests will die in the meantime? In view of the upside-down population pyramid of the Catholic clergy, it looks as though the celibate priesthood may die out in the foreseeable future.

But this is just another symptom of the dramatic loss of confidence the Catholic Church is facing. According to a study by the Allensbach Institute published in July 2010:

> ... the percentage of the general population that believes the Church to be capable of offering orientation on questions of morality has dropped from 35 per cent in 2005 to 23 per cent; between March and June 2010 alone it decreased from 29 per cent to 23 per cent. At the same time, the belief that the Church offers answers in the search for meaning has also declined. In 2005, around 50 per cent of the population still believed that; by March 2010 the figure was only 45 per cent, in June it was down to 38 per cent. (*Frankfurter Allgemeine*, 23 June 2010)

The latter figure is especially alarming because it concerns the Church's core mission, and figures such as these should galvanize the church leadership into taking immediate action.

However, at the Second Ecumenical Church Congress in Munich (May 2010) the bishops never even mentioned any of the numerous reform movements. Since then, numerous articles, comments, letters to newspapers and personal discussions have shown them the extent to which unrest, resentment, frustration and anger have spread among the church laity and clergy alike. And so there have been indications of a slow change of opinion within the German Bishops' Conference, and, if I am not mistaken, within other bishops' conferences as well. On the eve of the autumn plenary meeting of the German Bishops' Conference in Fulda in October 2010, the Bishop of Fulda, Heinz Josef Algermissen, who was hosting the conference, spoke of a 'bottleneck situation'. He indicated that many questions were ripe for discussion, from sexual morality to celibacy. Such topics can no longer be kept under wraps. In truth, apart from the virtually incomprehensible official catechism, it is the increasing backlog of reforms, halted for many decades and culminating in the cover-up of widespread sexual abuse, which constitute the main reason for the current wave of people leaving the Church.

Bishops Refusing to Enter into a Dialogue

Still, the massive opposition to dialogue on the part of the ultra-Roman wing of the worldwide episcopate should not be underestimated. Again I call attention to the situation in Germany as typical of that elsewhere.

In Cologne, the largest archbishopric, currently headed by the conservative Cardinal Joachim Meisner, only nine priests were ordained in 2009, and only four in 2010. The 221 parishes will soon be downsized to 180. The situation is the same in the Essen diocese under Bishop Franz-Josef Overbeck, another member of the conservative wing; there, only two new priests were ordained in 2009 and only one in 2010. He has amalgamated some 272 parishes (with roughly 350 church buildings still in ecclesiastic use) into 43 mega-parishes (information provided in 2010 by the art historian Dr Christel Darmstadt from the grassroots campaign 'Save Bochum's Churches'). Clearly, as role models for future priests, such conservative prelates alienate more than they attract.

The diocese of Limburg offers an especially alarming example of the damage being done by the narrow-minded, conservative prelates appointed under John Paul II and especially under Benedict XVI. There, in 2007, the widely admired, open-minded Bishop Franz Kamphaus was replaced by Franz-Peter Tebartz-van Elst, a protégé of Cardinal Meisner. Fully committed to the Roman line, he high-handedly set about streamlining his diocese. (See the report by N. Sommer in *Publik-Forum* on 3 December 2010 and also the report in *Spiegel online* on 15 November 2010.) He also ignored a public letter from ten of his priests accusing him of excessive spending, of dealing arrogantly with his clergy and of fostering a general climate of fear in the diocese (reported in *Frankfurter Allgemeine*, 17 September 2012).

Specifically, he has been taken to task for treating himself to an exorbitantly expensive and opulent episcopal palace to replace the modest housing of his predecessor. On his instructions, the new vicar general has warned the clergy to observe discretion and maintain secrecy, thus leaving them afraid to speak out and tell the truth about the prevailing conditions in the Church; the editors of church newspapers are being pressured to avoid controversial topics; every effort is being made to re-clericalize diocesan life. The candidates for the priesthood are once again inculcated with clerical arrogance, and, contrary to an explicit decision by the diocesan Council of

Priests, clerics who toe the line are once again being rewarded with Roman titles like 'Prelate' or 'Monsignor'. Meanwhile, lay people are being marginalized and are no longer permitted to act in the name of the Church, e.g. lay theologians serving in pastoral and liturgical roles are no longer called 'pastoral ministers'. Under no circumstances are remarried divorcees permitted to receive Holy Communion or homosexual couples to receive a blessing. The overall prevailing policy is to put an end to the parishes as they have existed for centuries and replace them with centres of worship staffed by the few remaining priests. This means that the diminishing numbers of practising Catholics must make ever-longer journeys to receive the sacraments at these centres.

Surely, one can understand the cry for help from the priests affected by such policies. In their open letter to their bishop they wrote:

> Are we old-fashioned models that are being phased out? We are pastors who wish to be close to and truly share in the lives of the people in their parish; priests who have come to love their parishes and who do not want to change and accumulate parishes as you would change your shirt; who are committed to a loving community of discussion and prayer ...; who are involved in parish councils; who have taken on responsibility and are increasingly finding themselves relegated to the margins as though they were just pieces of furniture ...; artists and intellectuals who perceive very clearly that their world is not the world of finery and tassels once again used by the Church for embellishment and adornment nor the world of glossy, puffed-up kitsch expressed in empty phrases ...

The letter could equally have been addressed to Bishop Georg Ludwig Müller of Regensburg, a former professor of dogmatic theology and friend of Ratzinger, who enjoys an even worse reputation than his colleague in Limburg, thanks to his authoritarian, anti-ecumenical church policies and hostility to the laity. But, already in February 2010, Müller was declaring that the Church had everything under control. He has repeatedly taken action against critical journalists, and, in August 2010, he denounced the public discussion of clerical sex abuse as 'stage-managed public criticism'. After all, he claimed, everything possible had already been done for the victims of abuse. In January 2013, Müller, now cardinal archbishop in Rome and Ratzinger's successor as head of the Congregation for the Doctrine of the Faith, had the audacity to suggest that the ongoing criticism of the 'Catholic Church' – by which he means the Catholic hierarchy – harks back to the former campaigns of the totalitarian ideologies against Christianity and evokes 'an artificially generated outrage these days that already reminds one of a pogrom atmosphere' (interview with Archbishop Müller: 'Deliberate discrediting of the Catholic Church', *Die Welt*, 1 February 2013). Not surprisingly, Bishop Müller showed little or no concern for the victims of sexual abuse in Catholic institutions when their representatives rejected the bishop's offer of monetary compensation. Instead of a four-digit lump sum paid out quickly, the bishops' 'round table' proposed a long, drawn-out, petty examination of every individual case.

On the other hand, the conservative wing of the German episcopate lost one of its most outspoken spokesmen in April 2010, when Bishop Walter Mixa of Augsburg was forced to resign under a cloud after a string of press reports exposed not only homosexual and alcohol abuse among his notoriously conservative seminarians but also a long list of personal failings, including child-beating, alcohol abuse, financial malfeasance, abuse of authority, etc., going back as far as his earlier years as parish priest and later as bishop in Eichstätt and Augsburg. When attempts to deny the charges and squash the reporting failed, the German bishops and even Pope Benedict XVI dropped him like a hot potato. His subsequent struggle for rehabilitation revealed a complete loss of any sense of reality. (For a summary of this sordid affair see the article by Anna Arco in *The Catholic Herald*, Friday 2 July 2010.) Statistics indicate the gravity of the crisis in his diocese: whereas in 2009 some 7,000 people left the Church in his diocese, as a consequence of the sordid affair surrounding his retirement the figure rose to 12,000.

In the wake of these recent scandals, resistance to any form of dialogue or reform by the conservative bishops in Germany seems to be weakening. Still, too many bishops hope to follow Rome's example and sit out the deep-seated church crisis as though it were a mere media smear campaign; with the blessing of the pope, they continue to rule as before. By acting in this manner, however, they are only making their Church more and more sick.

Unfortunately, in other countries, for example in the United States, the situation created by the papal policy of replacing independent-minded liberal bishops by line-toeing conservatives has produced similar disastrous results. In the words of the distinguished Jesuit Thomas J. Reese (see his report in the *Washington Post*, 16 November 2010), the Conference of Catholic Bishops in America has increasingly 'tilted to the right'. The former vice-president and current president of the American

Bishops' Conference, Cardinal Francis George of Chicago, now plays a particularly nefarious role. Already as a leading member of the International Commission on English in the Liturgy (ICEL), he had successfully edged out opposition to the new slavishly word-for-word translation of the Latin Mass into English. Cardinal George has also led the attack on President Obama's healthcare reform, claiming it would fund abortions, even though the Catholic Health Association disputes this claim.

In previous years, the US Conference of Catholic Bishops had had a number of outstanding presidents such as Cardinal Joseph Bernadin of Chicago, who worked in the spirit of the Second Vatican Council. But, under the bishops appointed by John Paul II and Benedict XVI, the direction taken by the Bishops' Conference has shifted radically to the right. Contrary to previous custom, these bishops successfully prevented the moderate vice-president of the conference from being elected the next president. Instead of reflecting the full range of Catholic social teaching, the American bishops now focus their attention almost exclusively on two moral questions: abortion and gay marriage. Ignoring the social issues emphasized by the Democratic Party, they have no scruples about supporting the Republican obstruction of all policies of the Obama administration. Like so many episcopal conferences, the American episcopate overlooks the need for fundamental changes in the crisis-ridden American Church, changes that would halt the general decline and end the self-chosen retreat into a ghetto situation.

In short, there is little or no hope that the illness affecting the Church will manage to heal itself without a radical turnaround on the part of the episcopate.

Diagnosis and Therapy

Given that the illness of the Church is hard to ignore, one might expect that within the worldwide Catholic episcopate, which together with the pope is responsible for the direction and 'cure' (possibly also the curative surgery) of the Church, there would be a widespread public debate about the principles which must guide such a radical cure, i.e. a debate which would go beyond mere superficial comments about mandatory celibacy and the like.

But we have not yet reached that point. In 2010, I had the same disappointing experience that Karl Rahner had had decades before, when he waited in vain for a response to his (confidential) 1970 letter to the German bishops. In 2010, I wrote an open letter to the bishops of the world. Copies were duly sent to each bishop, and the letter was widely publicized in the media worldwide and was endorsed by many readers. Not a single one of the approximately 5,000 bishops, some of whom I know personally, dared to answer, either in public or in private. Not only was there no positive reaction, but also no negative reaction, only complete and utter silence. Later on, I will attempt to explain the reasons for this silence.

Admittedly, people will ask me: what can individual bishops or theologians do, considering how gravely ill this Church is? I can only answer for myself: I am not a prophet or a miracle healer and I never wished to become a political agitator. So what can I do – I, who have always viewed myself as a professor of theology, philosophy and religious studies? I can, perhaps, offer services similar to those of a doctor or physician. Better yet – as suggested in the introduction to this book – those of a therapist who can help a critically ill patient, in this case the Church, not by offering superficial explanations and excuses but by providing a fundamental diagnosis that goes to the roots of the illness and by suggesting an effective therapy which will contribute a little to the patient's recovery.

- *The correct diagnosis* (Greek: *diágnosis* = 'discernment'): there must be no trivialization of the symptoms ('It's not as bad as it looks') but no alarmist dramatics either ('There is no cure!'). Instead, what is needed is an analysis of the history of the disease based on historical facts, a real pathogenesis which explains precisely how this centuries-old institution, the Catholic Church, got into such a lamentable condition. The medical term for this is *aetiology*: the search for the *aitía*, or cause.

- *Effective therapies* (Greek: *therapeía* = 'service, care, medical treatment'): what is necessary is not therapies which merely treat the symptoms or isolated aspects of the disease; antipyretic medication alone will not get the Church back on its feet. What is required is a therapy that goes after the root causes, one which penetrates through all the layers of forgetting, repression and taboo to reach the true causes of the disease and fight the pathogenic factors or processes at work. Maybe even surgery will be indicated in certain areas to root out specific cancers.

At this point, many people will probably demur that this will take too much time and effort and is not worth the trouble.

Medically Assisted Suicide or Reanimation?

No doubt, many people are of the opinion that the Catholic Church is irremediably, terminally ill and that it does not deserve to be saved. They believe that it cannot be reanimated. Recently, this erosion of faith in the Church's ongoing vitality has even begun to affect traditional Catholic circles. It has become increasingly clear that the number of people who consider the Church necessary – or even useful – has continually decreased since the peak of public approval at the time of the Second Vatican Council (1962–5), and under Benedict XVI it dropped to an all-time low. The results of significant surveys conducted in a number of Western countries show that this decline is not a development restricted to the 'recalcitrant' German-speaking countries.

In Italy, the land of the pope, less than half of the population still consider themselves to be Catholic, 20 per cent less than in 2004 (IARD RPS). This is despite the fact that more than 80 per cent consider religion to be important, a drop of only 8 per cent compared to six years previously. But many people want to have nothing more to do with the Church as an institution. Only 46 per cent still have confidence in the pope; six years ago the number stood at 60 per cent. Similar developments have been noted in such bastions of Catholicism as Spain, Ireland and even to some extent Poland. Three-quarters of American Catholics believe it is possible to be a good Catholic without submitting to the pope's authority.

Such a development of 'popular Catholicism' is not surprising, considering the restoration course of the hierarchy described above. In the last few years, numerous Catholics, including wrongfully penalized and marginalized theologians such as Eugen Drewermann and Gotthold Hasenhüttl, Matthew Fox and many others, have had enough of appealing in vain against the course charted by the church leadership and have left the Church: not, indeed, the Catholic community of faith as such, but the public corporation known as the Roman Catholic Church, the community of persons paying the church tax or otherwise conforming to church discipline. People who have left the Church in protest against the German church tax include the Freiburg professor for church law Hartmut Zapp and the Regensburg engineer Dr Andreas Janker. This can set a precedent and should serve as a warning to the church hierarchy – it is understandable that if you have lost your faith in the Church you do not want to continue paying the church tax.

What is more ominous is that a much larger number of Catholics have distanced themselves emotionally from the Church. They remain nominally Catholic, but they have lost all interest in the Church as an institution. I share the assessment of Thomas von Mitschke-Collandes:

> Many church members are reading up on how to leave the Church. This type of crisis is unique and unprecedented. Things have not yet calmed down. The numbers of people leaving the Church in 2010 could explode.

And the numbers did indeed explode.

In addition to the loss of faith in the Church among Catholics, we are seeing a growing hostility to the Church within secular society. All too many of our contemporaries feel the recent revelations of abuse have simply confirmed their view of the institutional Church as an unregenerate and power-hungry church hierarchy; they are convinced that local parishes and society in general have suffered immensely from the authoritarianism and dogmatism of church teaching, from the climate of fear the Church has generated, the sexual neuroses and the general refusal to enter into dialogue.

Some Catholics will of course object. Has not Rome recently 'asked for forgiveness' for its failures, its mistakes? Yes, but, as pope, Ratzinger did not personally admit his own wrongful involvement in the cover-up, and there were no practical consequences for the present and the future. The cases of sexual abuse and their cover-up have confirmed many people's impression that the church administration and the Inquisition continue to create new victims and new suffering.

It cannot be denied that hardly any major institution in Western democratic countries treats dissenters and critics within its own ranks so inhumanely. And none of them discriminates so strongly against women, for example by prohibiting birth control, forbidding priests to marry, by prohibiting the ordination of women. No other institution polarizes society and politics so strongly with its rigorously divisive positions on issues such as homosexuality, stem cell research, abortion, assisted suicide and the like. And while Rome no longer dares to proclaim formally infallible doctrines, it still envelops all of its doctrinal pronouncements with an aura of infallibility, as though the pope's words were a direct expression of God's will or Christ's voice.

Given this situation, it comes as no surprise that the more or less benevolent indifference to the Church that began some fifty years ago has in many cases slipped over into outright hostility, cynicism or even open enmity. Some would like to facilitate the demise of this terminally ill Church, to offer 'assisted suicide' so to speak. The media are continually serving up topics from the Church's 'criminal history' calculated to appeal to a mass audience, many of which had been described decades ago in the books of the formerly Catholic author Karlheinz Deschner. While we cannot deny that such portrayals may be correct, it is all too easy to forget that a similar method would make it equally possible to write a sensationalist criminal history of Germany, France, Britain or the USA – to say nothing of all the monstrous crimes committed by modern atheists in the name of the goddess of reason, the nation, the race or the party.

However, even in modern-day secular France, Voltaire's hate-filled dictum about the Catholic Church '*Écrasez l'infâme*' ('Crush the infamous thing') – no longer finds expression in overt persecution; instead, there and elsewhere, it leads simply to the marginalization of the Church. The European Parliament caused quite a stir when the majority refused to include any reference to God in the preamble of the European Constitution; an understandable decision, given the numerous non-believers and believers of other faiths in Europe. But the unwillingness to include any mention of Christianity at all as constituting part of Europe's cultural heritage alongside the legacies of antiquity and the Enlightenment is symptomatic of the growing malaise, and is incomprehensible in view of the undeniable epochal cultural achievements and humanitarian contributions of the churches in the past. Another example of such marginalization is the advertising campaign on London buses sponsored by militant atheists (admittedly in response to the threats of hell-fire flung at atheists by Christian fundamentalists): 'There's probably no God. Now stop worrying and enjoy your life.' Often, such reactions simply mirror the Church's own scaremongering, un-evangelical pronouncements, and the Church would do better to reflect on them critically as warning symptoms, instead of simply rejecting them out of hand.

A Case History of the Church's Pathology

The illness of the Catholic Church did not begin yesterday; it started long ago. The Church's medical history is so old and complex that a detailed anamnesis (Greek: 'remembrance') is required. It will be necessary to enquire into the preliminary events leading up to the outbreak of the illness. Just as the doctor, psychotherapist or counsellor attempts, in conversation with the patient, to uncover significant moments of the progress of an illness, so the theologian and historian can discover root causes of the present illness in the history of the Church's ailing body. However, for this anamnesis he or she will need a non-ideological, carefully diagnostic approach to history.

In any event, the optimistic, harmonious interpretation of church history created by theologians in the nineteenth century is not at all helpful for a serious diagnosis and therapy, although this, of course, is the version preferred and put forward by the church authorities to immunize themselves against all criticism that might suggest pathological developments. According to this version, the Church's 2,000-year history represents an organic growth of teachings, laws, liturgy and piety. This view allows the Church to justify novel Roman dogmas which in fact were only enforced in the second half of the nineteenth and the first half of the twentieth century: the doctrines that the pope enjoys immediate and absolute authority over the Church in all its parts (universal jurisdiction), and that he enjoys guaranteed freedom from error when he solemnly pronounces on matters of faith and morals (infallibility), are specific examples. Further examples are two doctrines on the Virgin Mary, namely her freedom from sin from the moment of her conception (Immaculate Conception), and her bodily assumption into heaven at the end of her life (Assumption). And at the same time, this harmonizing approach to church history makes it possible to explain and take for granted the personal foibles and systematic abuses of power on the part of iniquitous holders of office. According to this approach, the Church is an enormous healthy tree in a state of continual growth, development and refinement, even though it occasionally carries dead branches and discards rotten fruit.

Such an idealized historical account can serve as a palliative, helping to make the disease of the Church psychologically endurable, but it does not face up to the causes of the illness. Often it simply serves merely as a placebo, as pseudo-medication, useful because of its calming effect on pious churchgoers and rebellious reformers. Those who share the lopsided view of the history of the Catholic Church as an organic process of maturation are unable and unwilling to take note of obvious abnormal, pathological phenomena, even when they clearly infect the whole body of the Church. Because the official representatives of the Church have been the ones mostly and primarily responsible for these phenomena and because the Church's representatives cannot and do not want to admit their existence, over the centuries alarming relapses have occurred time and again, despite intermediate, quasi-miraculous improvements. And the popes in particular have been far from innocent in contributing to these relapses. Instead of admitting the papal involvement in such relapses, the Holy Fathers prefer to canonize even their quite 'unholy' predecessors such as Pius IX, Pius X, and perhaps also Pius XII – canonizations which at best can be viewed as a confirmation of the *simul iustus et peccator* (of the saint and the sinner in one)!

On the one hand, while I reject the optimistic, harmonious view of the Church's history, I also reject the hate-filled denunciatory interpretation, which does not have a single good word to say about the Church. I agree neither with the uncritical admirers nor with the resentful critics, as both groups see only one side of the Church. Because the history of the Church – like that of all other big institutions – is mixed, I propose instead to make the effort to differentiate.

A detailed anamnesis will start with the historical causes of the illness and at the same time explain how things could come to such a pass. Non-historians may also observe many things on the surface, but cannot explain them. Often, behind the efficient organization stands a powerful financial machine making use of quite worldly methods. The impressive mass celebrations of Catholic unity all too often manifest only a superficial form of Christianity lacking in substance. The conformist hierarchy often consists mainly of clerical functionaries always keeping an eye on Rome for orientation, servile to those above them and autocratic towards those below. Embedded in the closed system of doctrines and dogmas is an obsolete, authoritarian, unbiblical, sterilely orthodox theology. And even those proudly acclaimed Western cultural achievements ascribed to the Church have often been accompanied by excessive worldliness and a neglect of real clerical duties.

Already I can already hear the objections of the apologists of the church establishment: *Quo iure?* – what right have you to sit in judgement on the institution of the Church? I can only repeat: I am not a judge but a theologian–therapist; I do not wish to sit in judgement but to provide a diagnosis and suggest remedies like a doctor, a psychotherapist or a counsellor. Admittedly, my recommendations, expounded at length in so many books and substantiated there in detail, have not been appreciated by the authorities to whom, along with a larger public, they are addressed. The authorities have found my recommendations so uncomfortable because many of these people are themselves caught up in the pathogenic structures. And they do not want to hear about necessary surgical operations and reforms in the body of the Church.

But, the apologists exclaim, surely it is not just a matter of historical changes within the institution? No indeed, it is a question of something far more permanent, a question of the truth, of the eternal truth. And the question is: what must endure in the Church, what should be the criterion for the truth?

Is Tradition or Progress the Criterion of Truth?

Two opposing attitudes to the truth can be seen not only in the concerns about the physical well-being of an individual but also in the concerns regarding the welfare of a society. For one group, it is the 'old ways', the things that have withstood the test of time, tried-and-true knowledge that counts; in short, it is tradition that must take precedence. For the other group, it is instead what is new, up-to-date, scientific, innovative, progressive that counts. Which of them is right?

I value tradition but I am not a traditionalist. Yet, in the Church, and not just in Rome, there are people who swear by the old ways. While the 'good old ways' may often be a stimulus, they should never be a model *per se*. Such thinking assumes that God would have been present only at certain periods in the past, for example during the time of the Church Fathers (the era of patristic Greek and Latin theology and culture) or during the Middle Ages (the era of scholasticism, Romanesque and Gothic art) but would have had nothing to do with subsequent ages, in particular with the Reformation and the Enlightenment. These modern eras, the traditionalists believe, were times of 'decline', which they often describe in veiled, umbrella terms like 'de-hellenization', 'de-churching' (= secularization) or 'de-Christianization'. But this approach means surrendering to the debilitating myth of decline, which is averse to any form of progress.

Along these lines, Benedict XVI saw his task as consisting primarily in preserving rather than unfolding the truth, which, for him, meant preserving tradition. But, in asserting his supreme authority over all church teachings, he claimed to determine by himself – at best with reference to his more recent predecessors – what belongs to tradition and what does not. In this vein, his predecessor Pius IX replied to the bishops who challenged his impassioned insistence on his own particular definition of papal infallibility, which claimed to rest on the Bible and tradition, with the notorious riposte: '*La tradizione sono io*' ('I am the tradition!') In reality, this papal dictum represents an absolutistic understanding of truth not unlike the absolutistic understanding of the state expressed by Louis XIV's dictum: '*l'État – c'est moi!*'

And so, in the Catholic Church of the nineteenth and twentieth century a typical Roman Catholic traditionalism or fundamentalism developed, which believed that everything should and could be left as it was – or must be restored to what it once was. That the Church continually needs to be renewed, they understand, at best, only as a moralizing truism used to discipline individual believers, for instance, in calling them to adhere more closely to papal doctrines on sexual morality and to defend the privileges of the Church. This kind of traditionalism survives into our own day. Moralizing papal platitudes are given a cheering reception by the young people at the huge youth rallies with the pope, even as these same young people continue using the pill and condoms, leaving the vestiges behind on the very grounds where the day before they had so enthusiastically cheered the pope.

Unquestioning devotion to the past results in enfeebled creativity, mental impotence and anaemic scholasticism. No, traditionalism cannot be the Church's top priority. Rather than an unreserved commitment to some version of the past, the Church needs freedom, a freedom that also manifests itself in a critical sifting of the Church's own history. And such a critical attitude will therefore dissociate itself from the equally extreme alternative of fanatical Modernism.

I love what is new but I am not addicted to novelty as such. In modern society, many people swear by everything that is new. They demand an unconditional orientation towards the future, setting their sights on Utopia. In the twentieth century there were those who proclaimed the advent of a 1,000-year Reich (which perished in 1945 after only 12 years); others who proclaimed the emergence of a classless society (it had run its course and collapsed by 1989). But even in the twenty-first century, many still dream of a new shape that humanity could take as a result of technological or ecological evolution, or political and social revolution. But neither black, nor brown, nor red, nor green Utopian visionaries have succeeded in bringing forth the ideal 'new humanity' of which they dream.

The Catholic Church has also had its share of individuals, groups and movements who were so fascinated by modern Utopias that they demanded a modernization of the Church by conforming to the spirit of the age. Alongside such modernizers, there also exists an odd Catholic mystical fanaticism paired with an apocalyptic belief in the future. The adherents of this type of apocalyptic thinking invoke higher revelations, mostly of more recent date, which go beyond those given by the historical Jesus Christ: precise prophecies about when and how the world will end, about a coming great war, about the conversion of Russia and the like, and they often underpin these prophecies with intricate numerological calculations. In his latest book, Benedict XVI himself gives an example of this kind of apocalyptic mysticism in referring to the strange 'Secret of Fatima'. In short, these modern-day mystical prophets offer a medley of superstition and obscurantism – widely disseminated by the modern media – to satisfy the craving for miracles and religious sensationalism of people both educated and uneducated in religious teachings. But is this true Christianity? Surely not!

Christian Churches Need to Be More Christian

Catholicism, as it evolved historically, and particularly modern Catholicism in its current form, cannot be the yardstick by which the Church measures itself. Many within the Vatican and many external 'supporters of the Vatican' want to commit the Catholic Church to a *status quo* which is both comfortable and profitable to them. And so they reject – always with reference to a 'higher' (i.e. papal) authority – any proposals for change in the pathogenic course they have adopted for the Church, and they rule out any serious reforms to the Church's teachings and practice: if it is not Roman (i.e. does not toe the Vatican line), it is not Catholic.

But more and more Catholics are seeing through the knee-jerk reactions that have brought Rome more and more power and only worsened the Church's pathological condition. No one who has even the slightest idea of the real history of the Church can either ignore its flaws, ruptures and cracks, deny the many contradictions and inconsistencies in its history, or gloss over and excuse them.

Conversely, however, the question arises: can such things really be reformed and transcended? I admit that I have become increasingly sceptical, not just in view of the current, lamentable situation in the Catholic Church, but also in view of the epic upheavals and paradigm changes that mark the history of all three Abrahamic religions, and particularly the history of Christianity, which I have analysed in two decades of laborious research. Neither Catholic leaders nor church historians have taken seriously the consequences of such shifts for our present-day Church.

I will return later to the topic of paradigm change, those epochal changes in the overall mindset and way of doing things that, in the history of the Church, have led to the formation of separate confessional traditions and churches. But here, I want to highlight at least briefly some of the problems facing the Church as a result of such changes.

Anyone who knows the Church's history will ask themselves: can one seriously expect a Church so deeply rooted in a Medieval paradigm ('P III' in my terminology – see Editor's

Note, pp. 339–41) to embark on a new course in the future? Can one expect this of a Church which has largely forgotten the original Jewish–Christian paradigm of the Apostolic Church ('P I') and which only selectively accepts the early Christian–Hellenist paradigm of the first millennium ('P II')? Can one expect an adequate response to the current problems facing the Church from a Church that sees both the paradigm of the Protestant Reformation ('P IV') and the paradigm of Enlightenment and Modernity ('P V') only as a falling away from the true path of Christianity? How can such a Medieval, Counter-Reformation, anti-modernist Church manage the transition to a new, more peaceful, more just, ecumenical paradigm ('P VI') appropriate to the twenty-first century? Given the fact that, at the Second Vatican Council, the Catholic Church only partly managed to integrate the Reformation and modern paradigms and that currently a restoration of the pre-Vatican II paradigm is well under way, is such a Church at all capable of steering a path into the future that allows it both to preserve the original message of Christianity and express it anew?

And this brings us to the crucial point; the challenge to reform is addressed not only to the Catholic Church but to every church that considers itself Christian: the Protestant and the Orthodox churches are likewise not sanctuaries immune to similar criticism. The crucial question is always the same: Does one's church faithfully incorporate and reflect the original Christian message, the Gospel, which to all intents and purposes is Jesus Christ himself, to whom each church appeals as its ultimate authority? Or is it mainly a church system with a Christian label, be it Early Christian/Orthodox, Medieval/Roman, Protestant/Reformed or Modernist/Enlightened?

Without a concrete and consequent return to the historical Jesus Christ, to his message, his behaviour and his fate (as I described it in my book *On Being a Christian* [1977]), a Christian church – whatever its name – will have neither true Christian identity nor relevance for modern human beings and society. For Catholics, that means that all the many Roman Catholic institutions, dogmas, doctrines, ceremonies and activities must be measured according to the criterion of whether they are 'Christian' in the strict sense of the word or, at the very least, not 'anti-Christian', in short, whether or not they are in agreement with the Gospel.

This is what so many people in the Church are hoping for when they say to themselves: our Church must become more Christian again, must once again model itself on the Gospel, on Jesus Christ himself. And to ensure that such hopes are not dismissed as an unrealistic theological agenda, I want to illustrate this point so crucial for the survival of the Church with an – admittedly drastic – image.

An Ominous Snapshot

Few scenes in the recent history of the Catholic Church have troubled me as much as the one that took place on 8 April 2005 in St Peter's Square in Rome. The occasion was the opulent funeral for Pope John Paul II, staged with a degree of pomp and circumstance that would have befitted a Roman emperor. As always, the camera work had been pre-arranged between the Vatican and Italian television, ensuring that the ceremony was impressively broadcast to an audience of many millions all over the globe. During the ceremony, Joseph Ratzinger, head of the Congregation for the Doctrine of the

Faith and Dean of the College of Cardinals, and vested in festive crimson, came down the steps and took his place next to the deliberately chosen plain wooden coffin. Next to the coffin – placed there equally deliberately – stood a huge crucifix realistically representing the cruelly tortured body of the suffering and crucified Christ. I could not imagine a greater contrast. On the one side, one saw the opulently clad head of the Congregation for the Doctrine of the Faith, the modern name for the notorious, former *Sanctum Officium* of the Inquisition, which, with its authoritarian teachings and secret inquisitorial proceedings, has for centuries been responsible for the suffering of innumerable people within the Church and which to this day, more than any other papal institution, embodies the concentrated power of the new *Imperium Romanum* – a point underscored by the presence of 200 guests of state from all over the world, including, in the first row, the family of the war-mongering president of the United States, George W. Bush. On the other side, one saw the Man of Sorrows from Nazareth, who in his life had preached peace, non-violence and love, and who represents a last court of appeal for all those unjustly persecuted, tortured or suffering innocently.

Involuntarily, one is reminded of the figure of Christ in the famous chapter on the Grand Inquisitor in *The Brothers Karamazov* by Dostoyevsky. According to the tale, Jesus Christ has returned to sixteenth-century Spain and has been incarcerated by the Grand Inquisitor of Seville with the intention of burning him at the stake as a heretic because he dared to bring freedom to humankind, a freedom that, in the mind of the Grand Inquisitor, human beings are utterly incapable of living. Confronting Jesus, the Inquisitor demands to know: 'Why have you come to get in our way?' In response, the prisoner answers not a single word; instead, at the end of the Inquisitor's reproaches, he gently kisses the wizened old man on his bloodless, ninety-year-old lips. Touched by this incomprehensible gesture, the Grand Inquisitor, instead of pronouncing sentence, shows him the door, opens it and sends him away, saying: 'Go and do not come back ... do not come back at all ... ever, ever!'

But Jesus does come back – again and again. I have often thought how easy it would be to transpose this story from gloomy sixteenth-century Seville to the friendlier Vatican of the twentieth and twenty-first centuries. The subject of the freedom of Christians is as topical as ever. And this perhaps constitutes 'the fundamental feature of Roman Catholicism', as Dostoyevsky conjectured when he had the Inquisitor say to Jesus: 'It was all told to you by the Pope and so it is now all of it in the Pope's possession, and now we should appreciate it if you would stay away altogether and refrain from interfering, for the time being at any rate.' But then, to many people's astonishment and dismay, Ratzinger – the head of the Congregation that today, although no less authoritarian than its predecessor, uses more subtle methods of repression – was himself elected pope. In an initial charm offensive, he presented himself as a humane and charitable shepherd, but time and again he revealed his old face as the merciless head of the Inquisition. And after a time, many people noted how Pope Benedict XVI was following a disastrous course not unlike that pursued by George W. Bush. It was no coincidence that, at Bush's invitation, Benedict happily celebrated his 81st birthday in the White House, together with the autocratic president: both men, Bush and Ratzinger, proved themselves over the years to be incapable of learning anything, for example in their common stance on the issue of abortion. Both have exhibited an antipathy to serious reforms and a fondness for ostentatious public appearances. Both have ruled autocratically and without administrative transparency. Both have been intent on limiting people's rights and freedoms and justify this with the need to maintain 'security'.

As a corrective for poor or misguided leadership, the constitutions of democratic countries provide limited terms of office and regular elections. Unfortunately, the authoritarian papal monarchy makes no provision for such democratic correctives: not even the College of Bishops is empowered to curb an autocratic pope. The result is widespread alienation of a substantial number of believers and a moral dilemma for many of today's most actively involved Catholics. As one prominent Catholic recently put it to me, 'Ratzinger's Church is not my Church!' Many have already voted with their feet. Regularly, I receive suggestions – not just from indignant conservatives! – that I should imitate the many thousands who have left the Church in the last decades. Disappointed Catholics argue that in the eyes of the hierarchy and the conservative clergy and laity who increasingly set the tone in the Church, critical theologians are merely a 'source of irritation' to be ignored or silenced. In place of a truly broad, 'Catholic' Church reflecting the full spectrum of legitimate opinion and practice, Rome and its neo-conservative allies now dream of reducing the Church to a 'small flock' of 'true believers' unconditionally loyal to the pope and willing to follow Vatican directives.

But, then, before my mind's eye, very different images of the Catholic Church take form.

The Other Church

These are images that have little to do with the triumphal demonstrations of power in St Peter's Square, but instead reflect what can be experienced thousands of times over around the world. Everywhere I go, I meet deeply committed people in parishes and hospitals, schools and charitable institutions, who in their practical day-to-day involvement in church life are following in the footsteps and in the spirit of the man from Nazareth. They are people who – notwithstanding their personal foibles – do much good for their neighbours and for the community, both within and beyond the boundaries of the Catholic Church. When I look at these people, it becomes impossible for me to think only of the sexual abuse cases and their cover-up or of the other scandals that have recently come to light. All over the world, I have met clergy working on the front line, wearing themselves out in the service of others. I see innumerable men and women who offer support to young and old, to poor and sick people, to those who have been given a raw deal in life, to those who suffer under their own failures.

This is not an idealistic vision of the Church or a mere Utopian projection, but an empirical fact that is confirmed by many other Catholics and Christians generally, and that explains why they, too, do not wish to leave or do away with the Church. And this is the Church with which I can still identify: the global community of committed believers, a community that extends beyond the narrow boundaries of individual denominations. This community of faith is the true Church. Of course, I do not exclude popes, cardinals, bishops or all manner of prelates from this Church, nor do I exclude the dignitaries of other churches either. But, for me, all of these officeholders, who represent the Church as a concrete visible institution, are of secondary importance, since, according to the New Testament, they should only be the servants and not the masters: 'not that we lord it over your faith, but we work with you for your joy' (cf. 2 Corinthians 1:24). After all, it was not without reason that, in its constitution on the Church, the Second Vatican Council deliberately placed Chapter II on the 'People of God' in front of Chapter III on the hierarchical structure of the Church, although it could not prevent the Curia from scandalously tampering with the text of that chapter. This priority set by the Council should not merely apply in theory but also in practice. In the current reality of the Catholic Church, unfortunately, this is seldom the case.

For the time being, we must wait and see if Pope Francis will prove to be a pope in the tradition of Pope John XXIII, who better fitted St Gregory the Great's description of the papal office as 'Servant of the Servants of God' than the concept behind the customary titles of more recent origin, 'Holy Father' and 'Your Holiness', that set the pope above his episcopal confreres and give him a quasi-divine status. At the moment, Pope Francis is giving mixed signals. Although he has introduced a new, more simple and humble style into the Vatican, there are also indications that he will take the same hard line on dogmatic, moral and disciplinary issues that his immediate predecessors have taken. And, in the same vein, there are currently relatively few bishops who convincingly demonstrate that they are independent servants of their dioceses rather than compliant servants of the Roman Curia. In any case, I speak for myself and many others of like mind in saying that we are not Christians because of the church hierarchy and we are not Catholics because of the pope in Rome.

I give thanks to another and higher authority (and to many helpful fellow men and women) that my belief has remained unshaken: not my belief in the Church as an institution, but my belief in Jesus Christ, in his person and cause, which remain as the original core of the good traditions of the Church, of its liturgy and theology, and which, despite all of the undeniable decadence and corruption in the Church, have never disappeared and never will. The name of Jesus Christ is like a golden thread in the often torn and besmirched (and, therefore, constantly cleaned and rewoven) fabric of the Church in the course of its history.

And, therefore, at the end of this first chapter I will return to my initial question: 'Can we save the Catholic Church?' Yes we can, but only if the spirit of Jesus Christ moves our whole community of faith anew and endows the leadership of the Church with new credibility, understanding and acceptance. That, in turn, depends on those of us who together constitute this community of believers and who are open to the breath of the Holy Spirit, which moves where and as it wills.

Much of what prevents people from being open to the Spirit will be described in the next chapters. I will show how the church community is suffering under the Roman system of power. This system developed gradually, beginning in the first century AD, and was being claimed, theoretically at least, in Rome by the middle of the first millennium. Outside of Rome, however, it found little acceptance until around the end of the first millennium and the first centuries of the second millennium, and then only in the West – with fatal consequences for all of Christianity. It is necessary to soberly and precisely analyse this Roman system to discover whether the Catholic Church could not, perhaps, be saved if it ceased to be enslaved to this system.

CHAPTER 2

THE ROMAN SYSTEM

Seven Myths and the Problems They Have Caused

Whether academic or popular, criticism of the Church often lacks historical depth. Some things are described as 'fundamentally Catholic', even if they developed during a later stage of Catholicism, and, conversely, other things are dismissed as being utterly 'non-Catholic' even though they had been present from the beginning and existed for centuries. What is urgently required, therefore, is a well-founded historical analysis that can shed more light on the matter.

To make an accurate diagnosis of an illness, one must not merely look at the symptoms; one must get to the causes. A diagnosis of the Church's illness, therefore, must take into account the most recent scientific research: Catholic and non-Catholic historians alike now agree on many points that were once debated between Catholic apologists and non-Catholic critics. The no-longer-contested findings of modern historians make uncomfortable reading for the Roman Curia and their supporters, and so they continue to ignore them, not just in theory but also in practice, a fact eloquently documented by the many unheard, historically well-founded demands for reform. Hence, a comprehensive anamnesis – a re-membering

– of the Church's history, seeking to understand the origins and development of the Church's illness, is imperative. Without such an anamnesis there is no question of a cure.

During my years as a student in Rome, I dutifully listened as a tame, domesticated history of the Roman Catholic Church was recounted, and this left me unsatisfied. Since my early days as a young professor, I have repeatedly turned my attention to historical studies. My long project of anamnesis is reflected and documented, with abundant references and concrete details, in many of my books.

Many conservative readers, after reading this highly critical book, will no doubt object that I have not dealt with the positive sides of the Church, but the positive aspects of the Catholic Church have all been set forth at length in my previous books. To repeat them here would only distract from the problem at hand. In particular, my book *The Church*, published over forty-five years ago, is still considered topical and relevant and, translated into many different languages, is still used as a classic textbook in universities today. My books *Christianity: Its Essence and History* (1995) and *The Catholic Church: A Short History* (2001) present detailed, systematic accounts of the Catholic Church's overall historical development. The present book, therefore, does not deal with the history of the Church in general, but with the Church's specific medical history, and the causes of the illness of the Church. As already discussed, I will concentrate here on problems with the Church's constitution and with the central Roman institution of power, the papacy.

It is time to investigate a long and chequered history. Let us start at the beginning.

1. Peter – the First Pope?

Anamnesis

Rome, even papal Rome, was not built in a day. There is no doubt that, from early on, the Church located in the city of Rome, the capital of the Roman empire, and widely renowned for its efficient organization, effective charitable activities and numerous martyrs, played an important role. As a refuge of orthodoxy against Gnosticism and other heresies, it played a key role in formulating the baptismal creed, in limiting the canon of the works included in the New Testament, and, last but not least, as the city with the graves of the two chief apostles, St Peter and St Paul, in developing the tradition of apostolic succession.

But on a closer look, which of these elements can be verified historically? There is no word in the New Testament of St Peter himself ever having visited Rome. Nor is there any unequivocal reference to an immediate successor to St Peter (in Rome of all places). According to the writings of St Matthew, it was St Peter's personal faith in Christ and not that of his successors that was and remains the 'rock', the eternal foundation, on which Jesus built his Church (Matthew 16:18).

On the other hand, the First Epistle of Clement, dating from AD 96, and the letters of Ignatius of Antioch, written around the transition from the first to the second century, do explicitly state that Peter stayed in Rome and they testify to his martyrdom there. This tradition is therefore very old and, significantly, there are no rival witnesses to contradict it. Even in Antioch, while there is ample evidence in the Acts of the Apostles that St Peter stayed there for a lengthy period of time, no one has ever claimed that the grave of St Peter is located there. As yet, at least, it has not been possible to verify archaeologically whether the grave of St Peter lies underneath the current Vatican basilica, although there are significant indications. More importantly, however, there are no reliable early witnesses that St Peter, an uneducated Galilean fisherman called Simon, who stands in sharp contrast to St Paul, a Roman citizen fluent in Greek, ever functioned as the 'overseer' or *epískopos* (the term from which the word 'bishop' derives) of the Church in Rome. He was clearly the spokesman for the circle of disciples around Jesus before Jesus' death and resurrection, and he continued to exercise this function for some time afterwards, as long as the circle of disciples remained together in Jerusalem and later in Antioch and the surrounding regions. But there is no evidence of his exercising such a function from the city of Rome; under no circumstances can he be called 'Prince of the Apostles' in any modern sense of the term 'prince'. The evidence, on the contrary, indicates that the monarchical episcopacy was introduced only at a relatively late date in the city of Rome, probably shortly after the beginning of the second century, at least thirty years after Peter's martyrdom. However, already in around the year 160 monuments were raised to Peter and Paul, both of whom were presumably martyred during Nero's persecution of Christians in Rome around AD 64 to 68. It was the graves of the two chief apostles that served, in the first centuries, as the principal justification for the claim to a limited primacy accorded to the church of Rome, although *not* yet to the bishop of the city.

But does that make Rome 'the mother of all churches' as is proclaimed in the pretentious inscription adorning the basilica of St John Lateran, the original cathedral church of the Diocese of Rome: '*Caput et mater omnium ecclesiarum urbis et orbis*' ('Head and mother of all the churches of the city and of the earth')? By no means! The head and mother church of early Christianity was incontestably Jerusalem, not Rome. And to this day there still exist any number of churches in the East such as Antioch, Ephesus, Thessalonica, Corinth and others that were founded by apostles completely independently of Rome and its bishop. To this day, these churches insist on their apostolic origin and heritage.

There can be no question, during the first centuries, of the diocese of Rome and its bishop enjoying any jurisdictional primacy over the whole Church, or even of a biblically based claim to primacy without any jurisdictional authority. The Petrine promise of the Gospel of St Matthew (16:18), which, from the middle of the first millennium, has customarily been cited as the biblical justification for the papal claim to primacy – 'You are Peter and upon this rock I will build my church' – and which ostentatiously adorns the interior of St Peter's Basilica in enormous black letters on a golden background, finds no corroborating mention in any of the other Gospels. And, with one exception, these words were never quoted, in full at least, in any of the Christian writings before the middle of the third century – the exception being a text by the controversial church father Tertullian who quoted the passage not with reference to Rome and its bishop but with reference to St Peter. It was only in the middle of the third century that Bishop Stephen of Rome (254–7) cited the promise made to Peter to assert his authority in quarrels with bishops in Spain, the Province of Africa and Asia Minor. But he met with vigorous opposition led by Bishop Cyprian of Carthage, who rejected not only Stephen's decisions and the theology behind them, but also his claims to possess the better apostolic tradition and to exercise jurisdiction over other churches. As it happens, Stephen's positions on the readmission of lapsed Christians to the sacraments and the validity of baptism performed by heretical and excommunicated priests eventually prevailed, but not by virtue of any decisive papal authority over the other churches. On the contrary, the idea that one church could exercise authority over all the others was generally rejected by bishops and theologians outside of the Roman sphere for centuries to come.

Thus, Rome enjoyed no jurisdictional primacy during the first centuries, and that is understandable, because jurisdictional primacy belonged to the emperor alone. As *pontifex maximus*, the emperor enjoyed a monopoly on legislation that extended even to church matters (*ius in sacris*). After the Christianization of the Roman empire in the fourth century and for many centuries to come, it was the emperor who exercised the highest legal authority in the Church as in the State. He was the highest administrative instance with supervisory authority that extended even to the Roman community and its bishops. Without previously consulting any bishops, much less the bishop of Rome, Constantine, also known as Constantine the Great, convened the First Ecumenical Council in 325 at his new residency in Nicaea, east of Byzantium/Constantinople, and he issued laws, professions of faith and other prescriptions regulating the order of the Church. He confirmed the decisions made at the Council of Nicaea and enforced them throughout the empire. He also revamped the organization of the Church to conform to that of the empire, with the bishoprics of each civil province being placed under the authority of the 'metropolitan' bishop ruling in the provincial capital city.

Roughly four centuries after Constantine, a document was forged based on legends invented in the fifth century, bearing the title *Donation of Constantine*. According to this forgery – widely accepted at face value in the West for centuries – Constantine, in 315 or 317, conferred on Pope Sylvester and his successors explicit supremacy over the ancient patriarchal sees of Alexandria, Antioch, Constantinople and Jerusalem, as well as over 'all the churches of God in the whole earth'. In addition to administrative rights over estates owned by individual churches throughout the empire, it gave the pope authority over the city of Rome and over the whole Western part of the Roman empire, implying a right to appoint and depose civil rulers there. Finally it gave him the right to various imperial insignia. Although this forgery soon found its way into collections of canon law, surprisingly, it was cited in support of papal claims only from the middle of the eleventh century on, particularly in the struggles of the popes with the Holy Roman emperors and with other secular leaders. It is the prime example of a whole series of far-reaching forgeries, which, even when they did not originate in Roman circles, were used effectively to justify and promote the ascendancy of the Roman see and its bishop to a position of monarchic primacy in the West. In the East, however, where the Eastern Roman emperor continued to rule, this process of papal self-inflation was met only with incomprehension and incredulity.

First Diagnosis

The fact that, during the course of the first Christian centuries, first the church in the city of Rome as a whole, and then only later, and gradually, its bishop came to enjoy a central position in the Church is incontestable. From the history of the rise of Rome and its bishop to leadership in the Church, we can learn to appreciate how a papal ministry of service to the unity of the Church centred in Rome and founded on the traditions of the two chief apostles, St Peter and St Paul, could still benefit Christendom in the twenty-first century, provided that the role played by this centre is exercised in the spirit of the Gospel. But there is nothing in the New Testament or in the early history of the Church that supports a claim to domination or jurisdictional primacy by either the Apostle Peter or the church in Rome, and much less by its bishop. In fact, as we shall see later, most often the exercise of this claim promoted neither unity nor harmonious interaction, but increased dissension and even led to schism. In the twenty-first century there is even less likelihood that any claim to primacy in a jurisdictional sense will find acceptance in Christendom. Nor does the constant repetition and pompous celebration of the Roman ideology of primacy and power help when the claim itself is built on sand. The only thing that might help to restore the credibility of this institution is a frank, self-critical reflection on the humble and often fallible role played by the biblical figure of Peter and on the unpretentious services performed by the early Roman church, in the form of what Ignatius of Antioch, in his *Letter to the Church of Rome*, written probably around AD 110, called a 'primacy of love'. In short, the Church needs a Petrine ministry, not a Petrine primacy.

2. Early Assertions of the Roman Claim to Primacy

Anamnesis

There was never a 'Donation of Constantine'. What did happen was that, in AD 330, Emperor Constantine I transferred the imperial capital from 'old' Rome on the Tiber to 'new' Rome on the banks of the Bosporus, initiating a gradual decline of Roman imperial power in the West and even in the city of Rome itself. This shift of the centre of power towards the East was accompanied and intensified by the movement of Germanic tribes into the growing power vacuum in the West, resulting, in the year 410, in the first sack of the proud 'eternal city' of Rome, which had not been conquered since the times of the Roman Republic. Taken together, these two developments created a power vacuum in the West. In the fourth and fifth centuries, certain power-hungry Roman bishops capitalized on this vacuum and used it to expand their authority, aiming at universal primacy in the ecclesiastical sphere and universal sovereignty in the political sphere.

Let us briefly look at the changes that gradually became church law *per viam facti* (i.e. as a result of concrete actions of individual popes and their supporters). For the most part, they are still contained in canon law today, despite the fact that they lack biblical or theological foundation:

- Rome declared itself to be the general court of appeal for the whole Church (Bishop Julius in the middle of the fourth century based this claim on an erroneous interpretation of the Council of Nicaea in 325).

- The popes and their supporters began to interpret Jesus' singling out of Peter, and especially the words recorded in Matthew 16:18, in a strictly juridical sense and used them to bolster Roman claims to supremacy. At the same time, they laid claim to the title 'Apostolic See' (*sedes apostolica*) as an exclusive Roman privilege, completely ignoring the existence of other 'apostolic sees' in the East (Bishop Damasus in the fourth century).

- The bishop of Rome began to call himself 'pope': 'papa', from the Greek *pappas*, was an affectionate honorific for one's father, and had long since been one of the names used for all bishops in the Eastern part of the Roman empire, but in the West it was now appropriated by the bishop of Rome, who claimed exclusive right to its use. At about the same time, the popes also began to adorn their own decrees ('*statuta*') with the attribute 'apostolic', and adopted the style and terminology customarily used in the official civil documents issued by imperial Rome. Thus, inquiries sent to Rome by other bishops were now answered by curt *decreta* and *responsa* (Bishop Siricius at the end of the fourth century).

- The popes now demanded that every important matter, after it had been discussed and resolved in a synod of bishops anywhere in the West, must now be submitted to the bishop of Rome for his review and given binding authority by his approval and proclamation (Bishop Innocent at the beginning of the fifth century).

- All further appeals against Roman decisions were barred; judgements passed by the bishop of Rome were to be accepted as final and binding (Bishop Boniface in the fifth century).

And thus began the gradual process of the church in Rome, and particularly its bishop, monopolizing titles and legal rights that had originally belonged to many churches and their bishops or to the civil rulers, a process which continues to the present day. However, it should be noted that, during this early period, all of these historical 'facts' remained little more than empty claims. Particularly in Constantinople, where ultimate authority still rested solely with the emperor and where the city of Rome was generally looked down upon as merely the run-down capital of former times, such claims were completely disregarded. Thus, all attempts made by the bishops of Rome in the fourth and fifth centuries to assert and to exercise a divinely ordained, ruling primacy (*iurisdictio*) extending to the whole of the Church, based on Jesus' choice of Peter and the promise made to him, had little or no real effect.

Even Augustine, that brilliant contemporary of many of these Roman bishops, who was himself bishop of Hippo Regius in North Africa and by far the most important theologian in the West, and one, moreover, who was positively inclined towards Rome, gave no more credence to the Roman bishops' claim to universal jurisdictional primacy than did his great North African predecessor, Cyprian, the great bishop of Carthage, 200 years earlier. In Augustine's final major work, his monumental *City of God*, the pope plays no role at all. For Augustine, all bishops were essentially equal. Although he regarded Rome as the centre of the empire and of the Church, Augustine gave no encouragement whatsoever to papalism, and he did not believe that Rome could legitimately claim supremacy or jurisdictional primacy over all the churches. For Augustine, the foundation of the Church does not rest on the person of Peter, much less on the persons of his successors, but instead on Christ and belief in Christ – a point that the young Joseph Ratzinger himself quite openly discussed and even defended in his 1953 doctoral dissertation on Augustine. For Augustine, the highest authority of the Church did not rest with the bishop of Rome but instead – in complete agreement with the entire Christian East – in the ecumenical council bringing together the bishops from all over the world. Moreover, not even to such an ecumenical council did Augustine ascribe any infallible authority.

Second Diagnosis

On its own turf in the West, Rome increasingly laid claim to having a special and separate tradition. The Church was now viewed primarily, in a legal sense, as a monarchically structured, absolutistic and centralistic unified Church, grounded, for the most part, in Roman canon law and on (largely forged) Roman decrees that were completely unknown in the Eastern part of the empire. In contrast, the view which prevailed in the other churches, especially in the east and in North Africa (Tertullian, Cyprian, Augustine) was the notion, based on the New Testament, of the Church as a *koinonia* or *communio*, i.e. a community of believers and of local churches and their bishops in a collegially organized group of churches sharing common sacraments, liturgical arrangements and symbols of belief. Outside the Roman sphere of authority and influence, this notion has remained in force up to the present day.

3. The First True Pope and His Rome-centred Ideology

Anamnesis

In the generation following Augustine, the leading figure was Pope Leo I (440–61), a sound theologian and jurist, a fervent preacher and pastoral minister, and a highly capable states- man, who came to be known as 'Leo the Great'. He was the first Roman bishop to whom historians give the title 'pope' in what has become the classical sense of the term.

Filled with a sense of Rome's mission, Leo forged the classic synthesis of the idea of Roman primacy. Contrary to the bibli- cal text, Leo interpreted the Petrine passages in the New Testament in a strictly legal sense as a 'fullness of power' (*plen- itudo potestatis*) given to St Peter and thus as a primacy conferred on the bishop of Rome, making him head of the entire Church. Leo's idea of the bishop of Rome as the succes- sor to St Peter was based on a (forged) letter purportedly sent by Pope Clement to St James, the brother of Jesus, in Jerusalem. According to this epistle Peter, in a final testamentary disposi- tion, had appointed Clement to be his sole legitimate successor. Using the Roman law of hereditary succession, Leo defined the legal status of Peter's successor more precisely. While Peter's successors did not inherit his personal attributes and merits, they did inherit the official authority and function conferred upon him by Christ. Thus, even an unworthy pope could be a fully legitimate successor of Peter and could act as such. Leo was the first bishop of Rome to adorn himself with the pagan priestly title of *pontifex maximus*, which only shortly before had been discarded by the Byzantine emperors in

Constantinople. In 451, Leo the Great, seconded by a delegation of Roman notables, succeeded in deterring the Huns massed in Mantua under the leadership of Attila from conquering Rome. Four years later, however, he was unable to prevent the Vandals from sacking Rome.

Notwithstanding the profound influence that Leo the Great enjoyed in the West with his Roman theology and politics, his ideas carried no weight at all in the Eastern Catholic Church, which, at that time, was still the more important one. Nowhere is this more evident than in Leo's bitter setbacks at the Fourth Ecumenical Council at Chalcedon (451). His demand that his legates should preside over the Council was refused outright. In the face of this explicit prohibition, Leo's *Tome* – an official letter setting forth the Roman position on the union of divine and human natures in the one person of Christ in terms reminiscent of Augustine – was first examined by the Council to determine whether or not its teaching corresponded to orthodox faith. The fact that the Council, after this scrutiny, enthusiastically approved Leo's formulations with the acclamation, so triumphantly cited by Vatican apologists, that 'Peter has spoken through Leo!' must not be overrated. This acclamation was not a blanket acknowledgement that the pope is *a priori*, i.e. always and everywhere and of his nature, the (infallible) mouthpiece of Peter; instead, it applied only to this particular case at hand and then only *a posteriori*, namely after the Council's own examination of the matter had confirmed it. Similarly, the Council's request that Leo confirm its decisions was not an admission that these decisions had no binding force without such papal confirmation, but was only the usual polite request to the patriarch of Rome, who had not himself taken part in the Council except through his delegates, that he now personally concur with the conciliar decisions and enforce them in the West.

In fact, the Council neither acknowledged nor granted Leo any special privileges or prerogatives extending his authority to the whole Church. Instead, it declared that the ecclesiastical rank of a city should depend upon its civilian status in the empire. Thus, it accorded to the see of Constantinople, the New Rome and contemporary imperial capital, the same honour and authority that the see of ancient Rome, the former imperial capital, had enjoyed from antiquity. In this huge assembly with its 600 members, the vigorous protests of the Roman legates against this act of conciliar autonomy went unheard, and Leo's subsequent personal protests against this decision fell on equally deaf ears in the East. In short, although the bishop of Rome emphatically had claimed here to exercise a juridical primacy, this claim was not accepted by the more important, Eastern half of the Church.

Leo was the first bishop of Rome to be buried in St Peter's. His successors continued to act along the same theological and political lines. In the pontificate of Gelasius I, at the end of the fifth century, the Roman claim to papal supremacy experienced a brief apogee, but this was only possible because the pope enjoyed the protection of the Arian Ostrogoth king of Italy, Theodoric. Thus he was able to unfold his notion of papal power along the lines of Augustine's doctrine of the 'Two Kingdoms', developed in his famous *City of God*, into a claim that the papacy is entirely independent of the emperor in Byzantium. According to Gelasius' theory, emperor and pope have two different functions within the same community; the emperor possesses only earthly, temporal authority; whereas the pope enjoys sacerdotal, spiritual authority. But the spiritual authority is superior to the temporal authority of the emperor, because it is responsible for the sacraments, and it bears responsibility for the temporal rulers before God. This doctrine entirely withdrew the clergy from the temporal order and from the jurisdiction of temporal courts. This combined Leonine/Gelasian doctrine has been called the *Magna Carta* of Medieval papacy by the great Medieval historian Walter Ullmann.

Third Diagnosis

The concept of papal primacy as outlined by Pope Leo I represents the classical formulation, in the patristic period, of the Roman claim to supreme authority. From that point on, it was constantly reiterated, defended, cast into diverse forms of canon laws, and finally, some 1,500 years later, in 1870, it was solemnly defined to be a dogma of the faith by the First Vatican Council. But the truth remains: the massive legalistic reinterpretation of a 'fullness of power' (*plenitudo potestatis*), purportedly bestowed by Christ himself on Peter as a reward for Peter's faith, has no solid foundation in either the New Testament or the great traditions of the universal Church of the first millennium. There are even fewer foundations for a claim by the bishop of Rome to be the heir of such a 'fullness of power' over the whole Church. The epistle quoted by Leo I purporting to have been written by Pope Clement to James, brother of Jesus, in Jerusalem is nothing more than a crude second-century forgery, which had been translated into Latin only in the fourth or fifth century, roughly at the time of Leo the Great himself.

In the Middle Ages, the teachings of Popes Leo and Gelasius were elaborated into the doctrine of two distinct, divinely established powers, regal and sacerdotal, symbolized by the 'two swords' mentioned in Luke 22:38. For some 600 years the precise relationship between these two powers by divine right remained unclear: only in the eleventh-century investiture struggle, when the German Emperor Henry IV appealed to this doctrine to justify his unlimited authority in worldly affairs, did the popes reply with the counter-assertion of the superiority of the sacerdotal–papal power over the regal, e.g. in the thesis paper entitled *Dictatus papae* found in the Vatican archives for 1075 under Pope Gregory VII. The assertion of absolute papal supremacy reached its apex in the bull *Unam sanctam*, issued by Pope Boniface VIII in 1302 against the king of France, Philip IV the Fair, in the struggle over the control of the French clergy.

Nevertheless, these claims, controversially discussed by the theologians and canonists of the Middle Ages, remained for many centuries merely an expression of Roman wishful thinking. Only much later, in the wake of the Reformation and the Enlightenment, did it develop its own historical dynamic. Thus, the call for a 'Catholic state' curtailing civil liberties, which was a hallmark of Roman political theology until the mid-twentieth century, when it was overthrown by the Second Vatican Council, rested on this doctrine, which completely ignored other factors essential to an adequate theology of the Church–State relationship.

4. Erring Popes, Papal Forgeries and Papal Proceedings

Anamnesis

The inflation of papal claims to power during the period of the Germanic migrations in the fourth and fifth centuries met severe setbacks in the sixth and seventh centuries. In the sixth century, Emperor Justinian, who ruled from Byzantium-Constantinople, effected a sweeping restoration of the authority of the Imperium Romanum even in Western regions like Italy, the Balkans, southern Spain and North Africa. He ordered the building of the Hagia Sophia cathedral in Constantinople as the great church of Christendom, and he re-established the principle of a state church subject to the emperor.

He let the bishops of Rome clearly feel the emperor's juridical supremacy. The new Rome enjoyed not merely equal footing with the old Rome, but, in important respects, was accorded a rank superior to that of old Rome. While the patriarchs and metropolitans of the Eastern Catholic Church accepted the pope as the bishop of the old imperial capital and as the sole patriarch for the Western Church, they regarded him as merely *primus inter pares* ('first among equals'), not by virtue of some biblical promise or juridical transfer of power, but solely because old Rome was the place where the two chief Apostles, St Peter and St Paul, were buried.

Even in Rome itself, during this period, no one considered the bishop of Rome to be infallible; the errors committed by popes of the time were only too much in evidence. Even 1,500 years later, at the time of the First Vatican Council in 1870, two famous cases of erring popes were still being fiercely discussed, and, at the Council itself, the Tübingen church historian and bishop of Rottenburg Karl Joseph von Hefele cited them as a conclusive argument against the notion of papal infallibility. But his arguments were ignored by the powerful Curia and the majority of the Council fathers. The first case was that of Pope Vigilius, who lost all credibility at the Fifth Ecumenical Council in Constantinople (553) due to his vacillating theological positions and was therefore denied burial in St Peter's Basilica and remained proscribed for centuries, even in the West. The second case was that of Honorius I, pope from 625 to 638, who, some forty years after his death, was condemned as a heretic at the Sixth Ecumenical Council of Constantinople (681), not just for holding false theological opinions but for promoting heresy by his official actions as pope. This condemnation was explicitly affirmed by Pope Leo II, 682–3, when he confirmed the acts of the Council, including the condemnation of Honorius's actions as pope, and officially propagated this in the West in letters written to the king, the bishops and the nobles of Spain. Honorius's condemnation was reaffirmed by the Seventh Ecumenical Council of Nicaea in 787 and by the Council of Constantinople (869–70) – the Eighth Ecumenical Council according to Roman Catholic reckoning – both of which also received papal approval. Furthermore, from the eighth to the eleventh centuries, all new popes had to swear, before taking office, that they affirmed the condemnation of Honorius pronounced by the Sixth Ecumenical Council. Evidently, popes can err, even when they act officially as pope!

Despite such embarrassments, the popes resolutely continued to expand their claims to power with the aid of three major forgeries:

1. The *Donation of Constantine* has already been mentioned above. It is based on a completely fictitious legend, fabricated in the fifth or sixth century, about Pope Sylvester I, of whom little is known except that he reigned from 314 to 335. The document itself was forged, probably in the eighth century, and proved to be a very effective instrument in the assertion of papal supremacy, especially in the thirteenth and fourteenth centuries, until it was finally exposed as a forgery by the Italian priest and humanist scholar Lorenzo Valla in 1439–40. According to the legend, Emperor Constantine, in gratitude for being cured of leprosy, received baptism at the hands of Pope Sylvester in 315 or 317 and as a reward conferred on the see of Peter authority over the city of Rome and the whole Western part of the Roman empire. He granted the pope the use of imperial insignia and vestments (the imperial purple), and permitted him a princely retinue commensurate with his imperial rank. Furthermore, Constantine is said to have given the pope supremacy over all the other churches, in particular over the patriarchal sees of Antioch, Alexandria, Constantinople and Jerusalem. The only historical truth behind the tale is that Constantine handed over to the bishop of Rome the Lateran palace (formerly the residence of Roman officials and later the property of his second wife Fausta Flavia Maxima), together with the refurbished basilica of St John the Lateran and the new basilica of St Peter's on the Vatican, the construction of which Constantine himself had ordered.

2. The Symmachean forgeries are a collection of documents produced in the papal Curia of Pope Symmachus (498–514), the second successor to Pope Gelasius. Among other things these forgeries coined the fateful dictum: '*prima sedes a nemine iudicatur*', which asserts that the *prima sedes* ('the principal see'), i.e. the pope, can be judged by no other authority, not even by the emperor or any civil or ecclesiastical court. The historical truth, however, is that the popes were repeatedly judged by secular as well as ecclesiastical authorities. For example, the Ostrogoth king Theodoric the Great, himself an Arian Christian, summarily threw Pope John I into prison after he failed to accomplish the mission in Constantinople that the king had sent him to perform there, and the pope eventually died in prison. The Emperor Justinian, in the course of his 40-year reign, summoned the bishops of Rome to appear at his court whenever he deemed it necessary and monitored the orthodoxy of their beliefs. After Justinian's decree of 555, the election of every bishop of Rome required the imperial *fiat* ('Let it be done!'), a practice that continued up to Carolingian times. Again and again in the sixth and seventh centuries, popes had to face formal court proceedings brought against them by the emperor, by the clergy, or even by the people of Rome (who still enjoyed the right of electing the pope!). These proceedings often ended with the deposition of the indicted pope. And such cases persisted until the fifteenth century.

3. The pseudo-Isidorian decretals, ascribed to the learned encyclopaedist St Isidore of Seville (*c.* 560–638) or to an otherwise unknown Isidore Mercator, were probably

fabricated in France in the ninth century at the time of the decline of the Carolingian empire by a group of talented clerical forgers. In the most widely received version, these forgeries comprise more than 700 closely printed pages. They include 115 complete fabrications passed off as decrees of early Roman bishops and 125 authentic documents that have been falsified by later interpolations and amendments. The aim of the forgeries was to weaken the authority exercised by the rulers over the churches and their bishops, including the popes, and the authority of archbishops over the other bishops within their territories; the effect, however, was to give an enormous boost to papal hegemony.

In Carolingian times, however, there was still no trace, even in the West, of any generally recognized juridical primacy enjoyed by the popes. Juridical primacy belonged to the Frankish rulers, as it had previously belonged to the Byzantine emperor, and the Frankish rulers saw themselves and behaved as the Church's divine right rulers. Scarcely half a century after Charlemagne, however, Pope Nicholas I (*c.* 800–867) appeared on the scene with a full-blown 'Petrine' understanding of the importance of his office. Boldly, he attempted to put an end to the age-old autonomy of the national churches and to bring them under the central authority of Rome. Not surprisingly, and probably not entirely in good faith, he embraced both the notorious pseudo-Isidorian forgeries and the forged *Donation of Constantine*.

Fourth Diagnosis

The forgeries are particularly nefarious because they create the fatal impression that, from earliest times, the Church had been governed by Rome down to the last detail. This meant an unprecedented inflation of papal power, which found expression in the new title of 'lord of the whole world' and was reinforced by an increasing number of papal decrees and judgements. The popes now claimed the exclusive right to convene and confirm synods, a right formerly exercised by the emperor. Bishops condemned for wrongdoing could now appeal to the pope, to whom the final decision on all 'matters of serious import' was now reserved. Even civil legislation that ran contrary to the canons and decrees of the pope was declared null and void.

The forgeries thus provided justification both for the absolutist rule of the pope over the Church and for the autonomy of the Church *vis-à-vis* the State. They clothed the papal claims, which in fact had only emerged after the middle of the fifth century, with an aura of venerable antiquity. The forgeries should not be seen as mere curiosities of a by-gone age; they provided precisely the theological–juridical legitimization that the papal claims had previously lacked. From then on, the Church in the West and the whole of Western canon law became entirely centred on Roman authority.

Pseudo-Isidore's collection soon spread over all of Western Europe and was incorporated into Gratian's *Decretum* of the twelfth century, which became not only the standard textbook of Medieval university courses in canon law, but also the opening document of the *Corpus Juris Canonici*, by which the Catholic Church was governed until the official codification of canon law in 1917. The authority of these forgeries remained unquestioned for centuries: even Luther appealed to some of the forged canons to disprove claims to papal and conciliar infallibility. Only around the middle of the sixteenth century did the team of Lutheran historians known as the Magdeburg Centuriators clearly demonstrate their falsity, but this had no consequences for subsequent Catholic canon law and did not even prevent individual provisions stemming from them from being taken over uncritically into the 1917 codification. Even in the Middle Ages, the papal chancellery itself should have been capable of recognizing the spurious character of these forgeries; already at the turn of the first millennium, Emperor Otto III had branded the *Donation of Constantine* as a forgery. But why should the Curia have done so, when the forgeries so eminently served Roman interests? The Curia was evidently less interested in historical truth than in protecting and expanding its own power. From a historical perspective, even the *Codex Iuris Canonici* promulgated by Pope John Paul II in 1983 has dubious authority, because it retains many provisions that originally trace back to this collection of forgeries. Honesty would demand that such canons either be expunged or at least be explicitly identified as resting on forgeries.

5. Unholy Fathers and Reforms

Anamnesis

'Holy Father' or 'His Holiness' are the most frequent titles used to address or refer to the pope. They reflect the attempt within the Vatican to surround all things papal with an aura of sacredness. The terms 'holy' and 'sacred' are attached to any number of Roman Catholic institutions, offices, objects and even persons, thus wrapping them in a cloak of eternal radiance. Those who take such honorific titles all too literally might be reminded that many popes, not only in the distant past, but also more recently, were anything but 'holy', and that the lifestyle of the papal court often failed to impress contemporary witnesses as being particularly saintly. The power-mongering Nicholas I, who had so loudly claimed Roman primacy, was succeeded by a series of weak and even downright corrupt popes.

Small wonder that the tenth century in church history is called the *saeculum obscurum*, not inappropriately translated as the 'dark age'. Over dozens of gory pages, honest histories of the papacy describe the innumerable intrigues and conflicts, murders and acts of violence committed by the popes and the papal court during this period. Popes alternated with anti-popes stemming from the rival families of the Roman aristocracy. Think of the dreadful and bizarre posthumous trial of Pope Formosus (891–6) at the notorious 'Cadaver Synod' of 897. Nine months after Formosus's death, his successor once removed, Pope Stephen VI (or VII), ordered his exhumation and staged a mock trial of the putrefying corpse, dressed in full papal regalia and propped up on the papal throne, which resulted in the annulment of his election and all of his acts, the hacking off of the fingers of his right hand by which he had conferred sacraments and blessings, and the uniceremonious disposal of his corpse in the Tiber. Equally notorious is the reign of terror from 924 to 933 of the '*senatrix*' Marozia, described in contemporary records as being the mistress of one pope (Sergius III), the murderess of a second (John X) and the mother of a third (her illegitimate son John XI). She kept the latter prisoner in Castel Sant'Angelo in Rome until she herself was overthrown and imprisoned in 932/933 by her son Alberic from a previous marriage. Alberic then ruled Rome for two decades as '*dux et senator Romanorum*', with the popes acting as his submissive tools.

The popes of the tenth century were clearly unable to pull themselves out of the swamp of corruption by their own boot-straps. This task was undertaken by the increasingly powerful rulers of the Eastern Frankish empire, who now styled themselves 'Holy Roman Emperors of the German Nation'. Inspired by his role model Charlemagne, the Saxon Emperor Otto I the Great (912–73) called a Roman synod in 963 to depose the youthful Pope John XII for dishonourable conduct, insurrection and refusing to take an oath of obedience to his imperial authority. In John's place, Otto engineered the election of a layman, who took the name Leo VIII and who within a single day received all the required sacraments and consecrations, following a procedure which remained legal up until the new *Codex Iuris Canonici* of 1983. For centuries to come, depositions and appointments of popes by either the Roman populace or the emperor remained the order of the day, resulting in an alternating series of popes and anti-popes, not a few of whom either murdered their rivals or were murdered themselves in their turn.

The urgently needed reform of the papacy began only at the end of the first millennium, led, for the most part, by members of the monastic reform movement that began at the Abbey of Cluny in Burgundy at the beginning of the tenth century. This movement was marked not only by its strict observance of the Benedictine rule but also by its centralized organization, which transformed the hitherto loosely organized Benedictine family into the first religious order in the modern sense, well-suited to acting as an agent of Roman ecclesiastical politics. In exchange for direct subordination to the pope, exemption was granted to the Cluniac order as a whole by way of a papal privilege which freed the individual monasteries from the supervision of the local bishops – in direct contravention of a decree by the Council of Nicaea – but also entailed payment of an annual fee to Rome. This institution provided the papacy not only with enormous revenues but also with a close-knit network of prosperous operational bases across much of Europe.

The reform of the papacy, however, was actually carried out not so much by the Cluniac monks acting on their own, but rather by the German kings and emperors. It was King Henry III who had three rival popes deposed at the synods of Sutri and Rome in 1046. Bishop Suidger of Bamberg was then nominated by King Henry III and, according to tradition, he was then elected pope by the clergy and people of Rome; he took the name Clement II but ruled for only a year until his untimely death in 1057. Thus the sordid series of corrupt popes stemming from and created by the Roman aristocracy was followed by a series of mainly German popes loyal to the emperor and open to reform. Unwittingly, however, it was this series of good popes who would go on to create the basis for the papacy as the greatest rival to the Holy Roman emperor.

Fifth Diagnosis

The papacy has gone through phases of appalling decadence, relieved by phases of reform. The reform impulses often came from outside the papacy itself. Theologically, during the times when unworthy popes held office, apologists for the papacy resorted to distinguishing between the 'objective' office and the 'subjective' officeholder. Augustine had already introduced this distinction in order to repel the Donatists, who held that all baptisms and sacraments performed by bishops or priests who had fallen away from the faith during the time of the Diocletian persecutions (the so-called *lapsi*) were automatically invalid. In contrast, Augustine argued for a differentiation between a person and his office: thus even personally unholy popes could validly perform holy actions, not only sacramental, but also administrative, which meant that even unworthy popes could theoretically keep the institution of the papacy alive.

In summary, the papacy has only ever been kept alive by repeated reforms. The decadence of the tenth century was followed by the Gregorian reforms of the eleventh century, much as the decadence of the papacy during the Renaissance in the fifteenth century was followed by the Reformation in the sixteenth century, which, unfortunately, split the Church because Rome refused to carry out the reforms that were really needed. Thus the Reformation was followed by a Counter-Reformation, which, despite its impressive achievements in politics, Baroque art and the reform of pastoral care, only confirmed and cemented the Medieval *status quo* with regard to the papacy, the liturgy, theology and church discipline.

6. From the Roman Principle to the Roman System

Anamnesis

Under the Lotharingian Pope Leo IX (1049–54) – himself a relative of the Holy Roman Emperor Henry III – leadership of the reform movement passed to the pope himself. In five hectic years, Leo reformed the Roman urban clergy and made the cardinals (from the Latin *cardines*, i.e. the hinges of a door), who were the suburban bishops and the principal priests and deacons of the urban churches, into a kind of official papal senate. He also made cardinals of intelligent and highly motivated advocates of reform from beyond the Alps. Among these, the Lotharingian, Abbot Humbert, later cardinal-bishop of Silva Candida, stands out as a learned theoretician and shrewd promoter of absolutist papal supremacy. Another prominent figure was Archdeacon Hildebrand, who as the pope's legate travelled extensively in Italy, France and Germany, and for the first time brought home to the clergy in these lands the power of Peter's successor on earth.

It was the jurist and theologian Humbert of Silva Candida in particular who, as the pope's closest confidant, and as an adroit, often sarcastic stylist, laid out the full programme of papal claims in a broad range of publications and defended them in numerous papal writs and bulls. Humbert was an astute champion of the Roman principle, namely, that the papacy was the source of and standard for all laws, the highest instance with the right to sit in judgement on all others, but itself subject to no one's judgement. Humbert compared the role of the pope in the Church to that of the hinges of a door, the foundations of a building, the source of a stream and the mother of a family. The Church was to the State what the sun was to the moon, the soul to the body and the head to the limbs.

This Roman principle, making the papacy the source and measuring stick for all ecclesiastical (and in some versions even civil) legislation and in all cases the ultimate court of appeal, provides, to this day, the ideological basis for the Roman

System. A system (from the Greek: 'organized whole') is an entity compounded of interdependent components. A social system involves mutual interdependence of persons and institutions within an internal structure clearly set off from external factors and structures. The Roman System is an ecclesiastical system of power and domination in which the pope enjoys and exercises over the people and the institutions of the whole Church a monopoly of power and the right to determine what counts as truth. The foundations of this system were laid in the large-scale forgeries of the early Middle Ages and subsequently developed and implemented during the High Middle Ages.

The battle for absolute papal power was fought using the rallying cry *'libertas Ecclesiae'* ('the liberty of the Church'). This, however, by no means meant the freedom enjoyed by every Christian, which was such an important theme for St Paul, but rather was shorthand for the freedom of Church institutions, particularly the papacy, from any responsibility to or control by secular powers. The struggle of the popes to promote and defend the *libertas Ecclesiae* focused on two particularly sensitive areas: the appointment of bishops and other clergy by the laity and the issue of clerical marriage versus celibacy.

The traditional appointment of bishops by laymen, i.e. by the emperor or other rulers, which involved their investiture with secular rights and duties, was now denounced as 'simony', i.e., the sale or purchase of sacraments, sacred offices and privileges in the Church in return for remuneration, named after Simon Magus (whose story is recounted in Acts 8:9–24). The upshot of this struggle was an unprecedented growth of clericalism, giving the clergy not only predominance and pre-eminence within the Church itself, but also entailing numerous direct or indirect claims to clerical privilege within civil society as well.

The traditional marriage of priests was now condemned as 'concubinage' (from the Latin term for the illegal cohabitation of two persons of the opposite sex living together as man and wife) and was prosecuted accordingly. This reflected an ideal of pan-monasticism, which sought to impose monastic ideals and ways of life on the entire clergy. Viewed at a deeper level, however, it is a sign of broadly institutionalized misogyny and general hostility to human sexuality.

Together, this constituted a papal monopoly on power and truth, reinforced by juridicism and clericalism, institutionalized misogyny and hostility to human sexuality, and enforced, when need be, by cruel and brutal violence (inquisition, burnings, wars, crusades). This newly created system was pushed through radically and ruthlessly by Hildebrand, who ruled as Pope Gregory VII from 1073 until 1085 and who, as mentioned above, had for decades played a back-stage role as Roman archdeacon and papal legate to synods and on visitations. After Gregory became pope, he was so driven by his passionate convictions and adamant will that no resistance or opposition could thwart or deflect his efforts to put the Roman Catholic paradigm (P III) into concrete ecclesiastical and political practice, using all the means at his disposal to push through the system he himself had helped to develop. The 'Gregorian reforms', initiated already in part before he became pope, rightly bear his name today, but that name is also associated with the sordid history of the 'Investiture Controversy' between the papacy and the imperial power and with the humiliating, but politically shrewd, penitential trek of King Henry IV to Canossa.

Sixth Diagnosis

The Gregorian reforms amounted to a Gregorian revolution: a revolution from above. They gave birth to the absolutist papal monarchy of the following centuries, which had nothing to do, except in name, with the original collegial constitution of the Church described in the New Testament or with the federated church order that had prevailed throughout the previous millennium. This new order was propagated with the help of Roman policies, ideology and propaganda, purporting to represent the older order of the Church, but in fact resting on forged documents and, when need be, pitilessly implemented by physical force.

It took over 600 years, interrupted by innumerable setbacks and periods of decline, before the papacy was able fully to transform the original Latin Catholic paradigm, first outlined by Augustine and the fifth-century bishops of Rome, into the Roman System, thereby realizing the programme conceived in principle by Popes Leo I and Gelasius I: the sole and absolute reign by the pope over Church and State, allegedly harking back to St Peter, and ultimately to Jesus Christ himself.

In the eleventh century, the Church became 'Roman' through and through. As such, the church in Rome now demanded recognition as the mother (*mater*) and head (*caput*) of all the churches and as the one and only church to whom obedience and submission was due. At this time, a Roman mysticism of submission began to take form that still haunts the Catholic Church to this day, with submission to God meaning submission to the hierarchy, meaning submission to the pope; putting, in effect, the pope over God himself as he exercises his governing role in the world. Understandably, the consequences have been grave and disastrous.

7. The Roman System Splits the Unity of Christendom

To prevent any misunderstandings, let me make three things clear at the outset:

- The Roman System did, of course, have several positive aspects and real achievements. The Gregorian reforms made the Church visible and audible as an institution endowed with its own law, its own constitution and its own goals over and against the State.

- Major schisms in church history never have a single religious cause; they also have political, economic, cultural and psychological roots.

- The focus on the role of the papacy is a natural consequence of the central position of the bishop of Rome within the fabric of the Church. This focus is not meant to denigrate or obscure the other aspects of the Catholic Church: its liturgy, spirituality, charitable and cultural services. The aim is not to put exclusive blame on anybody, but to identify those who bear the principal responsibility for the first great schism that divided the Church at the beginning of the second millennium.

Anamnesis

For centuries, a separation of the Eastern and Western churches had been taking shape in the form of growing mutual alienation. This split, however, was boosted by the steady expansion and display of papal claims as described above, an expansion completely at odds with the early Christian tradition and with the traditions of the Eastern Church as a whole. Of course, cultural, religious, social and psychological factors played important roles in alienating the two parties: different languages (Greek versus Latin); different cultures (the Greeks appeared haughty, nit-picking and perfidious; the Romans ignorant and uncivilized); and different practices (different liturgical ceremonies and practices with regard to piety, theology, ecclesiastical law and organization).

But these cultural and religious differences, of themselves, need not have led to a schism. In the last analysis, it was the political differences within the church organization, above all the menacing growth of papal power, that was responsible for the schism. And, to this day, the papal claim to supremacy stands as the only serious obstacle to the re-establishment of an ecclesial communion reflecting once again the 'Church of the Seven Councils' (Nicaea I, 325, to Nicaea II, 787).

Seventh Diagnosis

A pope-centred notion of church unity remains to this day an unacceptable innovation in the eyes of the Eastern Church. The Eastern Church has never requested definitive papal decrees or responses; it has never requested papal exemptions for its monasteries; it has never tolerated the imposition of bishops by papal appointment. And it has certainly never recognized an absolute and direct juridical authority of the bishop of Rome over all other bishops and believers. But Rome, however, indefatigably continues to attempt, with all the means at its disposal – canonical, political and theological – to override the old church constitution, to extend its juridical supremacy to all the churches, including those of the East, and to push through a centralist constitution tailored to Rome and the pope.

The political conflict between East and West escalated in the seventh and eighth centuries. In 753/54 Pope Stephen II travelled to the King of the Franks to request military aid and to obtain guarantees for a papal state, created at the expense of former Byzantine territories. Later, on Christmas Day, 800, Pope Leo III – himself cleared only a few days before of charges of unbecoming conduct – high-handedly crowned Charlemagne, the King of the Franks, with the pompous title 'Charles, serene Augustus, crowned by God, peace-bringing great emperor ruling the Roman empire, and by the grace of God King of the Franks and the Lombards'. This title meant more than a mere restoration in the West of the ancient double empire; it was based on the claim that Constantinople had now lost its right to the imperial title, by reasons of heresy and the ascendency of a woman, Irene, who from 797 on had been ruling in Constantinople as sole 'emperor' (not 'empress'!) after dethroning her son and co-emperor. And the imperial office was conferred on Charlemagne by the grace of the pope, a hitherto unprecedented expression of papal claims to supremacy.

Later on in the ninth century, the arrogant Pope Nicholas I (858–67) wilfully and unjustly excommunicated the saintly Byzantine Patriarch Photius, a distinguished theologian and pastorally minded bishop, venerated in the East, for defending the traditional patriarchal autonomy against Roman encroachments and for resisting the unilateral Western insertion of the 'Filioque' clause into the universally accepted creeds formulated by the Councils. Under the successors of Nicholas, this schism was soon patched up and Photius enjoyed Roman recognition during his second term of office. But the next schism, that of the eleventh century, would not be patched up at all, and it has persisted to this day.

How Can This Open Wound Be Healed?

On 16 July 1054, the papal legate to Constantinople, the aforementioned Cardinal Humbert of Silva Candida, interrupted a liturgical celebration in the Hagia Sophia cathedral to deposit on the high altar a papal bull teeming with falsehoods and unfounded charges, which excommunicated the ecumenical patriarch of Constantinople, to which the patriarch replied by excommunicating the papal legates. Neither the fact that the patriarch was not entirely innocent in the foregoing conflict, nor the fact that the excommunications explicitly mentioned the individual persons of the patriarch and the papal legates, mitigates the fact that this arrogant assertion of papal supremacy – in fact invalid, because the pope had died in the meantime – inflicted a grave wound on the body of the Church which has still not healed even today, not even after the dramatic but merely symbolic act of 1965 in which Pope Paul VI, moved by the example of Pope John XXIII and the Second Vatican Council, joined with Patriarch Athenagoras I of Constantinople to nullify the mutual anathemas of 1054 and officially to 'remove [them] both from memory and from the midst of the Church' ('Joint Catholic–Orthodox Declaration of Pope Paul VI and the Ecumenical Patriarch Athenagoras I', 7 December 1965). Since then, the sorrowful history of growing estrangement that led to an outright separation 900 years ago is being reappraised by theologians and historians, and a modicum of accommodation and *modus vivendi* is being achieved. The popes and the patriarchs now exchange tokens of respect, meet regularly, and even pray together in the context of Eucharistic celebrations, but they have refrained from taking the next logical step of celebrating the Eucharist together.

After the sentences of excommunication had been withdrawn and after so much had been done to improve relations, it would have been consistent to officially re-establish the *communio*, i.e. the full fellowship of the Eucharistic celebration. Vatican II had already laid the foundations for this:

- According to the Council, the differences between the churches do not weaken the unity of the Church but strengthen it. In principle, the Eastern churches have equal standing with the Western church. They have the right and the duty to maintain their own independent liturgy, canonical laws and spirituality. This could be the basis for a new ecclesial fellowship between West and East.

- According to the Council, the ancient rights and privileges of the Eastern patriarchs already in communion with Rome have been confirmed or re-established.

But the disputed issue concerning Roman claims to primacy, which continue to be a point of contention between the Western and Eastern churches, must finally be discussed openly and brought to an ecumenical solution based on the seven ecumenical councils which are accepted by both sides and on the consensus of the early Church Fathers.

It should not be forgotten that, notwithstanding all points of contention, a basic consensus already exists: the Eastern churches continue to acknowledge a primacy of the Roman church and of its bishop based, according to tradition, on the two chief Apostles St Peter and St Paul. Thus, from the beginning, the possibility of a pastoral primacy exercised by the bishop of Rome has always existed as a real option, provided that the bishop of Rome seriously tries to serve the whole community of the Catholic Church as a rock of faith (Matthew 16:18), to strengthen the brothers and sisters (Luke 22:32) and to care for the sheep of the Lord like a good shepherd should (John 21:15); in short, by offering his pastoral ministry to the whole Church while following in the footsteps of St Peter, without the Roman System of power and domination.

Here ends the first stage of my diagnosis of the illness currently afflicting the Catholic Church. The anamneses in this chapter have brought to light seven stages in the growth of disease that over the course of the first millennium led to a state of multi-morbidity that I will investigate more closely in the next chapter. Before going on, however, it will be useful to give a brief résumé of these seven stages here:

1. From the second century onwards, a tendency began to project into the Apostolic Age institutions and practices that in fact arose only at a later date and became what they are today only over the course of a long-drawn-out history. Three such projections must be distinguished:

- St Peter was not given a primacy of jurisdiction by Christ, nor did he exercise one in the Apostolic Church. Neither did he pass his special role in the Apostolic Church on to a direct historical successor.

- The special position enjoyed by the local church of Rome in the early Church rested on its being the burial place of the two principal apostles, St Peter and St Paul, not on a supposed Petrine authority inherited by the city's bishop apart from the Roman ecclesial community as a whole.

- There were growing claims of the bishops of Rome to embody, in their person and office, the leading role enjoyed by the local Roman church as a whole and to be the legal heirs, by direct historical succession, to a jurisdictional primacy conferred on St Peter himself.

2. As far back as the third century, inflated claims were raised by the bishops of Rome to exercise personally an autocratic monarchical power over the other churches, but these claims were not accepted as such.

3. In the fifth century, a 'fullness of power' ideology emerged, claiming to set the bishop of Rome above all of the other bishops and their churches and even above the rulers of the State, but again the claim found virtually no acceptance and remained largely a dead letter in practice.

4. In the sixth to the eighth centuries (despite undeniable historical evidence for the limitation of papal authority by ecclesiastical synods and by civil rulers, culminating in the solemn condemnations of popes Vigilius and Honorius as

heretics), fictitious legends and forged documents were invented in support of papal claims to universal authority and immunity from all other authorities.

5. In the eighth and ninth centuries, repeated relapses into corruption and disorderly conduct required the intervention of the civil authorities to overcome them and to discipline the popes who were guilty of them.

6. In the eleventh and twelfth centuries, an absolutist papal monarchy emerged as a result of the Gregorian revolution 'from above', and set the papacy at loggerheads with the Holy Roman emperors.

7. In the eleventh century, the festering alienation of the Eastern (Greek) Church, resulting from the continuing attempts to exercise papal control over it – epitomized by the papal excommunication of the patriarch of Constantinople in 1054 – led, in the course of the following century, to a full-blown schism between the two halves of the Church; a Latin Church autocratically ruled by a papal monarch and an Eastern Greek Church retaining the traditional church order of synodical rule by bishops under the patriarchs and answerable to the Byzantine emperor.

The most appropriate name for this condition of multi-morbidity is 'the Roman System', since it involves a whole complex of legal, administrative and financial institutions and routines, ideologically justified by a theology of papal primacy. The point here is not to question the motives of those who contributed to its elaboration: by no means were all of the popes and curialists power-hungry or corrupt; often they responded in good faith to real dangers in the light of genuine concerns and honestly attempted to use the (mis)information available to them, e.g. the falsified documents circulating as canon law. The result, however, was nonetheless catastrophic.

Thus, any effective treatment of the disease now afflicting the Catholic Church must continue the diagnosis by showing how this Roman System further developed in the centuries that followed. That will be the task of the next two chapters, to lay open the root of the disease, and that will not be a pleasant task.

CHAPTER 3

SEEDS OF A CHRONIC ILLNESS

Findings and Therapies

Admirers of the Catholic Middle Ages, with its magnificent cathedrals, impressive monasteries and universities, brilliant syntheses of theological speculation and beautiful examples of Romanesque and Gothic art, will no doubt be dismayed at my critical analysis of the Roman System. They may well be disheartened or angered to learn how characteristic features of the eleventh-century Gregorian reforms became the roots of malignant growths that, after repeated bouts of disease and partial recoveries in the following centuries, eventually led to a massive, incurable outbreak of disease at the time of the Reformation and to the amputation, once again, of a substantial portion of the Church. The problems that we see today are, in fact, much older; they go back in essence to the Middle Ages. In this chapter, as in its predecessors, I have no intention of questioning or belittling the many positive, often beautiful and, in any case, impressive aspects and achievements of the Middle Ages; I have great respect for them, and I have described them elsewhere in detail. But here is the place to focus on the malignant elements that deformed the countenance of the Church then, and that continue to cause disease in the Church today.

Nowhere is the problem clearer than at the turn of the twelfth to the thirteenth century, during the pontificate of Innocent III (1198–1216), arguably the most brilliant pope in the Church's history. Elected at the age of 37, he showed himself not only to be a shrewd jurist, a capable administrator, an astute diplomat, a brilliant theologian and an eloquent orator, but also a born ruler with an instinct for power. Significantly, he was never canonized as a saint, and popular belief held that he would burn for centuries in purgatory before entering heaven. He indisputably represents the apex of the Medieval papacy, but also its turning point.

Under Pope Innocent, the Romanization of the Catholic Church reached its summit. Seven distinct processes became entwined to form permanent features of the Roman System, a system which persists to this day and causes great harm and suffering within the Catholic community. The medical term for such a condition is multi-morbidity. The symptoms indicate that there are several *foci* of disease. All of them already existed under Innocent III and, already at that time, they were perceived by many Christians of the West as open wounds calling for a cure. To all intents and purposes, however, these wounds remained untreated, and they have continued to proliferate, ultimately becoming pathogenic structures in themselves.

This chapter will discuss these seven distinct roots of disease. Although I am not looking at things through rose-tinted spectacles, neither am I a prophet of doom. In any case, I have never followed the dreadful injunction of St Ignatius of Loyola 'to hold that the white which I see is black, if the Hierarchical Church so decides it' (Rule 13 in the final chapter on 'Thinking with the Church' in the *Spiritual Exercises* of St Ignatius), and, by the same token, I have always refused to see black as white.

1. Roman Monopoly of Power and Truth

The Findings: The Pope as an Absolutist Monarch, the Papal Church as Mother

Unlike the Eastern churches, since the times of Gregory VII and Innocent III the Catholic Church in the West has been entirely geared towards the pope in terms of belief, canon law, discipline and organization. It is fixated on an absolutist monarch who reigns supreme over the Church as its sole ruler. This fixation conforms neither to the New Testament nor to the early Christian models of the Church.

Instead of the older title 'Vicar of St Peter', Innocent III preferred the title 'Vicar of Christ' ('*Vicarius Christi*'), which he claimed as an exclusive Roman prerogative, although, up until the twelfth century, it had commonly been used for every bishop or priest. He saw himself, as pope, as standing in the middle between God and the people. For Innocent, St Peter (the pope) was the father and the Roman Church was the mother (*mater*) of all Christendom. The term 'mother' was now used, ambivalently, to refer both to the Church generally as the mother of all believers but also and more specifically to refer to the Roman Church as the mother, the 'head' (*caput*) and the 'teacher' (*magistra*) of all the other churches. Indeed, the universal Church became virtually equated with the Church of Rome, and it comes as no surprise that, as late as the mid-twentieth century, the social encyclical of John XXIII issued on 15 May 1961 bore the title *Mater et Magistra* ('mother and schoolmistress'). Scarcely a half century after Innocent III, a pope who ascended the papal throne in 1243 under the name Innocent IV would have the audacity to call himself '*Vicarius*

Dei' ('Vicar of God'). Not surprisingly, this same Innocent IV was responsible for introducing the use of torture by the Inquisition.

I have already described how Rome had early on supplanted the original 'mother church' of Jerusalem, claiming to be (according to the ancient inscription of the Lateran Basilica) the 'Mother and Head of all the churches of the city and of the world' (*omnium urbis et orbis ecclesiarum mater et caput*). For the Jews in Europe, this would have catastrophic consequences. Roman Christendom wanted nothing to do with the children of Israel living in its midst. Papalism allied itself with anti-Judaism.

In 1215, Innocent III convened an 'ecumenical' council in Rome; in fact, however, it was no more than a papal synod, despite its roughly 2,000 participants, including almost 500 archbishops and bishops; the Greek Church was not represented at all. This most brilliant synod of the Middle Ages was as much a massive demonstration of papal power as it was a shabby manifestation of the irrelevance of the episcopate. Against the Jews it passed a series of resolutions that anticipated the downright anti-Semitic sanctions of later periods: Jews were required to wear special clothing setting them apart from normal citizens; they were prohibited from holding public office or even leaving their houses during the three Easter holy days; and, notably, they were compelled to pay a special tax to the local Catholic clergy.

The Therapy: Instead of an Absolute Primacy of Domination and Rule, a Pastoral Primacy of Service

None of the three crucial claims about the existence of a primacy exercised first by St Peter himself, then about the continuation of this Petrine primacy as an enduring office in the Church, and finally about the title of the bishops of Rome to succeed to this Petrine primacy, is confirmed by exegetical and historical research. Even Catholic commentators today admit that the definition of the Petrine primacy of the popes as formulated by the First Vatican Council rests on shaky foundations. At the same time, however, Orthodox and Protestant theologians have come to admit that a primacy exercised by an individual within the Church does not stand in contradiction to the teaching of Scripture. However weak may be the evidence to justify the authoritarian claims of such an institution, there is nothing in the Bible that would preclude the existence of a primacy of service in the Church. Indeed, both Orthodox and Protestant Christians could in all likelihood accept primacy within an ecumenical Church when such a primacy theologically and practically conforms to biblical teaching. In fact, even most of the original Protestant reformers, including the younger Luther, his colleague Melanchthon and even the more rigorous Calvin, thought along such lines. That is an indication of hope that a therapeutic reform of the papal office could be effective.

What counts is not the historical pedigree of the papal succession; even if it could be established without question, by itself it would prove little. What counts is the succession in spirit: i.e. in the spirit of the Petrine mission and task as outlined in the New Testament and in the spirit of St Peter's historical witness and service.

111

Even if a pope were to incontestably prove his historical lineage by demonstrating that he and all of his predecessors were the legitimate successors to the historical St Peter, and to prove that the first person in this succession had been explicitly 'appointed' by St Peter to be his juridical successor with all the rights and privileges claimed by the popes today, would that count for anything, if this pope himself failed to follow in the spirit of St Peter's mission, failed to perform the tasks commissioned by St Peter, failed to bear witness and to serve the Church as St Peter had done? Such a merely historical succession without a succession in spirit would be of no avail to himself and of no avail to the Church.

Conversely, if a pope cannot, at least for the early centuries, establish a chain of juridical succession with absolute historical certainty, but if he personifies the Petrine functions as described in the Bible, fulfilling the duties and tasks laid upon him and offering the Church the kind of witness and service ascribed to St Peter in the Scriptures, then the question of the accuracy of the historical 'pedigree' of such a true servant of the Church and emulator of St Peter would be of secondary importance. Even today, the pope does not receive his office by a special laying on of hands: he receives it by election, not by consecration, and even his 'installation', later transformed into an 'enthronization', is only a secondary, non-sacramental act. What would count is that such a pope, even without an impeccable pedigree, would have his special charism, the gift of *kybernesis* (1 Corinthians 12:28), a Greek term describing the function of the helmsman (a person who steers, but who is not necessarily the captain of the ship). Can anything more be demanded?

2. Juridicism and Clericalism

Findings: The Church Becomes a Juridical and Clerical Institution

In the paradigms of the Early Church and the Byzantine Church, the Church was always legally subject to imperial law. By contrast, in the West, from the Middle Ages onwards, an 'imperial' Roman Catholic Church produced its own canon law and jurisprudence, rivalling the imperial code of law in terms of both complexity and sophistication. Western canon law focused on the pope as the absolute ruler, legislator and judge of all Christendom; according to the Roman ideology, the emperor and all other secular rulers were subordinate to the pope.

At the time of the Gregorian reform, a number of professional compilations of laws in the spirit of the Roman Church were collated in Rome. The twelfth-century popes issued more laws for the whole Church than all their predecessors put together. The different compilations and the laws contained in them were often inconsistent and at times even contradictory. To resolve the resulting issues, a more systematic textbook was needed, which not only collected the laws together but also discussed the emergent issues to resolve them. Thus was born a textbook, bearing the name *Decretum Gratiani*, which quickly found broad acceptance. According to legend, the work was compiled and written by a Camaldolese monk named Gratian, who taught at the University of Bologna; it is more likely, however, that several authors were involved in its composition. Fatally, 324 passages purporting to hail from popes of the first four centuries were taken over uncritically from the pseudo-Isidorian decretals, and of these at least 313 have been proven to be forgeries. Given the influence of these forgeries, it is small wonder that the professional church lawyers and professors of church law, i.e. the canonists, became in effect papal lawyers who, naively assuming the validity of the forged 'papal' decretals, became invaluable ideological supporters of the Roman System, not only in Rome, but in chanceries, ecclesiastical tribunals and university faculties all over Europe.

In the course of the following centuries, three voluminous official collections of decretals emerged to supplement and update the *Decretum Gratiani*, and these, together with additional unofficial compilations, were compiled into a collection known as the *Corpus Iuris Canonici*, by which the Church was governed until the laws of the *Corpus* were codified into the official *Codex Iuris Canonici* of 1917/18, a revised edition of which was produced in 1983. In a classical example of papal autocracy still at work at the end of the twentieth century, this codified Latin law served as the model for a codification of Eastern Church law that was drawn up and promulgated in Rome in 1990 as the norm for the life of the Eastern churches in communion with Rome. Useful as such a codification might be in practice, and despite attempts to take earlier Eastern legislation into account, this Roman action ran contrary to all Eastern Church traditions.

The need to harmonize the contradictions between different laws and to define their application in difficult situations gave birth to an army of legal scholars, who enabled the papal monarchy, in the absence of any substantial military force of its own, to extend and to enforce its control over the everyday life of all of the churches throughout Europe outside of the Greek and the southern and eastern Slavic territories.

Needless to say, this legal system admitted no separation of powers. The pope was at the same time the supreme ruler, the absolute legislator and the final judge, who at will could overthrow the decisions of any and every other authority. Already under Innocent III, however, such appeals led to serious abuses, generating a system of privileges, despotism, partisanship and greed. This sordid Roman 'tradition' has also survived in the Roman Catholic Church down to the present.

More than anything else, however, it was the imposition of clerical celibacy (about which more will be said later) that established a new social order, in which the clergy and the hierarchy, set off as priesthood and prelacy, now became a class apart from and elevated above the people or laity. This unheard-of clericalization assumed such proportions that 'Church' and 'clergy' came to be used synonymously, leaving the laity completely excluded from the power structure of the Church. The clergy became the sole custodians of the gifts of grace by which the Church is constituted. Hence, 'Church' came to mean the clergy, organized hierarchically and monarchically as a pyramid with the pope at its apex.

Under Innocent III, monasticism too became clericalized, making it into a hierarchically organized structure parallel to the hierarchical structure of the secular clergy (*saecularis* means 'being in the world' or 'worldly'). In earlier times, the monks, as a rule, had been laymen rather than priests; they were set apart from other laymen only by their ascetic lifestyle. Some lived as hermits, but the majority lived in monasteries, where they practised a common life under the authority of an elected abbot. In either case, they were subject to the local bishop. No overarching organization existed; the monasteries were linked with each other by sharing a common 'monastic rule' – the Rule of St Benedict in the West and the Rule of St Basil in the East were the most important – and by their shared customs (*consuetudines*), often set forth in the form of written constitutions which applied and interpreted the rule. Alongside the monks of this classical type in the West, the clergy attached to the cathedrals and other major churches often lived together as canons in semi-monastic chapters or priories according to the Rule of St Augustine written for clerics.

The reform movement of the eleventh and twelfth centuries radically changed the organizational pattern of both the monks and the canons, transforming their loose federations into centrally organized religious orders. The principal monastic orders were those of Cluny, Citeaux, Chartreuse and Camaldoli, in which priest–monks now played the principal role, and were served by lower-ranking lay brothers, who performed the more menial tasks. The principal order of canons was that of Praemontré. The tight organization of these orders made them effective instruments not only for promoting church reform generally, but also for extending papal power.

Parallel to these new monastic and canonical reform orders founded in the eleventh century, around the beginning of the thirteenth century, a new kind of religious order came into being. Collectively, these new orders are known as mendicant orders, because, unlike classical monks, they supported them-selves by begging instead of by living off the fruits of their manual labour and the rents of their often extensive monastic properties. They differed from the classical monks in another respect as well: they were not bound to their monasteries by the rule of stability; thus, they could be sent out on apostolic preaching missions. Their members were mainly priests, and, aside from their characteristic practice of begging and their engagement in public preaching, their lifestyle and organizational pattern resembled that of the canons. Many followed the Rule of St Augustine.

The mendicant orders emerged out of a movement of religious renewal among the laity, known collectively as the Poverty Movement, which, towards the end of the eleventh century, suddenly appeared on the scene in southern France and northern Italy, with echoes in adjoining Spanish and German regions. It was initiated by Peter Waldo, a layman who in around 1070 in Lyon began preaching an apostolic way of life in simplicity and poverty. His movement quickly attracted a large following, but its criticism of clerical corruption and its theologically unsophisticated, direct biblical preaching in the language of the people evoked the suspicion of the bishops and eventually led to outright persecution. The ideal of apostolic life, however, also appealed to many priests, and they were soon joined by laymen who willingly accepted priestly ordination. By giving papal approval to these orders, Pope Innocent III effectively domesticated the Poverty Movement and, at the same time, called into being a powerful agent to promote Roman influence.

The Dominicans and the Franciscans, founded at the beginning of the thirteenth century in southern France and central Italy, became the archetypes of this new type of religious community. At their centres were confraternities of priest-religious, who, in imitation of the example of the apostles (*vita apostolica*) lived together in small, democratically ruled communities called 'priories', practising evangelical poverty and simplicity. Using the newly emergent urban centres of Europe as their bases, these friars (from *fratres*, i.e. 'brothers') preached in the streets as well as in the churches, using the language of the people. Trained and teaching at the new universities springing up all over Europe, they became the vanguard of the Church's intellectual life, helping to establish theology as a scientific academic discipline and engaging in learned dialogue with Jewish and Islamic scholars. Moreover, the local priories of priest-religious became the focal points for a much larger community of lay women and men seeking to practise and promote the Gospel. Some of the women lived as nuns in monastic seclusion, but the majority of the women and men belonging to this so-called 'third order' lived as celibate or as married individuals in the world, where they sought to live out their familial and professional lives according to the Gospel.

Innocent III quickly recognized the potential of these mendicant orders and gave them papal approbation, which removed them from episcopal supervision and shielded them from the efforts of the secular clergy to curtail their influence. Looking directly to the pope for direction, the priests of these orders and the laity associated with them contributed enormously to strengthening papal authority and influence throughout Europe and later in the mission lands. The theologians of these orders became the outstanding ideological apologists for papal claims, but also the principal agents of the notorious Inquisition, at first merely *ad hoc* tribunals instituted by Innocent III to repress dissent in the Church, later institutionalized under Innocent's successors as permanent tribunals with sweeping powers to hunt out and murder those convicted of heresy or witchcraft.

Therapy: Instead of Hierarchy and Domination, a Community in Freedom, Equality and Brotherhood/Sisterhood

The constitution of the Church as a clerical hierarchy organized on monarchical principles completely inverts the original ordering of the Church as described in the New Testament. If we wish to make today's Church more Christian, we need to recover the original order of the Church as outlined in the New Testament. In the New Testament, 'church' stands for the entire community of faith. According to the New Testament, the Gospel is propagated not by aloof hierarchs or learned theologians, but by simple and humble witnesses, both ordained and non-ordained, who give living witness to the person and message of Christ more by their deeds than by their words. It is the community of faith taken as a whole that inspires belief in Jesus Christ, shapes Christian commitment and ensures the enduring, effective presence of Christ's Church in the world by faithfully following Christ in daily life. Not just a select few, not just bishops, clergymen, monks and nuns, but every Christian, whatever his or her standing in the Church or in society, is called to spread the Christian message by living a life according to the Gospel. All have been given the same gift of baptism in Jesus' name, the same gift of Eucharistic Communion as a celebration of remembrance, thanksgiving and union, the same assurance of forgiveness for their sins. Day-to-day service and active responsibility for our fellow men and women, for the ecclesial community and for the world as a whole constitute a duty laid upon all. This ideal of apostolic life had inspired the Medieval Poverty Movement and the mendicant orders it gave birth to. Recovering it means not only reconnecting with the New Testament tradition but also with the best traditions of Medieval Christianity.

3. Hostility to Sexuality and General Misogyny

Findings: Denigration of Sexuality and Marriage

Even in the first centuries, women were increasingly being kept away from positions of leadership in the Church. In the fourth and fifth centuries, in his campaign against Pelagianism and its emphasis on free will, Augustine, now Bishop of Hippo Regius, sharpened the theology of sin and grace. In Augustine's theology, everyone was born into sin, and Augustine accounted for this inheritance by tracing it back to the biblical story of Adam's fall. Following a false Latin translation that completely misrepresented the original Greek text of Romans 5:12, Augustine understood Paul to be teaching that sin came into the world via Adam, because 'in him' – i.e. in Adam's own 'original' sinful act – all human beings descended from Adam personally and formally became guilty of sin, not, as the Greek text actually states, merely by 'following his [Adam's] example'. With this interpretation, Augustine historicized, psychologized and sexualized Adam's original fall. Reading St Paul's remarks on human sinfulness in a tendentious manner, Augustine then interpreted Adam's fall as a sexually coloured original sin that enslaved human beings to their carnal, self-centred appetites. This sin was passed on through the act of sexual intercourse, so that every newborn infant is doomed to eternal death unless freed from original sin by baptism.

Through this interpretation of the biblical teaching on the Fall, Augustine, who had a brilliant capacity for analytical self-reflection far exceeding that of any other author of antiquity, effectively poisoned the entire Western Church with his doctrine on original sin, which is rejected down to this day by the Eastern churches. This doctrine has given rise to a fatal denigration and denial of sexuality. In this view, even the slightest sexual desire or overt action, even when meant as a token of affection, becomes a grave sin, unless it is performed within marriage and motivated by the intention to produce children. Human sexuality becomes a demon to be repressed and if possible purged, since carnal pleasure makes a person impure. The expression of sexuality is permitted only as an instrument for the propagation of the race, and it should be accompanied by as little carnal pleasure as possible. This attitude, only slightly mitigated in secondary aspects, shapes papal teaching down to this day (see the 1968 encyclical *Humanae vitae* of Paul VI, repeatedly reaffirmed and elaborated on by Popes John Paul II and Benedict XVI).

Augustine's theology of original sin had a profound influence on Medieval morality and penance. Because original sin was passed on through sexual lust in the consummation of marriage, an austere sexual ethic became the norm. Sexual abstinence, indeed celibacy, i.e. the abstention from marriage as such, was now demanded of the clergy and even recommended to the laity. Conversely, the laity were forbidden to touch holy objects with their impure hands, especially the sacred bread and wine of the Eucharist. Male sperm, like menstrual blood, having intercourse and giving birth to a child, made a person ritually impure and excluded the affected person from receiving the sacrament for a longer or shorter time. Thus it was taught that married couples should refrain from sexual intercourse on Sundays and high feast days, as well as on the eves of such feast days and the eight days following them; likewise on certain days of the week (for example, Fridays) and generally during Advent and Lent. Behind this drastic containment of sexual expression even within marriage lay archaic, magical ideas entirely foreign to the spirit of the Gospel.

By associating sexuality with women, this theology fostered misogyny and contributed to the further marginalization of women in church life. Women were seen as the weaker sex, not only physically, but also morally and intellectually, and were thus disqualified from holding offices of leadership. In marriage they were subjugated to their husbands, and in the Church to the male clergy. Rule by women, even in the political and social spheres, was denounced as an evil; at best, women gained recognition only as perpetual virgins or chaste widows.

In the eleventh century, the church leadership, under the pressure of male celibates, pushed through the prohibition of marriage for all priests in the Western church. In the Eastern church the clergy, with the exception of bishops, can marry to this day and thus tend to be closer to the community and better integrated into the social fabric. The clergy of the Western church, by contrast, were separated from the laity by their celibate state, implying a higher moral perfection making them superior to the laity and better qualified to rule.

Under the influence of the monks Humbert and Hildebrand, Rome enforced a kind of pan-monasticism upon the whole clergy, requiring unconditional obedience, renunciation of marriage and family, and the practice of communal life. Especially in northern Italy and in Germany, massive clergy protests against the prohibition of marriage resulted. Hildebrand, as Pope Gregory VII, incited the laity to boycott the ministries of married priests. Abhorrent witch-hunts and persecution of the wives of priests occurred. After the Second Lateran Council of 1139, marriages of priests were declared invalid and the wives of priests were treated as concubines. The children of priests were reduced to slaves owned by the Church. Thereafter, universal compulsory celibacy was the rule in the Western church, but in practice this rule was often ignored, even in Rome, up until the time of the Reformation.

Therapy: Renounce the Augustinian Doctrine of Original Sin, Abolish the Law of Celibacy and Improve the Status of Women

The requirement of celibacy is not a tenet of faith. It is a Medieval canon law that should have been abrogated long ago in response to the well-founded criticism of the sixteenth-century reformers. It should not have been tabooed at Vatican II but should have been discussed openly and then abolished. Today the overwhelming majority of the Catholic clergy and laity call for the abrogation of the celibacy rule and the restoration of women to positions of leadership in the Church. The traditional arguments against preaching by women and the ordination of women are not merely outdated, they are also theologically dubious and untenable..

4. Propensity to Violence and Crusader Mentality

Findings: Theological Vindication of the Use of Force and of War

Like the Western Church, the Orthodox Churches of the East also participated in the political and military actions of the temporal powers. In many cases they provided the theological legitimization for the use of military force, and at times they inspired and abated individual wars. But it is only in Western Christianity that a theory of the legitimate use of force to achieve spiritual aims developed, and this theory became the justification for using force to spread Christianity and to suppress internal dissidence.

Once again, Augustine played a critical role. Initially he wanted to leave the separation of the wheat from the chaff to the ultimate judgement of God; later, however, confronted with the proliferation of dissenting groups in North Africa and impressed by the success of their forceful persecution, he came to believe that the use of violence against heretics and schismatics could be justified theologically. He seized upon a passage within the Parable of the Wedding Feast (Luke 14:16–24), which in the Latin version became gravely overstated by calling the host a *dominus* ('ruler') and having him say in v. 23, '*Coge intrare*', ('compel [them] to enter'), although the Greek term used here means only 'urge them'. The same Augustine, who could speak so eloquently of the love between God and humanity, who could define God as 'love itself', in this way became, for ages to come, the chief ideological supporter of forced mass conversions, of inquisitorial persecution of suspected dissenters and of holy wars waged against all those who refused to bow to Roman Catholic authority. Nothing similar occurred in the East.

Augustine's theory became the inspiration of the Medieval crusades. Already, Gregory VII had toyed with the idea of personally leading a massive military invasion of the Byzantine Empire to assert Roman primacy there and end the schism. Ten years after Gregory's death, Pope Urban II launched the First Crusade as a 'holy war' against the infidels under the sign of the victorious cross. As the mouthpiece of Christ, the pope personally called upon Christians to 'take up the cross', i.e. to take up arms in the name of the cross. Without genuine religious fervour and the conviction, at times boarding on mass psychosis, of acting in Christ's name and authority, the crusaders would never have been able to bear the sufferings and exertions of fighting their way through thousands of kilometres of enemy territory with inadequate provisions and exposed to guerrilla attacks and then, on arrival in the Holy Land, having to wage long sieges to make their conquests.

Innocent III became the initiator of crusades directed against fellow Christians. The prime example is the catastrophic Fourth Crusade (1203–4). From the beginning of his pontificate in 1198, Innocent had been calling for a new crusade to reassert Western Catholic control over the Holy Land. Although Innocent explicitly forbade violence against fellow Christians, when the crusaders began by sacking the Dalmatian city of Zara in 1202, he quickly acquiesced and withdrew his excommunication of the majority of the participants. The same thing happened after the atrocious capture and plundering of Constantinople in 1204, which was followed by the establishment of a Latinate emperor in Constantinople, the partition of Byzantine territories among Latinate rulers, and the subjugation of the Greek Church under a Latin patriarch and Latin bishops. After an initial angry protest, Innocent gladly accepted the stolen goods, pardoned the leaders responsible for the atrocities and recognized their usurped titles. At the Fourth 'Ecumenical' Council of the Lateran in 1215, he welcomed the intruding Latin prelates from the East, confirming their authority over the Greek Church. The ancient dream of Roman hegemony over the Eastern Church appeared at last to have attained its goal. But, as Innocent himself realized in a rare moment of insight expressed in a letter of 1205, the atrocities of the Fourth Crusade in fact had the opposite effect: instead of healing the schism, they put the final seal on it.

In 1209, Pope Innocent initiated the first official crusade against Christians in the West. The object, this time, was the Albigensians, adherents of a neo-Manichean underground church, who called themselves 'Cathar' (from *katharoi*, i.e. the 'pure'), which flourished in the Languedoc region of southern France. The grisly 20-year-long Albigensian wars led to the extermination of whole villages and towns and the subjugation of the more cultivated population of Occitania to the imposed domination of less cultured rulers intruding from the north.

In later centuries, the example of these crusades would be invoked to justify the violent *Reconquista* of Spain under the banner of the Apostle St James the 'Moor Slayer' (*Matamoros*) and the forced conversion or expulsion of the Jews and Muslims who had lived there for almost a millennium.

These wars in the name of Christ represent a monstrous abuse of the symbol of the cross and a profound perversion of Christianity. No wonder that, with Innocent, the notion was born among dissenters that the pope is in reality the antichrist.

Therapy: Instead of Violence and Crusades, Bearing the Cross in Daily Life

Even in the Middle Ages, many people questioned whether the Jesus of the Sermon on the Mount, harbinger of non-violence and advocate of loving one's enemies, would have approved of such belligerent undertakings in his name. Instead of inspiring Christians to bear their crosses in daily life, the cross – stitched on the crusaders' outer garments – became an excuse for bloody violence inflicted on others.

But already at the time of Innocent III, a clear alternative to the Roman System became visible at a historic meeting of the pope with St Francis of Assisi in 1209. Francis, the *poverello*, i.e. 'little poor man', showed the papal autocrat by his whole way of life what living in imitation of Christ is really about:

- *Poverty*: Innocent III stood for a Church of wealth and splendour, of greed and financial scandals. The alternative would be an unpretentious, open-handed Church with transparent financial policies, a Church exemplifying inner freedom from material possessions and outward Christian generosity.

- *Humility*: Innocent III stood for a Church of power and domination, of bureaucracy and discrimination, repression and inquisition. The alternative would be a Church marked by humility and humanity, social solidarity, brotherhood and sisterhood, a Church encouraging dialogue and offering hospitality even to non-conformists, whose leadership practises unassuming ministry, not clamping down on new religious impulses and ideas from below but welcoming them and putting them to fruitful use.

- *Simplicity*: Innocent III stood for a Church with overly complex dogmas, nit-picking moralistic casuistry and legalistic tutorism, i.e. the moral principle of always playing on the safe side of the law whatever the cost. All of this was laced together in an all-pervading canon law, an all-knowing scholasticism and an all-pervasive fear of novelties. The alternative would be a Church proclaiming joyful tidings, a theology guided by the Gospel and willing to listen rather than indoctrinate, an institutional Church not set over and above, but rather joined in partnership with, the Church of the people of God.

Regrettably, the popes failed to follow the example of St Francis, and their self-inflation was followed by their humiliation.

5. Reversal of Papal Worldly Power into Papal Impotence

Findings: Collapse of Political Power and Monetization of the System

At the beginning of the thirteenth century, at the height of the papal dominance under Innocent III, no one could have imagined the depths of papal abasement and impotence at the end of the same century. Admittedly, the ends met by Gregory VII and Innocent III were bad omens: Gregory died in exile abandoned by his supporters, while Innocent died unexpectedly and his corpse was found in the Cathedral of Perugia stripped naked and robbed by his own servants.

The dramatic reversal of papal fortunes at the end of the century, however, was the work of Boniface VIII (1294–1303). In his autocratic bull of 1296, *Clericis laicos infestos* ('The laity are in a high degree hostile to the clergy'!), he declared taxation of the clergy to be the sole prerogative of the pope and threatened France and England with excommunication if they did not comply. Four years later, he ostentatiously staged the first 'Holy Year' in 1300 by issuing a special jubilee indulgence that generated vast cash revenues for a Curia always in need of more money.

The following year, Boniface provoked a quarrel with the French king Philip IV the Fair, and then in the bull *Unam sanctam* proclaimed the most extreme formulation of the papal claims to supremacy, defining obedience to the pope 'as absolutely necessary for salvation for every human creature'. This astute jurist and ruthlessly power-hungry pope, who suffered from Caesar-like delusions of grandeur, planned to excommunicate the French king on 8 September 1303 and, in imitation of Gregory VII, to release Philip's subjects from their oath of loyalty. But times had now changed – Boniface was arrested in his castle at Anagni by armed agents of the French king and the Colonna family and imprisoned. Although he was soon released from imprisonment by the townspeople of Anagni, he was a broken man and died one month later in Rome. His second successor, a former Archbishop of Bordeaux, was no longer enthroned in Rome but in Lyon, and moved the papal court to Avignon under the protection of the French king.

The period of French domination of the papacy known as the 'Babylonian Captivity' of the popes in Avignon lasted some

70 years. It represented a dramatic shift of power. The hierocratic papacy, denuded of its moral credibility as a result of its megalomaniac power politics, was now a 'declining system' (see Walter Ullmann, *The Growth of Papal Government in the Middle Ages* [1970]), in sharp contrast to the 'ascending system' of rule by law of the emerging nation-states.

But the popes learned nothing from history. The enormous papal palace in Avignon was expanded and embellished at great cost; the corrupt papal bureaucracy, the venal financial administration and ostentatious papal ritual were inflated and nepotism flourished. The growing need for supplementary revenues caused the burden of papal taxation to be felt with increasing weight throughout Europe as the Church was exploited for Roman ends. Thus, in the late Middle Ages, the Roman papacy lost its religious and moral leadership, becoming instead the first great financial power in Europe. Monetary impositions were collected by the popes with all means at their disposal, by direct force and by the threat of excommunication and interdict. Despite enormous pastoral damage, Germany had to live for almost two decades under an interdict prohibiting all ecclesiastical ministrations.

Small wonder that, under such circumstances, opposition to the papacy grew enormously in the fourteenth century: in universities, colleges and schools, in the emergent urban middle classes, and among influential writers and journalists, from Dante Alighieri, who condemned Boniface VIII to hell in his *Divina Commedia*, to the influential pamphlet *Defensor pacis*, published in 1324 by Marsilius of Padua, a former rector of the University of Paris. In it, he formulated a theory of the State making the authority of the State independent from that of the Church, the bishops independent from the pope and the parishes independent from the hierarchy. Marsilius pointed to the papal 'plenitude of power' (*plenitudo potestatis*) with neither a biblical nor a theological foundation as being the main cause of discord in Europe.

Therapy: Reform of the Head and the Branches

In this depressing situation, the catchphrase echoing throughout Europe at the end of the fourteenth century was the call for 'a reform of the Church from the head to the members'. Only a general council, it was commonly believed, could re-establish the unity of the Church and carry out the needed reforms. Unlike the Medieval papal synods, such a council would receive its authority not as an outflow of the papal 'plenitude of power' but as a representation of all of Christendom. This conciliar theory – later discredited as 'conciliarism' by papal apologists – was not, as opponents commonly asserted, taken over from heretical writings of Marsilius and Ockham, but was based on the entirely orthodox, official canon law theory of the twelfth and thirteenth centuries (see Brian Tierney, *Foundations of the Conciliar Theory* [1998]) and beyond that on the patristic accounts of the first ecumenical councils as the representations of the Church.

6. Refusal to Reform

Findings: All Attempts at Reform Failed

The chaotic situation in Italy in the fourteenth century eventually resulted in a papal schism marked by the rise in 1378 of

two competing lines of Catholic popes mutually excommunicating each other; a third line emerged in 1409 as a result of
an unsuccessful attempt to resolve the schism. A radical solution was needed, and this became the principal task of the
Ecumenical Council of Constance (1414–18), called to
re-establish the unity of the Church and tackle the necessary
reforms.

Outside Rome it was generally felt that the Council, rather
than the pope, was the highest institution of the Church. In its
famous decree *Haec sancta*, the Council of Constance solemnly
invoked the principle dating back to the early Church that 'the
Council stands above the pope'. As a legitimate convocation of
representatives of the universal Church assembled in the Holy
Spirit, the Council derives its authority directly from Christ.
Everyone, even the pope, is obliged to obey the Council in
matters pertaining to faith, the eradication of schism and the
general reform of the Church.

The defeat of the Roman System, which had brought the
Catholic Church in the West to the edge of ruin, appeared to
be sealed. But the new pope elected and installed by the
Council, Martin V Colonna, a former Italian curial cardinal,
initiated an astonishingly rapid restoration of papal autocracy.
With all the means available, the desperately necessary reforms
of the Church and of its constitution were thwarted. Following
a directive of the Council of Constance, subsequent councils
met in Pavia, Siena and Basel, but their reforming actions were
circumvented by the Curia, which exercised a tight grip on the
reins of day-to-day church government.

Undeterred by the decrees of the Council, the popes renewed
the Medieval claims to supremacy. On the eve of the
Reformation, at the Fifth Lateran Council in 1516, Leo X

Medici bluntly spoke of 'the currently reigning Roman pontiff, enjoying authority over all the councils …'. This extreme papalism, subject to no conciliar control, opened the floodgates for the manifold abuse of the papal office by the Renaissance popes. With their enormous building projects and their magnanimous support for the arts, these popes attempted to demonstrate that the centre of Christendom was also the centre of art and culture.

But the price of these extraordinarily expensive projects was the adamant refusal to reform the papal system, for that would have required a fundamental change in the attitudes of these thoroughly secularized papal rulers and their courts. That the Renaissance did not result in a rebirth of the Church was unequivocally the fault of these popes, who behaved like ordinary Italian Renaissance princes, living lives of immense luxury, indulging in unrestrained hedonism and uninhibited profligacy and promoting in the first place the interests of their families:

- The corrupt Francisco della Rovere, later Sixtus IV, a strong supporter of the dogma of the Immaculate Conception of the Virgin Mary, provided for a host of his nephews and favourites at the expense of the Church, appointing six of his relatives to be cardinals, among them his cousin Pietro Riario, one of the most scandalous libertines of the Roman Curia, who succumbed to the effects of his debauched lifestyle at the early age of 28.

- Innocent VIII Cibo, who moved into the Vatican palace accompanied by his son and daughter and who, through his papal bull, enormously contributed to the hysterical persecution of witches, publicly recognized his illegitimate children and celebrated their marriages with great pomp and ceremony in the Vatican itself.

- The astute politician Alexander VI Borgia, the role model for Machiavelli, obtained the papal throne through massive bribery and favouritism; he fathered four children with his mistress (and additional children with other women during his time as cardinal). He excommunicated the great preacher Girolamo Savonarola and was jointly responsible for the subsequent burning of the popular preacher at the stake in Florence.

- Leo X Medici, who became cardinal at the age of 13, was a great lover of art, enjoyed life, and concentrated most of his energies on procuring the Duchy of Spoleto for his nephew Lorenzo. He barely noticed the epochal event of 1517 which was soon to put an end to the universalist papal claims in the northern half of Western Christendom. In that year, Martin Luther, a hitherto unnoticed German Augustinian professor of New Testament theology at the University of Wittenberg (who a few months earlier had personally witnessed Roman corruption during a visit to the city as an agent of his Order), published 95 critical theses criticizing the sale of indulgences used to finance the construction of the sinfully expensive new Basilica of St Peter's. To this day, the admonition given me by my spiritual director during my own seminary years in Rome rings in my ears, 'When you see the magnificent dome of St Peter's, never forget that!'

7. The Reformation: a Radical Answer to the Church's Unwillingness to Reform

For centuries, Rome had blocked all serious reform; the payback for this was the Reformation, which, once alight, quickly developed an enormous religious, political and social dynamic. For Rome, which had already lost the Church in the East, this was a second catastrophe which cost it most of the northern half of its surviving Imperium Romanum. Thus, the Roman System led to a split in Western Christianity as well. Soon, Catholics would be referring to their Church as 'Roman Catholic' without noticing that the qualification 'Roman' effectively stood for a disavowal of the term 'Catholic', being, so to speak, a contradiction in terms like 'wooden iron'.

Luther's personal impetus to reform the Church and the immense explosive impact this reform would develop came from the single basic conviction that the Church must return to the Gospel of Jesus Christ, as Luther had personally experienced it in the Holy Scripture and in particular in the writings of St Paul. In practical terms, this meant:

- Over and against all the traditions, laws and authorities which had accumulated over the centuries, Luther emphasized the primacy of Scripture – 'by scripture alone' – as the ultimate norm for the correct interpretation and application of all the other secondary norms of faith and practice in the Church.

- Instead of the thousands of saints and numberless official intermediaries between God and man, Luther insisted on the primacy of Christ: 'through Christ alone', since Christ is the focal point of Scripture and the point of reference for all interpretations of the Bible.

- Instead of all the pious religious actions enjoined by the Church and the effort of believers to achieve salvation by meritorious 'works', Luther re-asserted the primacy of grace and of faith: 'by grace alone', i.e. in virtue of the favour of the merciful God as he has shown himself in the crucifixion and resurrection of Jesus Christ – and 'by faith alone', i.e. the unconditional hopeful trust in God's loving promises.

Therapy: Take Luther's Demands for Reform Seriously

If the Vatican had been able to see the 'signs of the times', the split could probably still have been averted, even at the eleventh hour. Luther, and the reformers in general, wanted to remain Catholics; they did not want to leave the Catholic Church. The rapid implementation of three popular demands for reform would probably have brought about a turning point:

- use of the vernacular in the liturgy (encouraged by the Second Vatican Council and now generally practised);

- distribution of Holy Communion from the chalice to lay persons (permitted in principle by the Second Vatican Council but not everywhere practised);

- abolition of compulsory clerical celibacy and admission of married priests (excluded by papal intervention from discussion during the Second Vatican Council and still adamantly opposed by the popes and the Curia).

At the outset, Martin Luther was by no means the un-Catholic rebel that centuries of Roman polemical historiography have made him out to be. As I showed in my dissertation *Justification: The Doctrine of Karl Barth and a Catholic Reflection* which originally appeared in 1957 and was translated into English in 1964, Luther's understanding of the justification of sinners, the centre of his theology, could, already in the sixteenth century, have been understood and affirmed within the context of a broader understanding of Catholic tradition as expressed in the works of the great Medieval scholastics. The results of my pioneering study have been confirmed and endorsed by theologians on both sides of the confessional divide, and they found official confirmation in the Joint Declaration issued by the Pontifical Council for Promoting Christian Unity and the Lutheran World Federation and solemnly proclaimed at a public ceremony in Augsburg in 1999.

Luther's personal experience of justification through faith, which implies placing one's trust in God, not in human works or institutions apart from God, formed the basis of his public call for the reform of the Catholic Church. He called for a reform in the spirit of the Gospel, which aimed less at reformulating the teachings of the Church and more at regenerating Christian life in every area. His reforming tract *To the Christian Nobility of the German Nation Respecting the Reformation of the Christian Estate* was a sharp attack on three arrogant assumptions of the Roman System (the three 'walls of the Romanists') which stood in the way of Church reform, namely:

1. that the spiritual power of the pope had absolute authority over the temporal power;

2. that the pope had the sole authority to interpret the Scripture;

3. that the pope alone had the power to convene a council and confirm its decrees.

It should hardly come as a surprise that this last principle, giving the pope arbitrary control over the Council, which to this day is anchored in the *Codex Iuris Canonici* and remains in force after the Second Vatican Council, rests on six references to earlier legal sources, of which three are taken directly from the pseudo-Isidorian forgeries and the other three are deduced from them.

Then came the fatal mistake: instead of responding to the reformers' demand that the Church 'return to the Gospel of Jesus Christ', a demand that necessarily would have meant fundamental changes in the system, i.e. a paradigm change, Rome refused to rethink its power structure and the ideology supporting it in terms of the Gospel. Instead, hostile to any serious reform from below, Rome reacted by demanding Luther's unconditional submission. And when this submission was refused, Rome replied in January 1521 with the sentence of excommunication, excluding him from the communion of the Church and placing him under imperial ban. But by then it was too late. Luther's message has spread throughout Germany and attracted a large following, including powerful princes willing to protect him and to carry out the needed reforms in their own territories even against Roman and Imperial opposition.

Anyone who has honestly studied the history of this tragic affair is compelled to admit that it was not the reformer Luther, whatever his faults and tactical errors, but rather Rome and its hostility to reform, abetted by its alliance with the Habsburg Emperors and with some German princes, that bears the chief responsibility for the fact that 500 years after the schism between the Western and Eastern Churches, a new schism opened between northern Europe, which became largely Protestant, and southern Europe, which became aggressively Roman Catholic. In the course of the colonial expansion of the European powers, this schism was imported into the New World and later spread into Asia, Africa and Oceania. In this way, a second festering wound opened, this time in the body of Western Christendom.

Here ends the second stage of my diagnosis of what ails the Catholic Church. A careful investigation of the seeds of disease has exposed seven specific *foci* of disease that remain virulent within the Church up until the present day. Naturally, the question arises: can this wound be healed in time? Is there still hope for recovery? Before answering this question, we must now examine further obstacles to recovery in the following chapters.

CHAPTER 4

REHABILITATION AND RELAPSE

Forces Driving and Opposing Reform

In the wake of Luther and the Reformation, there was widespread agreement, even in Catholic countries like Italy and Spain, that the Roman Catholic Church needed a radical cure. After the Reformation, the papacy was on the defensive and reaction replaced leadership. Meanwhile, the historical focus shifted from the Mediterranean countries to northern and central Europe. The famous '*Sacco di Roma*', a three-day sack of Rome by marauding imperial troops in 1527, symbolized the end of Renaissance culture in Rome. Yet the Roman Church would remain unreformed for years to come, although, even in Rome itself, more and more people saw the need for change.

A Severely Ill Patient in Need of Rehabilitation

Medically speaking, rehabilitation (from the Latin *rehabilitare*: 'to restore to a former capacity') goes hand in hand with prevention. Rehabilitation includes measures to restore damaged bodily functions, to facilitate early diagnosis of setbacks and thus to prevent relapse. At the beginning of the new epoch, in the sixteenth century, the Roman Catholic

Church was suffering from two festering wounds: the break with the Eastern Church a half century earlier and the contemporaneous break with the Protestant churches of northern Europe. Soon it would be exposed to entirely new forces and energies that would further ravage the body of the Church and result in additional infections instead of a cure.

A programme of comprehensive rehabilitation was desperately needed to restore the Church's ability to deal appropriately with new challenges and to reintegrate into modern society. In the political sphere, the term 'rehabilitation' describes the restoration of the political reputation of someone who had suffered under a previous regime and acknowledgement of his legitimate concerns; normally it occurs only as a consequence of paradigm shifts. Real reform of the Catholic Church in the sixteenth century would have meant rescinding the ecclesiastical and political measures that had cut off the Orthodox and Protestant churches and their members and correcting past mistakes. As recent political history shows, changes of this sort usually mean radical revision of the nomenklatura (from the Russian: 'the list of key administrative positions and people in leading positions'); thus, major changes in the papal power structure were needed. Nothing of this sort took place; the rehabilitation efforts concentrated only on symptoms, and so, instead of a thorough-going restoration of the Church's health, only a superficial recovery occurred, cosmetically embellished by magnificent manifestations of Baroque art and culture.

Although in his personal life Pope Paul III (1534–49) was still very much a Renaissance pope who ruled with his children and grandchildren serving as cardinals, he was nevertheless the first pope to lay the foundations for a modicum of reform by appointing capable and deeply religious leaders of the reform party to the College of Cardinals. Even more importantly, he supported and confirmed the creation of a new type of religious order composed of clerics living an active life in the world without the remnants of the monastic lifestyle that still marked the mendicant orders. Well-educated not only in theology but also in the secular humanities and sciences, and tightly organized in military fashion, these 'soldiers of God' became the elite vanguard of a movement known in church history as the 'Counter-Reformation'. In the forefront were the Jesuits, the 'Compañía de Jesús' founded by Ignatius of Loyola and his six companions in 1534 and approved by Pope Paul III in 1540.

Pope Paul III's third, and perhaps most important and enduring, contribution to the process of church reform, however, was his convocation of a General Council in 1537 – almost three decades after the Protestant Reformers had begun calling for a reforming free General Council to meet in Germany and just two years before Luther's death. After years of delay, caused mainly by curial opposition to a meeting on German-speaking territory, the Council finally met in 1545 in the imperial city of Trento at the fringe of the German-speaking area. Renewed efforts to move the Council to Italy caused long interruptions between 1549 and 1551 and again between 1552 and 1562, so that this Council of Trent came to a close only in 1563, going into Catholic history books as the Nineteenth Ecumenical Council. Regrettably, it was dominated by Italian and Spanish prelates who had little or no appreciation of the genuine motives behind the Protestant Reformation or of German concerns and mentality.

A Pretence of Rehabilitation: the Council of the Counter-Reformation

Without question, the serious reforming efforts of this Council, and above all its correction of the most glaring abuses and its reform of priestly training by the creation of seminaries as cadre factories, would have a great impact in the decades and centuries to come, but they were not sufficient to produce any true convalescence of the Church.

At the Council of Trent, nothing was said about the urgently needed reform of the papacy – too great was the fear of reawakening the slumbering decree *Sacrosancta* of the Sixteenth Ecumenical Council of Constance (1414–18) that had unmistakably declared the superiority of the General Council over the pope. The conciliar fathers made little or no effort to understand the biblical and historical theology of the Protestants; instead they contented themselves with reaffirming traditional scholastic theology and anathematizing the Protestant positions as heresy. Instead of extending a hand of reconciliation, the Council demanded abject submission. In short, the Council of Trent marked the beginning not of rehabilitation but only of reaction.

The programme of the Council of Trent was of Counter-Reformation – in essence, a revival of the Medieval Catholicism clothed in new anti-Reformation trappings. Nowhere is this clearer than in its reform of the Mass. It eliminated the worst outgrowths of the past, only to reaffirm and refine the lopsided understanding of the sacrament that had developed in the Middle Ages. It summarily dismissed the demands of the Protestants for celebration in the language of the people and for the admission of the laity to communion from the chalice.

It reaffirmed the Medieval notion of the Eucharist as an act performed alone by the ordained celebrant, and concentrated on the moment of turning bread and wine into the Body and Blood of Christ ('transubstantiation') and re-enacting the sacrifice of Christ on the Cross. In this view, the rest of the Mass, including the Liturgy of the Word (centred on reading and praying the Bible) and even the act of taking communion, became little more than decorative accoutrements. As in the Middle Ages, the laity were mere spectators: their presence could be dispensed with ('private' Masses) and their reception of communion, with the exception of the once-a-year 'Easter duty', was not encouraged, since they were presumed to be unworthy without an immediately preceding confession and absolution of their sins. The reform of the Mass by Pope Pius V in 1570 not only restored the Medieval Latin Mass but at the same time abrogated almost all of the regional and national variations, imposing on the universal Church, with exceptions, the form traditionally used in the city of Rome and now regulated down to even the smallest gesture.

The worldwide Catholic Church was not only ruled by Rome; it now became Roman in a cultural sense. Everything was loaded with Baroque ceremony and decoration in Roman style. The liturgical celebration, especially the Pontifical Mass, became a grand religious spectacle for an audience of awed spectators, a theatrical performance acted out in a theatre created by magnificent Baroque architecture, on an elaborate stage dominated by a Baroque high altar and orchestrated with the intricate counterpoint of Baroque music. All this pageantry expressed the renewed papal claim to the power and authority of an '*ecclesia militans et triumphans*', a militant and triumphant Church symbolized so eloquently in the monumental St

Peter's Basilica with its towering dome and breathtaking Bernini plaza, whose open circle of four rowed colonnades reaches out as if to enclose the whole world.

Guided entirely by narrow ecclesiastical interests, the Council initiated a programme of European re-Catholicization to be achieved by political means where possible, and by military force where necessary. The refurbished Roman Inquisition and the new *Roman Index of Prohibited Books* enforced internal discipline. In the second half of the sixteenth century, internal repressions, diplomatic complications and military aggressions produced a deluge of religious conflicts and religious wars, which ravaged Germany and France in particular; there were numberless atrocities on both sides.

In a scandalous abuse of religious faith, tiny Protestant groups were ruthlessly suppressed in Italy and Spain. France suffered through eight civil wars against the Calvinist Huguenots; in Paris, in a single night in 1572 (the infamous 'St Bartholomew's Day Massacre') 3,000 Protestant men, women and children were cruelly murdered, and in the following days an additional 10,000 Protestants were butchered in the provinces. On hearing of the atrocities, Pope Gregory XIII celebrated a solemn *Te Deum* and struck a commemorative medal. In the Netherlands, the Dutch Calvinists revolted against the Spanish reign of terror; the ensuing Spanish–Dutch War lasted over 80 years. In Germany, the terrible Thirty Years' War (1618–48) reduced cities and countryside to wasted, depopulated ruins swept over by alternating waves of German Catholic and Protestant armies and their Danish, Swedish and French allies.

Exhausted by three decades of warfare, the Catholic and Protestant rulers finally resolved their differences in the Peace of Westphalia (1648), which granted parity to the Lutheran and Catholic Churches and officially recognized the Calvinist Reformed Church. The religious rights guaranteed by this accord have largely persisted up until the present day. In addition to regulating religious affairs within the empire, the treaties formally recognized the independence of Switzerland and the Netherlands.

Thus ended an era shaped by the Reformation and Counter-Reformation. Religious fervour had reached its apogee and was now largely spent. But it was not the papacy that led the warring nations out of the hell of religious warfare. The religious clashes in which each side laid exclusive claim to the truth were repeatedly rekindled and stoked by the papacy, and it played a nefarious role not only in the Thirty Years' War. Peace was eventually made not by a religious dialogue leading to consensus but by a political decision to ignore the differences in belief. The inability of Catholics and Protestants to achieve true religious peace discredited Christianity itself and led to its losing its traditional function as the religious, cultural, political and social glue holding Europe together. Divided within itself and beholden to personal and national interests, Christianity itself would hasten the process of religious disaffiliation, the separation of religion from the State and the cultural and economic marginalization of religion – developments that taken together would make up the secularization process characteristic of the modern age.

Retreat into a Parallel World of Its Own Making, Shut off from the Modern World

Around the middle of the seventeenth century, a new global and political constellation began to emerge:

- Spain, once the pre-eminent Roman Catholic power made rich by its conquests and exploitation of the gold, silver and other resources of Latin America and parts of Asia, had exhausted itself in numerous wars, fought to defend its possessions and, by the second half of the seventeenth century, was on the way to losing its place among the great European powers.

- Both Germany, exhausted in the wake of the Thirty Years' War, and Italy, weakened by constant internecine warfare and foreign invasions, became negligible players on the global political stage.

- The papacy, deprived of its traditional role as an international power broker at the Peace of Westphalia, was not replaced by any other supra-national institution for maintaining or restoring peace; simultaneously, the aggressive drive of Protestantism became blunted as the Protestant churches became absorbed into the administrative apparatus of the national states.

- An age of royal absolutism followed the age of religious dissension: France, under Cardinal Richelieu and Louis XIV, became the dominant power in Europe, but the subsequent French kings proved weak and so this age ended in 1789 with the French Revolution and the execution of the French king and queen and many of the nobility at the guillotine.

- Simultaneously, a new cultural constellation began to emerge. Epochal paradigm shifts resulted from socio-political, ecclesiastical and theological–philosophical modernization efforts, but, for the most part, they occurred outside the areas under Roman Catholic control. In Catholic territories, institutions like the Inquisition and book censorship more or less successfully repressed efforts at modernization, especially in the religious and intellectual spheres. Constrained by its Medieval straitjacket, the Roman Catholic paradigm, so innovative during the Middle Ages, became now increasingly sclerotic, an enemy to innovation of every kind. Nowhere is this fear of everything modern better illustrated than by the opposition of Pope Gregory XVI (1831–46) to simple technological innovations like gas lighting and railways out of fear that they would strengthen the up-and-coming middle class, help spread liberal ideas and undermine the papal monarchy and clerical rule in the Papal States.

Despite all its Baroque trappings, Counter-Reformation Catholicism was essentially a conservative-restorative religion with a strong appeal to the economically, politically and cultur-ally stagnant rural populations of the Romance and Slavic nations and to the nobility who ruled over them. By contrast, in the cities with their upward-striving bourgeoisie and in enlightened circles of the nobility, more liberal views prevailed, and individual rights and duties were stressed. In Catholicism, the pope alone claimed to decide on the correct interpretation of the Bible and Tradition and to lay out the course to be taken in practice as well as in theory, tending to treat with scepticism and even intolerance innovation of every kind. In Protestantism, by contrast, the emphasis on the Pauline 'freedom of every Christian' contributed substantially to the focus on personal responsibility and autonomy which became characteristic of the modern age.

Science, technological progress, democracy and industrialization were the dynamic forces behind the emergence of modernity. From the sixteenth century until the 1960s, the official Catholic Church consistently opposed modernization and the dynamic forces behind it. This opposition to modernity transformed the Medieval and Counter-Reformation paradigm into an anti-modern fortress with a strong appeal to the supporters and beneficiaries of reactionary political and social institutions and movements. Controlled until the mid-nineteenth century more by the Roman Curia than by individual popes who came and went, entrenched Roman Catholicism used all of the holy and unholy means at its disposal to launch rearguard counterattacks against the emerging modern culture and to inoculate the loyal Catholic masses against the viruses of Modernism. Fanatical devotion to tradition gave birth to the viruses of hostility to science, hostility to progress, hostility to democracy and support of reactionary movements. These virus infections began at the onset of the modern era in Europe and spread rapidly. With regard to science and education, both so fundamentally important for modern men and women, this anti-modern Catholicism did little to raise the general level of education of the Catholic masses beyond a basic minimum; instead it concentrated its efforts on indoctrinating a small elite of educated Catholics with militant anti-Modernism to make them the vanguard of political and social reaction. The overall result was repeated recurrences of the Catholic malaise in the eighteenth, nineteenth and twentieth centuries down to the present day.

The First Virus: Church Hostility to Science

The paramount revolution of the modern age was one affecting the mind. Science became the pre-eminent superpower of the dawning new era. Scientist–philosophers like Galileo, Descartes and Pascal, followed by Spinoza, Leibniz and Locke, Newton, Huygens and Boyle helped lay the foundations for a new appreciation of the superiority of reason. They relied on ongoing logical deduction and empirical observation rather than venerable authorities. They used refined instruments, systematic experimentation and mathematical models to enhance and verify their empirical observations and to construct new theories to achieve mathematical certainty. Instead of reacting positively to this new science, the Church, fearing a threat to its monopolistic power to control truth, reacted negatively, mobilizing the instruments of prior censorship such as the Imprimatur, the *Index of Prohibited Books* and the Inquisition to repress intellectual novelties. So strong was the power of the Inquisition that it often even intimidated individual popes who showed themselves to be friendlier to the new science than the reactionary inquisitors in the Curia.

The virus of hostility to science is nowhere better illustrated than by the Church's reaction to the Copernican Revolution that culminated in the famous trial of Galileo. From antiquity, European thinking had been dominated by a geocentric–anthropocentric worldview, with the earth at the centre of the universe. This view had been developed by Aristotle as a physical theory and refined by Ptolemy as a mathematical astronomical model; it appealed to common-sense experience and appeared to be corroborated by the Bible. In 1543, Nicolaus Copernicus, a cathedral canon of the prince-bishopric of Warmia/Ermland in modern Poland, published a revolutionary alternative theory. Based on his own astronomical observations and calculations, Copernicus proposed a heliocentric world system with the sun near its centre and the earth and other planets revolving around the sun. Initially Copernicus's theory was challenged as a physical explanation of the universe by some Protestant theologians on biblical grounds and, more importantly, by many natural scientists on the scientific grounds that it could not be unequivocally and empirically verified, and did not fit with other scientific beliefs or with common-sense experience. Nevertheless, the new theory quickly found wide acceptance as a mathematical hypothesis useful for astronomical calculations.

According to an unverifiable report in his *Table Talks*, Luther rejected Copernicus's theory because it appeared to contradict the Bible; Melanchthon initially opposed it, but later came to admire it. Among sixteenth-century Lutheran scholars, it soon found wide support as a useful mathematical model, and sometimes even as a physical theory. Not surprisingly, it was perfected by the Lutheran Johannes Kepler in his *Epitome astronomiae Copernicanae* (1616–21).

In the Catholic Church, however, the theological argument soon gave rise to a *cause célèbre* with longstanding consequences: the trial of Galileo. In 1610, the Italian Catholic scientist Galileo Galilei began publishing evidence – gained by his personal observations using the newly invented telescope and by his methodical experimentation – that challenged the prevailing Aristotelian–Ptolemaic world view and supported the new Copernican theory as being a physical fact and not just a mathematical model. The priest-astronomers at the Jesuit Collegium Romanum in Rome were willing to give Galileo's ideas a hearing, but in 1615 the great Jesuit Cardinal Robert Bellarmine, the leading theologian of the day, argued that the new theory could not be interpreted as a physical explanation of the universe until convincing scientific evidence for the movement of the earth around the sun could be presented.

Meanwhile, Galileo's work was formally denounced to the Roman Inquisition by two Dominicans in 1613 and 1614 on the grounds that it contradicted the Bible. To prevent a condemnation of heliocentrism as heresy, Galileo decided to go to Rome personally. In 1616 a formal trial took place. The theological commission voted to condemn Copernicanism as 'foolish and absurd in philosophy, and formally heretical', but, under the influence of Cardinal Bellarmine, no such formal condemnation was issued, although the works of Copernicus, Galileo and other authors defending heliocentrism were put on the *Index of Forbidden Books*. Galileo himself does not appear to have been asked at this time to recant or even to cease publishing on the topic, as long as he contented himself with proposing Copernicanism only as a hypothesis.

Before continuing this sordid story, we should note that with others the Inquisition was not so mild and tactful. Giordano Bruno, who combined the Copernican world model with a pantheist, neo-platonic, mystical, Renaissance piety, was burned at the stake in Rome in 1600. The same fate befell the Italian natural philosopher Lucilio Vanini, who supposedly taught that God and nature were identical, in 1619 in Toulouse.

The anti-Aristotelian philosopher–theologian Tommaso Campanella endured crippling torture and mishandling in the prisons of the Inquisition from 1600 until his release in 1626 at the intervention of Pope Urban VIII. But even under papal protection he was not safe from the Inquisition, so in 1634, with the aid of powerful ecclesiastical friends, he found refuge in Paris, where he lived until his death in 1638 under the protection of Cardinal Richelieu and King Louis XIII.

In 1633, Galileo Galilei was once again summoned before the Inquisition to answer charges brought against his *Dialogue Concerning the Two Chief World Systems, Ptolemaic & Copernican*, published the year before. This time a formal sentence based exclusively on theological grounds was issued. It declared Galileo 'vehemently suspected of heresy, namely of having held and believed a doctrine which is false and contrary to the divine and Holy Scripture: that the sun is the centre of the world and does not move from east to west, and the earth moves and is not the centre of the world, and that one may hold and defend as probable an opinion after it has been declared and defined contrary to Holy Scripture' (Sentence of 22 June 1633 in the translation of M. A. Finocchiaro, from *The Galileo Affair: A Documentary History* [1989]). Galileo was required to 'abjure, curse and detest' those opinions. His book was forbidden and he was sentenced to imprisonment, later commuted to house arrest after he recanted his 'mistakes'. He spent the last eight years of his life under house arrest, although he continued to work even after he had gone blind.

Using instrumentally refined observation and controlled experiment, Galileo became the symbolic founder of modern science, beginning a new era of limitless exploration of nature and of the universe. Working at the same time as Galileo, René

Descartes, likewise a mathematician and scientist, became the founder of modern philosophy based on science. The new natural science relying on experimentation and rational construction subjected to controlled observation marked an epochal change in the notion of authority. According to the Medieval–Catholic paradigm the pope represented the highest authority, and according to the Reformation paradigm the highest authority was the text of the Bible. In the new paradigm of the modern age, however, the highest authority became human reason making use of the tools of science. Only what was rational and could be empirically verified was considered true, useful and binding. Now philosophy took precedence over theology: where Christian faith appeared to contradict what was held to be natural and humane, it was the latter that prevailed.

Galileo's conflict with the Church was symptomatic and set a precedent which poisoned the relationship between the young and aspiring sciences and the Church and religion at the very root. The sentence against Galileo was enforced in Catholic countries with the help of informers and inquisitors, creating an atmosphere of fear. In consequence, René Descartes postponed indefinitely the publication of his own treatise *The World, or, A Treatise on Light* (it was only published fourteen years after his death). The result was a silent withdrawal of scientists within the Church. The subsequent centuries saw few notable scientists working in Catholic countries.

The aftermath of the Galileo affair was almost as scandalous as the affair itself. Catholic scientists increasingly ignored the condemnations. In the face of mounting acceptance of Copernicanism, the Church began a cautious retreat, without, however, publicly admitting error. In 1744, it permitted a heavily censored version of Galileo's *Dialogue* to be published. In 1758, the new edition of the *Index* silently dropped the general prohibition of books defending heliocentrism, but failed to remove the works of Copernicus and Galileo from the list of works explicitly condemned. There the matter rested until 1820, when the official papal theologian and censor Filippo Anfossi, a rigorist Dominican fearful of novelty in any form and committed to restoring pure doctrine at all cost, refused to allow a book by Joseph Settele, a Swabian priest-astronomer teaching in Rome, to be printed on the grounds that heliocentrism had been declared heretical in 1633. Instead of seeking compromise, Settele appealed to Pope Pius VII, who ordered the Holy Office to review the matter. After the review, the pope officially decreed 'that no obstacles exist for those who sustain Copernicus's affirmation regarding the earth's movement in the manner in which it is affirmed today even by Catholic authors', suggesting that any difficulties that may have existed in the past had been resolved by subsequent confirming astronomical observations.

Despite the pope's explicit instructions, the rigorist Anfossi continued to argue that the issue had been settled once and for all back in 1633 as a matter of faith, and, to this day, some extreme Catholic traditionalists take this same line. Anfossi was officially rebuked by the pope and in the next edition of the *Index*, which appeared in 1835, the works of Copernicus and Galileo were silently omitted.

Finally, in 1979, 350 years after Galileo's death, Pope John Paul II announced that the case of Galileo Galilei would again be reviewed by an investigative commission. Although this resulted in a rehabilitation of Galileo, the pope, in his speech on 31 October 1982, avoided clearly acknowledging any guilt on the part of either his predecessors or the Sacred Inquisition (known today as the Congregation for the Doctrine of the Faith); instead he blamed it on the 'majority of theologians'. In the words of the historian of science Michael Segre, this was 'a rehabilitation, which did not take place'. Moreover, even after this rehabilitation, some Catholic apologists continue to argue, on a variety of historical grounds, that the actions of the ecclesiastical authorities were perfectly right and prudent in their day and remained so for centuries to come.

To this day, the Church has neither consistently nor emphatically moved away from its former hostility to science and it continues to deny even factual errors in dealing with scientific questions. Subsequent controversies would show that Rome learned little from the Galileo affair.

The Relapse: Charles Darwin

The Darwin affair was a second Galileo affair. As late as 1941, almost 100 years after the publication of Darwin's *On the Origin of Species*, Pope Pius XII claimed, in an address to members of the Papal Academy of Sciences, that the animal ancestry of human beings was completely unproven and that it would be necessary to await further investigations. Nine years later, in his reactionary encyclical *Humani generis*, Pius XII reluctantly and condescendingly signalled that the Church did not forbid scientific and theological investigation into the possibility (by no means yet proven) of an evolution of the human body, but he insisted that Catholics must continue to hold that the human soul is created directly by God and that all human beings are descended from one single original pair (*monogenesis*). Moreover, in all matters touching faith,

Catholics must submit to the judgement of the Magisterium. Subsequently, numerous Catholic theologians tied themselves in knots trying to give a sensible interpretation to these assertions, which for scientists were totally incomprehensible.

A few weeks later, Pius XII demonstrated just how remote and stubborn he was when, at a mass rally held on St Peter's Square on 1 November 1950, he solemnly proclaimed as an infallible dogma the belief – equally incomprehensible to scientists and attested neither in the Bible nor in early Christian tradition – that, at the end of her life, the body of the Virgin Mary was physically taken up into heaven!

The same year marked the beginning of the merciless purge under Pope Pius XII, otherwise so widely admired, of numerous theologians who attempted to bring Catholic theology in line with the results of biblical and patristic studies.

The Second Virus: Church Hostility to Progress

The scientific and philosophical revolutions produced in turn the cultural revolution of the Enlightenment, which eventually led to political revolution as well. For the first time in the history of Christianity, the impetus for a new comprehensive paradigm for the world, society, and the Church with its theology, did not emerge from within, but came from the outside.

The eighteenth century was marked by a strong decline in religious fervour, which accompanied a general cultural weather change. Particularly in Catholic France, traditional values such as 'order', 'authority', 'discipline', 'hierarchy' and 'dogma' were rejected and widely mocked. This marked the beginning of a process of secularization and emancipation which later spread, in milder forms, to Germany and other countries. This gradual drifting apart of culture and religion, society and the Church, would have far-reaching consequences.

The belief in the omnipotence of reason and in the capacity to master nature became the basis for the modern belief in progress. Eighteenth-century belief in the benefits of progress extended to all areas of life. History was thought to evolve rationally and progressively. Belief in progress – the belief that 'happiness' could already be achieved in this world – became the second guiding principle of the modern age. The vision of men and women being entirely self-determined combined with the belief in human dominion over the world of nature became for many people a secular pseudo-religion.

More and more, the use of coercion in religious matters came to be regarded as inhumane and unchristian. Catholic and Protestant belief in devils, demons and witchcraft were incompatible with the progressive age of reason, and the widespread practice of burning witches was condemned. The Flemish physician Johann Weyer and the Jesuit Friedrich von Spee were the first to attack the witch trials and burnings, soon to be followed by the Protestant jurist Christian Thomasius. Just as indulgences, pilgrimages, processions and monasteries had earlier come under fire, now obligatory celibacy and the Latin liturgy became objects of criticism even within the Church. With the exception of the enlightened Benedict XIV (1740–58), the popes of the eighteenth century were relatively insignificant figures and typically reacted to the challenges of their times by issuing sterile protests and undifferentiated condemnations. The Catholic princes, acting in their own interest in maintaining the *status quo*, often remained the papacy's sole supporters.

Catholic scholastic philosophy and theology were hardly touched by the cultural revolution of the Enlightenment, except that the lists of opponents to their theses grew ever longer. Biblical exegesis, however, which applied critical historical analysis to the study of the Scriptures, did begin to bud, only to be quashed before it could flower when the critical history of the Old Testament written by the Oratorian Richard Simon and printed in 1678 was immediately confiscated at the instigation of the famous French bishop and court preacher Bossuet. With the spirit of critical biblical scholarship within the Catholic Church extinguished, the intellectual avant-garde of theology also began to migrate out of the Church of Rome. It is due mainly to the immense labours of generations of Protestant exegetes that the Bible has become the most thoroughly studied book in world literature.

Religious tolerance was a concept originally as foreign to Protestants as it was to Catholics. Soon, however, it would become a keyword of the modern age. Increasingly detailed reports by European explorers, missionaries and merchants of far distant continents led to the dawning realization that the Christian religion was neither as unique nor as universal as Europeans had previously assumed. The intensification of international communication after the discovery and exploration of new continents, lands, cultures and religions brought the relativity of the European form of Christian religion increasingly to the fore.

For Protestants, this new awareness of other cultures and religions had few immediate consequences, since intensive Protestant missionary efforts began only in the eighteenth century and flourished only in the nineteenth and twentieth centuries, and by that time Enlightenment notions of tolerance and respect for other cultures shaped the Protestant missionary work.

The Roman Catholic missionary effort had already begun in the sixteenth century and was carried out especially in the lands conquered and colonized by Spain and Portugal. In general, a *tabula rasa* approach prevailed. Local cultures were swept away and native religious traditions and sensitivities were trampled upon. Catholic converts were forced to adopt Spanish and Portuguese lifestyles and forms of piety. In Eastern Europe, the Middle East, and especially in India, efforts were made not only to bring the ancient Orthodox churches of the East under Roman control but also to Latinize them as far as possible. To this intolerant policy there was one notable but short-lived exception, the Jesuit mission in China.

The Jesuit mission in China was initiated by the Italian Matteo Ricci in 1583. Impressed by the high level of Chinese culture and the need to accommodate missionary tactics to it, Ricci put aside his European clothing, language and behaviour to adapt to the Confucian lifestyle of the learned Mandarin elite and the imperial court. He was soon joined by other Jesuits who followed the same principle of assimilation and were greatly appreciated for their understanding of Chinese culture and for their services as scientists, astronomers, multilingual diplomats and importers of European technology, especially weaponry. So effective was their mission that, in 1692, the emperor Kangxi issued a decree of toleration giving legal status to Christianity alongside Buddhism and Daoism.

Initially, the Jesuit accommodation to Chinese culture was encouraged by the popes, even to the point of allowing the celebration of the liturgy in Chinese instead of Latin, but the Jesuits' success provoked the envy of the competing Franciscan and Dominican missionaries, mostly of Spanish or Portuguese origin, who rejected any accommodation to local culture or religious sensitivities and demanded that their converts completely assimilate to a European lifestyle, following the same *tabula rasa* principle that had marked their missionary activities in Latin America, India and the Philippines. Soon these rival missionaries denounced the Jesuit tolerance of traditional Chinese rituals and forms of expression – at stake was the translation of the Latin word 'Deus' into Chinese – to the Roman Inquisition. Rome vacillated for a time, but then, in 1704, Pope Clement XI heavy-handedly condemned the Chinese rites and other Jesuit accommodations and expressly forbade all further discussion. In 1715, he solemnly confirmed this decision in the papal bull *Ex illa die*, and in 1742 this decision was reiterated in a bull issued by Pope Benedict XIV. In effect, anyone who wished to become or remain a Christian would have to stop being Chinese! Not surprisingly, the Chinese emperor banned the Catholic missionaries in 1721 and his successor began active persecution in 1737. Not until the twentieth century would the popes begin a cautious retreat from this catastrophic position, as usual without any admission that the original papal action had been wrong. But by then it was too late, as we shall see later on in this chapter.

In the end, however, religious tolerance prevailed over rigorist confessionalism in Catholic as well as in Protestant countries. It proved impossible to maintain the monopoly of a single religion within the national state. Outside of the Papal States and the territories controlled by the Spanish and Portuguese empires, not even the Catholic rulers were willing to enforce the decisions of the Inquisition. Especially in the Protestant nations, new religious movements gave rise to new churches, and Christianity split into a spectrum of denominations forced to live side by side with each other. Commerce and immigration brought Jews, Muslims and members of other religions to the fore in Western lands. The civil authorities reacted first by proclaiming religious tolerance and later by granting legal status to the different Christian denominations, and later to the other religious communities as well. Despite Roman opposition which continued well into the twentieth century, enlightened Christians and even Catholics increasingly came to see the idea of mutual tolerance as a positive value rather than a mere grudging acceptance of an intrinsically evil situation that could not, for the moment at least, be overcome even by force.

Enlightened thinkers proclaimed freedom of conscience and freedom of religious practice to be basic human rights and called for their political implementation. From the French Revolution onwards, however, the popes, from Pius VI through Pius VII, Pius VIII, Gregory XVI, Pius IX, Leo XIII, Pius X, Pius XI and even Pius XII, consistently rejected any right to religious liberty, although they gradually came to grant that the conditions of modern times made the practice of tolerance by the civil authorities expedient for the sake of a higher good. Thus in Catholic lands and among staunch Catholics the idea of tolerance found, for the most part, only grudging acceptance as a lesser evil, and hostility to progress continued to prevail. This would not change until the decrees of the Second Vatican Council unequivocally affirmed religious freedom as an inherent human right (*Nostra aetate*) and affirmed the need to come to terms with progress (*Gaudium et spes*).

The Relapse: The Pill and the Campaign Against Modern Medical Techniques

In Europe, the Papal States were considered synonymous with hostility to progress. Their *monsignori* system of clerical rule made them the most socially backward states in Europe. The popes of the early nineteenth century rejected even technological advances like railways, gas lighting and suspension bridges as being unnecessary and even demonic when they promoted the spread of liberal ideas, the rise of the bourgeoisie, the curtailment of the privileges of the nobility and the overthrow of the papal monarchy.

Opposition to progress did not end there. In the twentieth century, questions of sexuality and reproduction became the litmus test for progressiveness. One of the most important inventions of the twentieth century is without a doubt the birth control pill, developed, ironically as the history of its Catholic reception would show, by two good Catholics, John Rock and Pasquale DeFelice. Within a few years, the Pill permanently changed the patterns of sexual behaviour and social coexistence between men and women. Since the 1920s, scientists had been investigating the role of hormones in pregnancy, and wealthy women financially supported the search for a pill that would prevent women from becoming pregnant. On the part of the Church, such research was at first ignored, but then, as it began to bear fruit, the pope reacted with emphatic rejection.

Some fifty years ago, on 9 May 1960, the first contraceptive pill was approved for use by the US Food and Drug Administration. It made a sexual revolution possible, but this revolution only really kicked off in tandem with the cultural revolution of 1968. The cultural revolution aimed at overthrowing established structures of power and thinking and called upon women to take control of their own sexual lives. Reliable methods of birth control allowed women to separate sexuality and reproduction, making possible sexual intercourse without fear of consequences and with enjoyment as its aim – exactly what St Augustine and the subsequent tradition had prohibited. Women were now free to decide for themselves whether and when they wished to conceive. Furthermore, the advent of birth control made it possible for more women than ever to go on to university studies – female students now often make up more than half of all university students in many parts of the world – and to pursue professional careers, gaining financial and social independence and making them true partners rather than inferiors in marriage.

In the same year that the cultural revolution broke out in Europe and America, in 1968, Pope Paul VI published his famous encyclical *Humanae vitae*, which reaffirmed the tradition of Catholic ethics going back to St Augustine and reinforced by Medieval physicalist notions of natural law, viewing sexuality as morally justified only for the purposes of reproduction. As I set forth at length in my book *Infallible?* (1971), the issue for Paul VI was not so much the question of human sexuality: it was the issue of papal authority and infallibility. Could Pope Pius XI have been mistaken when, in his 1930 encyclical *Casti connubii*, he contradicted the position taken shortly before by the Anglican Lambeth Conference, and condemned all forms of contraception as immoral? For Paul VI and a small coterie of conservative advisors, it was unthinkable that Pius XI could have been wrong. Thus, in 1968, Paul VI extended his predecessor's prohibition of mechanical and other forms of contraception to include the Pill. His decision flew in the face of the convictions of a huge majority of Catholic laity and theologians and even against the majority within the commission he had called to advise him on the matter.

De facto, this doctrine has been accepted only within conservative Catholic circles, but it was repeatedly confirmed by Paul VI's successors, John Paul II and Benedict XVI. Although now worldwide some 120 million women, including many Catholics, practise birth control using hormonal and other devices, the Catholic Church continues to reject the Pill fifty years after its invention. After the Galileo affair and the Darwin affair, this was now the third example of an epic mistake, which, this time, drove many women out of the Church or into silent internal emigration.

But the matter did not end there. After the development of the Pill, medical research went on to develop techniques of artificial insemination to help the many women unable to conceive and bear the child that they longed for, and techniques of embryonic stem-cell research were developed to discover new cures for diseases resistant to other forms of therapy. Admittedly, the morality of these techniques is debated not only among theologians but also among scientists, jurists and philosophers; however, the popes refused to give a hearing to the arguments of those scientists and theologians, many of them Catholic, who have come out in favour of a differentiated ethical evaluation of such practices. Instead, under John Paul II and Benedict XVI, the campaign against artificial contraception and the new reproductive techniques became part of the militant and undifferentiated crusade against abortion on the principle that a full human person is born at the moment of conception, when a human ovum is fertilized by a sperm cell; thus any act causing the destruction of even a single fertilized ovum, to say nothing of any of the subsequent stages by which it becomes a foetus capable of living outside the womb, is an act of infanticide, i.e. the cold-blooded murder of an innocent human person. Thus Rome protested loudly against the award of the Nobel Prize for medicine in 2010 to the pioneer of *in vitro* fertilization, Robert Edwards, whose work has enabled four million children to be born.

The development of life-prolonging technology in recent decades has opened up a further area of conflict between Catholic moral teaching and modern medicine, raising the question of a right to die. Caught in the trap of their own pro-life logic, the popes have increasingly come out in favour of postponing death at all costs, even if this means prolonging a mere vegetative state with no hope of restoring the person to conscious human life. A series of sensational cases involving Catholics, like the Karen Ann Quinlan and Terri Schiavo cases in the USA, have made the official Catholic moral stance appear absurd and inhuman even in the eyes of many Catholics.

Thus, today only a very small but vociferous minority of Catholics take the official opinion on bioethical matters seriously.

The Third Virus: Church Hostility to Democracy

The cultural revolution of the Enlightenment was followed by political, national and social revolutions. The epitome of all these revolutions was the French Revolution. Gone was the Medieval theocracy embodied by the pope; gone, too, was the authority of Protestant princes and patrician city councils. And, finally, gone were the absolute monarchies of the early modern period like those of Frederick II (Prussia) or Joseph II (Austria). The hour of democracy had come. The people (*demos*) were now the sovereign, represented by a national assembly, and the nation became the third guiding principle of the modern age.

After the storming of the Bastille on 14 July 1789, the path in France was clear for the *Declaration of the Rights of Man and of the Citizen* on 26 August 1789, influenced by the model of the American *Declaration of Independence* in 1776. The *Declaration of the Rights of Man* is the great Charter of modern democracy, one of the greatest documents in all of human history, and progressive Catholic clerics were significantly involved in formulating it. In the revolutionary National Assembly, these clerics were not alone in insisting that the declaration of human rights (*droits*) needed to be complemented by a declaration of human duties (*devoirs*). In fact, this idea was supported by almost half of all the delegates, but to this day it remains an unfulfilled desideratum not only in France.

In Rome Pope Pius VI, an aristocrat, declared the French *Civil Constitution of the Clergy* of 1791 invalid and condemned 'the abominable philosophy of human rights', particularly the freedom of religion and conscience, the freedom of the press and the concept of the equality of all people. It was a fatal decision for the Catholic Church, but, cost what it may, this condemnation was repeatedly confirmed by Rome in the nineteenth and even the twentieth century and the Church in France would pay a high price for its rejection of the Revolution.

The attempts to substitute a new 'Religion of Reason' for Christianity, however, failed. The new republican calendar making the revolutionary year 1792 Year I of a new era, assigning new names to the months and replacing the Judeo-Christian pattern of four seven-day weeks with three ten-day weeks per month proved complicated and unpopular and was abolished by Napoleon in 1805. The atheistic 'Cult of Reason' with ceremonies performed at an 'altar of liberty' culminating in the theatrical appearance of a woman representing the 'Goddess of Reason' ended effectively in 1794 and was officially banned by Napoleon in 1802. The Reign of Terror, 1793–4, with its mass guillotining carried out under Robespierre, shocked all of Europe. Nevertheless, many fundamental social changes introduced by the French Revolution survived and continue to influence the mentality of many people in France to this day. The secular character of the state and society and the programme of *laïcité*, officially formulated only in 1905, continue to govern France today:

- The creed yielded to the charter of the rights of man; church law gave way to the national constitution.

- The Cross yielded to the Tricolore; church ceremonies of baptism, marriage and burials were replaced by the civil registration of births, marriages and deaths. Teachers assumed the role previously played by the priest in the civil community.

- The altar and sacrifice of the Mass were replaced by the altar of the nation on which true patriots laid down their lives. Religious-sounding place and street names were often replaced by patriotic names.

- The veneration of the saints was replaced by the veneration of heroic martyrs of the Nation, the *Te Deum* by the *Marseillaise*.

- Christian ethics were replaced by the Enlightenment ethics of civic virtue and social harmony.

The result in France was a division between laicists and clericalists, culminating in the development of two mutually hostile cultures: on the one side, the predominating, often militant republican–secularist culture of the ruling liberal bourgeoisie; on the other side, the rearguard, clerical and royalist, later papalistic, counter- or subculture of a conservative Catholic minority. The march of the official Catholic Church into a cultural ghetto had begun.

Might there have been an alternative? From the start, Abbé Henri-Baptiste Grégoire, a zealous bishop and spiritual leader of the constitutional, i.e. pro-revolutionary, faction in the Church worked to promote reconciliation between the Church and democracy in the spirit of the ideals of early Christianity. But, against the determined opposition of the Curia and the traditionalist clergy allied to the nobility, this alternative had no chance. Thus, many of the issues raised by Grégoire found satisfactory resolution only after the Second Vatican Council. Only since the Council has it become safe for a Catholic to hold that the revolutionary ideals of 'liberty, equality and brotherhood' – demonized for so long by Rome – have early Christian roots that were later forgotten as hierarchical power structures were superimposed on the original constitution of the Church. Thus, the question to be faced today is: shall the Church continue to serve as a bastion of anti-democratic reaction or should it renew itself in the spirit of its founder, as a community of free men and women, essentially equal, a community of brothers and sisters (cf. Galatians 3:26–28).

It cannot be denied that the modern concept of nation-states gave birth to the calamitous ideologies and practices of nationalism and, quickly, imperialism allied with colonialism. Napoleon's wars of conquest cost hundreds of thousands of lives. In the nineteenth century, the dominant world power was no longer France but Great Britain.

Great Britain's predominance was linked to the technological and economic revolution which became the basis of the modern global economic system and a new global civilization. Caught in its opposition to innovation and democracy, the Catholic Church continued its rearguard opposition to the new economic system as well. In doing so, it often intervened in support of poor people who had become the victims of runaway capitalism, and Pope Leo XIII came out in defence of workers' rights. These positive contributions cannot be sufficiently lauded. On the other hand, the Catholic Church failed to take a lead in the battle against slavery, and, more often than not, it preached the moral duty of workers to submit to their masters. Thus the famous 'option for the poor and the oppressed' would have been more convincing if it had been linked with a clear 'option for democracy'. The oft-cited Vatican motto 'Pensiamo in secoli' – 'We think in centuries' – is a sign not only of Rome's haughty self-confidence but also of the fact that the Church frequently acts too late.

The Relapse: Preference for Authoritarian Regimes

Whenever public demands for church reform are voiced, Catholic opponents of reform recall the adage that the Church is not a democracy. Indeed, the popes of the nineteenth and the first half of the twentieth century were anything but impeccable democrats; more often they behaved as open or clandestine enemies of democracy. Towards the end of the Second World War, when the victory of the Western democracies was imminent, Pius XII could still only give a qualified endorsement to democracy, hedged under the condition that a sound democracy must be based not on the sovereignty of the people but 'on the immutable principles of natural law and revealed truth' (Christmas Address 1944); needless to say, only the pope and the Curia were qualified to interpret these principles. Pope Pius XII had no difficulty in working closely with dictatorships in Italy, Spain, Portugal and South America, as long as they protected the rights of the Church. In Italy, after the Second World War, Pius XII pleaded for the retention of the monarchy, discredited by its alliance with Fascism; a referendum decided otherwise. Imitating the nepotism of earlier times, Pius XII, the son of a bourgeois Roman family of lawyers in papal service, had his three nephews raised to princely rank and made them his principal advisors in financial matters. On the whole, he favoured a Catholic state and accepted religious tolerance only for pragmatic reasons, fearing negative consequences for Catholics living in Protestant countries.

John XXIII, and with him the Second Vatican Council, were the first to speak out clearly in favour of democracy and human rights. Pope Paul VI too was a staunch democrat because of his family traditions. But their reactionary Polish and German successors preferred to criticize Western democracy for its consumerism, dictatorship of relativism and negative tolerance, ignoring the fact that they themselves were the heads of an absolute dictatorship, often exercising no tolerance at all when Catholics differed on doctrinal and moral issues and not hesitating to exert political pressure to push through official Catholic positions. While still a cardinal, Joseph Ratzinger tried to pressure the German Bundestag to restrict counselling of pregnant women in conflict situations; in doing so, he alienated even the staunchly Catholic political party in his Bavarian homeland, the CSU. In Poland, where legislation strongly limiting access to the Pill was already in force, Pope Wojtyla attempted, in a threatening public address, to prevent the parliament from passing a more liberal law on abortion. Both attempts failed. These defeats signalled that the Roman Church leadership was steering a course with no future, and that brings us to the next viral infection.

The Fourth Virus: The Roman Catholic Enthusiasm for Restoration

After the Napoleonic wars, the political map of Europe was redrawn at the Congress of Vienna in 1814/15, dominated by the conservative 'Holy Alliance' of Russia, Prussia and Austria and masterminded by the Austrian Foreign Minister Prince Clement Wenceslaus von Metternich. For the Roman Curia, the congress brought the restoration of the Medieval Papal States that Napoleon had abolished. The traditional civil rule by clerical *monsignori* was immediately restored, and the legal system (*Code Napoléon*) was abolished and replaced by the pre-modern system of papal law. Some 700 cases of heresy were investigated by the Roman Inquisition.

Political theorists of the restoration, such as the Englishman Edmund Burke and the Frenchman Joseph de Maistre, who wrote a much-read book *The Pope*, supported these reactionary policies. Throughout Europe the Romantic era, originally a progressive movement, became increasingly reactionary, idealizing Medieval social structures and attempting to roll back the Enlightenment. But after the revolutionary wave of 1848, despite the temporary triumph of reaction, restoration and romanticism proved to be no more than a counter-revolutionary interlude. The only place where they persisted was in the Catholic Church; the second half of the nineteenth century became the high point of the neo-Gothic and neo-Romanesque revivals in art and architecture, the neo-scholastic revival in philosophy and theology and the Gregorian revival in liturgical music.

Democracy, however, continued its triumphant advance. The epic changes in economic and social living conditions known as the Industrial Revolution began to take hold. Behind these changes were evolutions in technology, production methods, energy production, transportation, agriculture, commerce and finance, but also in social structures and mentalities, called forth by the new market economy and a population explosion fed by an enormous increase in agricultural production and rapid urbanization.

Starting in England and propelled forward by science and technology in the nineteenth century, industry began to develop together with democracy. And industry became the fourth guiding principle of the modern age. This period is called the industrial age and it saw the emergence of a bourgeois–capitalist industrial society, characterized by the virtue of *industria* ('hard work') in sharp contrast to the indolence and indulgence of the agrarian feudal class. Admittedly, the capitalist industrial methods of production created new and dreadful class conflicts that brought forth fierce reactions from the industrial proletariat against oppression and exploitation by the capitalist owners and managers. Socialism and a manyfaceted Socialist Labour movement (see the *Communist Manifesto* of 1848) developed in the second half of the nineteenth century in response to the unbridled power exerted by the private ownership of capital.

For the Catholic, Protestant and Anglican churches, the break with tradition produced by democratization and industrialization proved a shock, but it also highlighted the need to win back the working classes, who had become alienated from the churches as a result of their alliance with the ruling classes. The nineteenth century witnessed a reawakening of religious fervour among the clergy and the laity. New religious orders with a charitable, educational or missionary orientation arose, foreign missions were revived and, above all, new forms of piety appeared. Church societies with a broad spectrum of religious, social and indirectly political initiatives flourished, particularly in Germany, where the *Volksverein für das Katholische Deutschland* (People's Association for Catholic Germany) became the biggest and most effective lay Catholic organization in the world. German Catholicism developed a momentous social dynamism. Bishop Wilhelm Emmanuel von Ketteler of Mainz made the Church a champion of poor people and the destitute lower classes. But even these social activities carried out under the roof of the Church eventually lost their credibility following the dispute regarding the definition of papal infallibility in 1871 at the First Vatican Council, a dispute which engaged the more educated members among the clergy and the laity especially in Germany.

The Relapse: an Index of Prohibited Books to Dull People's Minds

Since the Counter-Reformation, the basis of Catholic religious education for parish priests as well as the laity had not been the Bible, since individual readers might misunderstand it, but the Roman Catechism, commissioned by the Council of Trent and published in 1566 as the authoritative expression of the essentials of Catholic doctrinal and moral teaching. Translated into the vernacular and simplified for the laity, it became an instrument of indoctrination consisting of standardized questions and pat answers to be learned by rote. It was not intended to encourage personal reflection. In 1997, Pope John Paul II promulgated a new, thoroughly traditional *Catechism of the Catholic Church* put together by Joseph Ratzinger and his confidant and former student Christoph Schönborn. This catechism met with little success initially, but is now being disseminated more widely by the Pontifical Council for Promoting the New Evangelization set up by Benedict XVI in 2010.

In the nineteenth century, movements of Marian and Papal piety flourished. Marianism (a sentimental-emotional veneration of the Virgin Mary which developed in the Middle Ages) and Papalism (a triumphal-emotional veneration of the pope unknown even to the Middle Ages and the Counter-Reformation) became the two main instruments for keeping the flock on the true path of Catholic faith. In the nineteenth century, pilgrimage to the Holy Father residing 'beyond the mountains' ('ultramontanism' being the name of the extreme Rome-friendly movement in the Church) became increasingly frequent. At the same time, reports of Marian apparitions multiplied, being supported by dramatic accounts of miracles and by apocalyptic messages calling for doing penance and being loyal to the pope. Naturally, even critical Catholics have no objections to venerating the Mother of Jesus in a biblical framework. However, like the Second Vatican Council, which placed the discussion of the Virgin Mary within its *Constitution on the Church*, they reject the folkloristic and fundamentalist excesses which have come to dominate Marian piety.

Characteristic of the Roman opposition to innovation and its alliance with reaction is the infamous *Roman Index of Prohibited Books*, which was established in 1559 on the principle that Catholics might be easily misled and ensnared by publications contrary to Roman doctrine, and thus needed to be kept as uninformed as possible and remain an ignorant mass. The practice of banning and burning books began in the Middle Ages. However, the *Index librorum prohibitorum*, the official catalogue of books forbidden to Catholics, was introduced only during the Counter-Reformation and went through numerous revised editions, the last in 1948. It was officially abolished by Pope Paul VI in 1966. Over the centuries it grew to enormous proportions, effectively including one, several or even all of the books (*opera omnia*) of most of the leading intellects of the European modern age. In addition to innumerable theologians and critics of the Church, it listed the founders of modern science, Copernicus and Galileo; the leading philosophers of the seventeenth century: Descartes, Pascal, Boyle, Malebranche, Spinoza, Hobbes, Locke and Hume; the eighteenth-century thinkers Rousseau and Voltaire; Kant's

Critique of Pure Reason; and, later, the works of Victor Cousin, John Stuart Mill and August Comte. Likewise included were the great historians Gibbon, Condorcet, Ranke, Taine and Gregorovius; and the classical writers on constitutional and international law like Grotius, Pufendorf and Montesquieu. Also in the *Index* were the *Encyclopédie* by Diderot and d'Alembert and even the *Grand Dictionnaire Universel du 19ème Siècle* by Pierre Larousse. Finally, there is a prize selection of modern literature: Heine and Lenau, Hugo, Lamartine, Dumas *père et fils*, Balzac, Flaubert, Zola, Leopardi and d'Annunzio; and, more recently, Sartre, Simone de Beauvoir, Malaparte, Gide and Kazantzakis. Neither the Magisterium nor 'good Catholics' engaged in a critical–constructive dialogue with modern atheism and secularism; instead apologetic clichés, polemical distortions and blanket denunciations were used to ward off criticism.

As part of the reform of the Curia undertaken by Pope Paul VI in 1965, the Sanctum Officium (the Inquisition), which had become a well-organized intelligence agency of the papacy with an elaborate network of informants, was downgraded into a normal Congregation with the title 'for the Doctrine of the Faith'). It was no longer empowered to 'forbid' (*'prohibere'*) books, as Canon 247 § 4 CIC 1917 allowed, but only to 'disapprove' (*'reprobare'*) them. In a rather sheepish manner, the *Index of Prohibited Books* was effectively abolished in 1966: an equivocal notification issued by the Congregation for the Doctrine of the Faith declared that it continued to have moral force as a guide to conscience but no longer had legal force entailing automatic sanctions. Cardinal Alfredo Ottaviani, the widely feared head of the Congregation for the Doctrine of the Faith at the time, was forced to admit in an interview that the *Index* was now only a 'historical document'. In 1985, however, Cardinal Ratzinger, as head of the Congregation, reiterated the position that the *Index*, despite its dissolution, continues to bind morally. Despite these cosmetic changes, the Inquisition is still very much alive: no one is burned at the stake, but dissident theologians are disciplined by the imposition of periods of silence, withdrawal of the licence to teach and excommunication.

The Roman System Mounts a Frontal Attack on the Modern Age

Like Bishop Ketteler, the majority of bishops in the German and French episcopate together with many theologians fought fiercely, but ultimately in vain, against the proposal to proclaim a dogma of papal infallibility at the First Vatican Council in 1870–71. This discussion demonstrated the incompatibility between modern democracy, which had done away with absolutism, and the Roman System, which had emerged in the eleventh century and which clothed absolutism in a religious garb. Note the following contrasts:

- In modern democracies the traditional estates of the realm with the nobility and the clergy at the top disappeared; in the Roman System the estate of the clergy, crowned by the papal monarch, continued to hold sway.

- On the one side, the support of human rights and civil rights; on the other, the condemnation of universal human rights and the rights of Christians within the Church.

- On the one side, the sovereignty of the people in a representative democracy at all levels; on the other, the exclusion of the people and the lower clergy from the election of pastors, bishops and the pope.

- On the one side, the separation of powers (legislative, executive and judiciary); on the other, the concentration of power in the hands of bishops and the pope (primacy and infallibility).

- On the one side, equality before the law; on the other, a two-tier system with the clergy above the laity.

- On the one side, free election of office-holders at all levels; on the other, uncontrolled appointment by the higher authorities (bishops, the pope).

- On the one side, equality before the law of Jews and people of other faiths or no faith at all; on the other, the ideal of the Catholic state religion, to be realized whenever circumstances permit.

The short-sighted Roman strategy of opposing the modern world relied on internal consolidation and outward isolation. Under the leadership of Pius IX and his successors, every effort was made to strengthen the anti-modern, Medieval, Counter-Reformation Catholic fortress. Outside the fortress, the chill winds of religious indifference, anti-Catholicism and militant atheism could bluster at will; inside the fortress, traditional theology, Papalism and Marianism created a cosy atmosphere of emotional warmth and security. Catholic identity was expressed and reinforced by public demonstrations of piety like pilgrimages to Rome or the sites of Marian apparitions or, closer to home, by outdoor processions and mass assemblies. Good Catholics publicly showed their dissociation from the secular world not only by going to Mass on Sundays and Holy Days, but also by not eating meat on Fridays, by fasting during Lent and by practising various special devotions that brought them to church during the week; they used statues, devotional prints, medals and rosaries which served as tangible public badges of belonging.

In the second half of the nineteenth and the first half of the twentieth century, the Catholic believer was enclosed within what the German Catholic theologian and sociologist Karl Gabriel has called a specifically Catholic social form: a closed Catholic group-environment with its own worldview. Dazzled by ecclesiastical triumphalism coupled with demonstrative self-abasement on the part of the office-holder, the normal Catholic hardly noticed how bureaucratic and centralistic the official structures within the Church had become. The organizational structure of the Church was both modernized and sacralized, and the clergy, separated from 'the world' wherever possible, became more disciplined than ever before. All these factors combined to form an ideologically closed Roman Catholic system which legitimized the Church's distance from the modern world while it continued to justify the Church's claim to a monopoly on the ultimate interpretation of the world and morality.

The asynchrony between the developments within the Church and developments in modern society is striking. In 1864, six years before the First Vatican Council, Pius IX published his reactionary encyclical *Quanta cura*, together with a *Syllabus errorum modernorum*, a syllabus of modern errors expressed in eighty 'condemned propositions' citing earlier papal condemnations. The *Syllabus* represented an uncompromising defence of the Medieval and Counter-Reformation doctrine and power structures and a general attack on the values of modern civilization. It culminated in condemning the wish that the Roman pontiff should 'reconcile himself, and come to terms with progress, liberalism and modern civilization'. On 18 July 1870, after heated debate and against the protests of a substantial minority, most of whom left Rome before the final vote, the Vatican Council solemnly proclaimed the right of the pope '*ex sese*' ('by himself') to teach infallibly in matters of faith and morals. In the subsequent public controversy, the document's limitations on the exercise of this right were at first overlooked; only later would attention be called to them. In fact, the extreme papalists had failed to achieve their goals. Nevertheless, grave damage had been done.

Suspended as a result of the Franco-Prussian War and the Italian occupation of Rome, the Council was never reconvened; its reform programme was forgotten. Resistance to the new dogma on the part of the German-speaking bishops and university theological faculties soon collapsed. Karl Joseph von Hefele, the bishop of Rottenburg and highly respected Tübingen historian of the church councils, was the last to submit, waiting until April 1871. In a pastoral letter he called attention to the limitations imposed by the definition on the exercise of papal infallibility and indicated that he had no desire to join the newly forming Old Catholic Churches. Although only a small minority of Catholics actively joined the Old Catholic schism, a much larger number of intellectuals and workers left the Church or silently withdrew into internal emigration.

The immediate political consequences of the definition were dramatic and catastrophic. Otto von Bismarck used it as a pretext for his *Kulturkampf* (1874–9), a combination of repressive laws and direct persecution of clerics who refused to comply with them. Austria used it as an excuse to abrogate its concordat with the Holy See. The French government denounced it in a memorandum, which was supported by Great Britain, Spain and Portugal. In 1874 the English Prime Minister Gladstone published a pamphlet attacking the Catholic Church as an 'Asian monarchy' and charging the pope with planning to replace the rule of law by arbitrary tyranny and hiding its 'crimes against liberty beneath a suffocating cloud of incense'. In Italy, the consequences were more concrete. Already between 1859 and 1861 what remained of the Papal States, with the exception of the city of Rome itself, had joined the new Kingdom of Italy; the presence of French troops alone had saved Rome from the same fate. With the French troops withdrawn, in 1870, Italian troops occupied the city without meeting serious resistance. A month later, a Roman plebiscite [i.e. a direct vote by the electorate] overwhelmingly came out against papal rule, bringing to an end the 'Republic of St Peter' that went back to the eighth century. Pius IX refused to accept the loss of papal temporal power, and chose to become the self-described 'prisoner in the Vatican'.

While the Roman Catholic Church definitively opted against modernity, barely noticed by Rome, European history had long since given place to global history.

The Relapse: Rome and Communist China

I have already given an account of the Catholic mission to China in the sixteenth and seventeenth centuries and its pioneer Matteo Ricci SJ, and also of the wrong decisions taken by the popes at the time. Another wrong global political decision taken by the Roman Magisterium in the mid-twentieth century produced similarly grave consequences for the contemporary Church in China. The Chinese Communist revolution that culminated in Mao Zedong's *Proclamation of the People's Republic of China* on 21 September 1949 was more a response to European nationalism, colonialism and imperialism and the Christian proselytising associated with them than a mere product of Marxist-Leninist ideology. Focused, however, on Marxism, the Catholic rejection of the revolution proved a major catastrophe for the Catholic Church: thousands of foreign missionaries were expelled; all Church property, with the exception of church buildings, was confiscated; and many native clergy and laity were subjected to humiliation and imprisonment. In 1949, the country became officially atheist and the exercise of religion – to the extent that it was not explicitly forbidden – was placed under the supervision of the State Administration for Religious Affairs. Contact with outside ecclesiastical bodies including the Vatican was forbidden. Many Christians went underground, especially during the persecution during the Cultural Revolution (1966–76), and formed underground churches.

In 1951, a Chinese Protestant leader, Y. T. Wu, initiated the 'Three-Self Patriotic Movement' based on ideas developed by English and American Protestant missionaries some fifty years earlier. The new movement promoted 'self-governance, self-support, and self-propagation' to assure the Communist government that the churches would be loyal to the newly established People's Republic of China. Although during the Cultural Revolution public religious life in China was effectively banned, in 1979 the Protestant movement was officially reconstituted, not as a church in its own right but rather as a liaison agent for contact with state authorities; a year later, the China Christian Council, CCC, was founded as an umbrella organization for all the Protestant churches in China. Since then, Protestantism has flourished in China, despite continuing charges that the officially recognized organizations are used by the government to infiltrate, subvert and control Christian life.

The ideals of the Three-Self Patriotic Movement found echoes among Catholics as well, not only from opportunistic motives or due to direct government infiltration, but also out of conviction and genuine Christian concern. In his 1954 encyclical *Ad Sinarum gentem*, however, Pius XII declared that 'those persons who have adhered to the dangerous principles underlying the movement of the "Three Autonomies", or to other similar principles' cannot be 'considered Catholic or bear the name of Catholic', although he refrained from pronouncing a formal excommunication. In 1957, the Chinese Patriotic Catholic Association, CPCA, was established by the Bureau of Religious Affairs to exercise state supervision over mainland China's Catholics. In his 1958 encyclical *Ad Apostolorum Principis*, Pius XII condemned the association and declared that bishops who participated in the consecration of new bishops selected by the Patriotic Association were automatically excommunicated as schismatics. No such formal sentence was pronounced against those who merely attended CPCA-sponsored church services or otherwise accept CPCA directives, including those opposed to Catholic teachings; *de facto*, however, a schism did occur.

Pius XII's excommunications affected some 50 bishops who had been properly elected by the patriotic church. The Catholic Church in China split into an official patriotic church and an underground church loyal to Rome. Rome turned to Taiwan, supported the polemics of the opponents of the patriotic church, charging it with being merely an instrument of state infiltration and control, and encouraged the underground church. Thus, the relationship between China and the Vatican became hopelessly blocked.

Since Mao's death in 1976 the Chinese government and the Chinese Communist Party have pursued a more pragmatic religious policy. Many Chinese Catholics do not wish to have to choose between Beijing and Rome. They desire an alliance with the pope and the universal Catholic Church but are equally firmly rooted in their Chinese Church. They find the polemics on both sides unnecessary; in their view the Vatican is too fixated on the underground church and ignores how pluralistic Chinese society has become. According to official statistics, since 2004 some 100,000 Chinese have joined the official Catholic Church annually and 300 new churches have been built, so that the total number of churches has now increased to 6,300; 25 bishops have been ordained. Officially, there are currently 6 million Catholics in the People's Republic of China; many more if you also include the underground church.

True normalization of relations between the People's Republic and Rome will only be possible when the Vatican accepts the legitimacy of the validly ordained bishops of the official church. At a recent meeting with him in Beijing, the

Chinese minister for religions told me that the Swiss model of episcopal election described previously in this book could well be the solution for China; namely, election of the bishops in their own country, followed by their approbation by Rome.

Just as the situation of the Church in China differs from that of the Church in Europe, so too, do the situations of the Churches in Latin America, India, Indonesia or Africa differ from one another. This raises the question often posed, whether the analysis carried out in this book applies perhaps to the Church in Europe and North America, but not to other countries and cultures.

A Medical Analysis Only Applicable to the Western World?

It is true that the Medieval history of the Church and even the history of the Reformation are not as relevant for non-European countries as they are for Europeans and North Americans. Latin America, Asia, Africa and Oceania were at first merely the objects of European colonization and proselytizing; they were not active subjects engaged in developing an original, indigenous version of Christian spirituality, theology and life.

In the European modern era, the expansion of religious and economic interests supported by military force led to the wanton and systematic destruction, in the name of Jesus Christ, of other religions and cultures, particularly in Latin America. Many Christians now deplore this, but the Catholic hierarchy only rarely admits that this was the fault of the Church. Instead of clearly avowing his regret for the history of the Church's monstrous guilt in this process of cultural destruction and oppression, and for the Church's shared responsibility for the miserable social conditions in the countries he visited, John Paul II symbolically kissed the ground on each visit, but did not allow any questions to be put to him. Cynically and in defiance of historical truth, Benedict XVI, during his first trip to South America, went so far as to claim that in the sixteenth century the indigenous population of the continent had yearned for its proselytization and civilization by the Portuguese and Spanish conquerors. As prefect of the Congregation for the Doctrine of the Faith under John Paul II, Cardinal Ratzinger had disciplined many of the Latin American liberation theologians who had denounced the manifold social and cultural abuses and injustices in their countries that trace back to colonialism and to the continuing oppression of poor people by a Europeanized economic and political elite. Under the last two popes, bishops sympathetic to the cause of liberation theology were replaced by representatives of Opus Dei and other reactionary movements.

Open-minded Europeans and Americans of all denominations, however, are no longer willing to put up with Christian churches in other continents being led around by the nose. They reject a Roman imperialism that attempts to compel all churches to adhere to a Medieval system of thinking, spirituality and discipline and maintain obsolete forms of religious practice. In the twentieth century, especially after the Second World War, the countries of the southern hemisphere have become autonomous players on the global political stage, and they now compete politically and economically with the American and European powers. In short, the Eurocentric paradigm has given way to a polycentric one.

It is all the more important for Western theology, with its refined methods of scientific research, to demonstrate how the original Christian constitution of the Church and the original great Catholic Christian tradition of the first millennium in fact come much closer to the contemporary understanding of democracy than to the monarchical and authoritarian patterns of the past. In this way, the Church can learn from other religions and can increase the visibility of other cultures in a truly universal Church. By showing respect for the history of other cultures and religions, it can recover the riches of other cultures so often suppressed by Western colonialism and imperialism and use them to deepen its own understanding and practice of the Gospel. Without in any way falling into the trap of syncretism and indifferentism, the Church can integrate the different aesthetic, spiritual and cultic traditions of the non-Western nations and cultures and thus promote true Christian enculturation in each of the different contexts.

Rome must learn to permit and encourage a reasonable degree of autonomy in the different national, regional and local churches. Churches in other cultures must be allowed to take responsibility for shaping their own style of life and organization. This is absolutely necessary if they are to contribute to solving the immense social problems existing in these nations and continents outside the Western world.

According to United Nations statistics for 2012, the world population now exceeds 7 billion, 1 billion more than in 1999. Although the rate of growth has been dropping since the late 1960s, the world population is expected to reach 8 billion in 2025 and 9 billion in 2045. For the most part, this growth takes place in the less developed countries, where 82 per cent of the world's population now lives. The highest population increases are in Africa, where some 75 million women become pregnant unintentionally each year. Would it not be an inestimable help in attacking the roots of the enormous poverty in the developing countries if the pope and the bishops would promote access to sex education and contraception and announce that the use of condoms is permitted to combat the AIDS epidemic? Can anyone seriously claim that the questions of sexual ethics (in view of the problems of poverty rooted in overpopulation), of clerical celibacy (in view of the combined dangers of clericalism and the shortage of priests) or of divorce and remarriage (in view of the many polygamous traditions) are problems only for the Western world and have no relevance for the developing countries?

For all too long, Rome has preferred to ignore these grave social problems, focusing instead on maintaining and expanding traditional positions and power structures. Conflicts about the future course of the Catholic Church escalated after the First Vatican Council, which had been so abruptly suspended in 1870. Increasingly it would become clear that a new Council would be needed to tackle the problems left unresolved or made more complicated by its predecessor. But it would take almost 90 years until a pope, facing up to a completely changed global situation, would recognize that need and convene the Second Vatican Council.

CHAPTER 5

THE GREAT RESCUE OPERATION

Only Half Way to Reformation and Modernity

How Can We Save the Catholic Church? Between Modernism and Anti-Modernism

Christianity has an infinitely richer history than the Catholic Church which, in its turn, has an infinitely richer history than the papacy. But particularly in the nineteenth and twentieth centuries, the history of the Catholic Church became virtually synonymous with the history of the papacy. For decades after the end of the Papal State, the popes played the role of the much-pitied 'prisoner in the Vatican'. But it was only their stubborn '*non possumus*' ('we cannot') that prevented them from leaving the Vatican and coming to terms with the new situation of the Church in Italy. Despite all the positive achievements of the popes after Pius IX, their attitude to church reform remained ambivalent.

Leo XIII (1878–1903), the more open-minded successor to the infallibilist Pius IX, made no effort to wield papal infallibility. He ended the *Kulturkampf* with the German empire and similar reactions in other countries, and corrected Rome's negative stance towards modernity, democracy and civil liberties. No longer responsible for the socially backward-looking Papal State, he published, nearly half a century after the *Communist Manifesto*, a long overdue social encyclical, *Rerum novarum* (1891), as an expression of developing Catholic social teaching. But towards the end of his pontificate, reactionary tendencies once again manifested themselves, especially in measures taken against modern biblical exegesis.

Pius X (1903–14), respected as a pastoral pope, improved seminary studies and encouraged regular communion on the part of the laity. But, at the same time, he rigorously suppressed contemporaneous efforts to reconcile the Church with modern science and historical research and launched a rigorous campaign against reform-minded theologians, especially exegetes and historians branded with the defamatory label 'modernist'. A document of the Holy Office, *Lamentabili* (1907), named 65 heretical propositions, and the papal encyclical of the same year, *Paschendi*, presented a one-sided synthesis of Modernism, bringing together into an ideological system the amorphous views of a wide variety of theologians. To eradicate Modernism once and for all, a detailed *Oath against Modernism* (1910) was imposed on all Catholic clergy, and a secret spy ring called the Sodalitium Pianum (not unlike the modern Opus Dei) denounced bishops, theologians and lay leaders allegedly tainted with the heresy. The canonization of this 'holy–unholy Father' by Pius XII in 1954 speaks for itself.

Benedict XV (1914–22), a moderate man, eradicated the vicious anti-Modernist secret society. He made intensive, though unavailing, efforts to mediate between the adversaries during World War I. But, without seeking approval of the global episcopate, he also endorsed the new *Codex Iuris Canonici* (1917) that had been prepared by his predecessor and was aimed at legitimizing and safeguarding the centralized Roman system.

Pius XI (1922–39), a scholar and realist, solved the 'Roman Question', which had remained open since 1870, by concluding the Lateran Treaties (1929) with the Fascist leader Benito Mussolini. In these agreements, Pius XI renounced all claims to the greater Papal States, contenting himself with sovereignty over the mini-state of the Vatican. In return for renunciation of earlier rights, the Vatican received an enormous financial compensation that became the basis for the Vatican's current wealth. Pius XI supported indigenous clergy in mission territories but also the lay organization Catholic Action, which was intended as a political extension of the church hierarchy. At the same time, he published an anti-ecumenical encyclical, *Mortalium animos* (1928), stating his reasons for debarring Catholic participation in the great ecumenical conference in Lausanne. An even greater disaster was his encyclical against birth control, *Casti connubii* (1930), published as a reaction to a statement by the Anglican Lambeth Conference. This encyclical later became one of the principal arguments underpinning the 'infallible' consensus of the pope and the bishops with regard to marital ethics that served as the basis of Pope Paul VI's fatal encyclical *Humanae vitae* of 1968. The *Reichskonkordat* with Hitler's Germany, concluded shortly after Hitler came to power in 1933, gave an unprecedented boost to Hitler's international standing. But the German-language encyclical *Mit brennender Sorge* ('With Burning Concern') of 1937 condemned the National Socialist doctrines and policies and the numerous violations of the concordat. Eugenio Pacelli, Papal Nuncio in Germany and later Cardinal Secretary of State, was deeply involved in both the concordat and the encyclical. In 1939, on the eve of World War II, he became Pope Pius XII.

Pius XII – a Holy Pope?

Pius XII (1939–58) was the last uncontested representative of the Medieval Counter-Reformation/anti-Modernist paradigm. In keeping with the spirit of Pius IX, and despite numerous objections, he proceeded, in 1950, to define a new, completely unnecessary and historically unfounded, 'infallible' Marian dogma, i.e. the bodily assumption of the Blessed Virgin Mary into Heaven. At the same time, he banned the French worker-priest movement, and prohibited the most distinguished contemporary theologians, many of them French, from teaching theology; these included Teilhard de Chardin, Yves Congar and Henri de Lubac. However, from the very beginning of his pontificate, he avoided any public condemnation of National Socialism and anti-Semitism, and he refrained from excommunicating the Catholic Nazi criminals.

This decidedly Germanophile Catholic diplomat had by and large a legal/diplomatic mindset rather than a theological/biblical one, and he had enjoyed only limited experience of pastoral care. Correspondingly, his actions were not guided by pastoral considerations, but rather by the concerns of the curial institutions of the papacy. After his traumatic experiences as Nuncio in Munich during and after the short-lived Munich Soviet Republic (1918–19), he was obsessed by fear of physical contact and dread of Communism. On the whole, his attitude was authoritarian and anti-democratic, not unsympathetic to the kind of 'Führer-Catholicism' that was widespread in Germany at the time of the Nazi takeover. Thus he was predisposed to form pragmatic anti-Communist alliances with the Fascist regimes in Italy, Spain and Portugal, and even with totalitarian Nazism. One need not question his good intentions if one says that for Pacelli, the career diplomat, what counted was primarily the protection of the freedom and power of the church institutions, in particular the Roman Curia, the hierarchy, Catholic organizations, schools, associations, and the freedom of religious practice. Throughout his life, however, the concepts of human rights and democracy remained utterly foreign ideas.

For Pacelli, a scion of the city of Rome, Rome was the new Zion, the centre of the Church and of the world. He never showed any particular personal sympathy towards Jews; theologically, he viewed them as a people of God-killers and he held them responsible for the Bolshevist revolution in Bavaria in 1918–19. A triumphalist representative of Roman ideology, he considered Christ to be a Roman, not a Jew, and Jerusalem to have been replaced by Rome. This is one of the reasons why, like the entire Roman Curia, he opposed the founding of a Jewish state in Palestine.

Pacelli was very much aware of the affinity between his own authoritarian (anti-Protestant, anti-liberal, anti-Socialist and anti-Modernist) concept of the Church, and the authoritarian concept of the state held by the Fascists and Nazis. In his view, the concepts of 'unity', 'order', 'discipline' and the 'Führer principle' applied as much to the supernatural order of the Church as to the natural order of the State. Pius XII, who as pope was also his own secretary of state, greatly overestimated the power of diplomacy and concordats. Basically, he had only two political aims: fighting Communism, and maintaining the institutions of the Church. For him, the vexed question of the Jews was for the most part merely an irrelevant annoyance, and there is mounting evidence that he was fully informed as early as 1940 about the dimensions of the Holocaust. Only towards the end of the war did he use diplomacy and charitable assistance to save individual Jews or groups of Jews, particularly in Italy and Rome. In two speeches given in 1942/43 he briefly deplored in general and abstract terms the fate of 'unfortunate people' persecuted because of their race. But he never publicly uttered the word 'Jew' in this connection. Pacelli did not protest against the Nuremberg Race Laws (1935) or the so-called *Kristallnacht* pogrom (1938). Just as his predecessor had failed to protest against the Italian invasion of Ethiopia in 1936, he refrained from protesting against the Italian invasion of Albania on Good Friday 1939 and the German invasion of Poland on 1 September 1939, which triggered World War II.

It is often alleged that he intended to protest against the Nazi persecution of the Jews, but was dissuaded from doing so by Nazi reprisals against the Jews in the occupied Netherlands after the Dutch bishops denounced the Nazi deportation of Jews in mid-1942. However, even Konrad Adenauer, the postwar German Federal Chancellor, argued that a papal protest would not have been either pointless or counter-productive: as evidence he cited the success of Bishop Clemens August von Galen's protest against Hitler's euthanasia programme in 1941 and the support given by the Danish Lutheran bishops to the Jews of Denmark in 1943. Nevertheless, Pius XII avoided any form of public protest against anti-Semitism. Although he was in a perfect position to speak out, he remained silent on the subject of the notorious German war crimes committed everywhere in Europe, and on the Holocaust, the worst act of mass murder of all times. When he became pope, he failed to publish the encyclical against racism and anti-Semitism that had been drawn up under his predecessor.

This is not the place to pass judgement on the personal guilt of Pius XII in this area or on his positive achievements in other areas. But one can and must ask whether he should really be canonized as Paul VI, John Paul II and Benedict XVI have advocated. Did he really show the 'heroic virtue' that Benedict XVI attested in raising him to the rank of 'Venerable' on 19 September 2009? The canonization of Pius XII would be as problematical as that of Pius IX – an avowed enemy of Jews and Protestants, of human rights, religious freedom, democracy and modern culture. It would be another Vatican farce and a repudiation of all the recent admissions of past papal guilt. I well remember the words spoken to us as students at the Collegium Germanicum by Pacelli's loyal private secretary Father Robert Leiber SJ, at a time when the pope was still alive: 'No, he is not a saint, but he is a great man of the Church.' Despite Pius XII's efforts to prolong his life and his control of the Church with dubious medical practices, the last years of his pontificate, until his death in 1958, were years of lethargy and depression for the Church. The next pope, however, would be a complete surprise.

Reinvigorating the Church: John XXIII

Elected on 28 October 1958 as the successor to Pius XII, Angelo Giuseppe Roncalli, at the age of 77, was expected to be a 'caretaker pope', but quite the reverse was true: he became the pope of a momentous transition, or paradigm shift. He released the Catholic Church from its inner torpor and breathed new life into it. Not only in my opinion is he recognized as the most important pope of the twentieth century, and his pontificate, which lasted less than five years, proved to be a genuine Petrine ministry in the biblical sense. He wanted to 'throw open the windows of the Church'. In the face of massive opposition from the Curia, he showed the ailing Church, caught up as it was in a combination of the Medieval, the Counter-Reformation and the anti-Modernist paradigms, a way to true renewal. His motto was *'aggiornamento'*, proclamation of the Gospel in terms and structures appropriate for our times. It included coming to an understanding with other Christian churches, opening up towards Judaism and other world religions, seeking better relations with the Communist countries of Eastern Europe and Asia, promoting social justice (in his encyclical *Mater et magistra*, 1961), opening up to the modern world as a whole and clearly affirming the existence of human rights (his encyclical *Pacem in terris*, 1963). His collegial style of leadership helped to strengthen the role of the bishops. In every area, Pope John demonstrated a new pastoral understanding of the papacy.

Roncalli's attitude to Judaism was particularly historically significant, and stood in sharp contrast to that of Pacelli. While Roncalli was Apostolic Delegate in Turkey he saved the lives of thousands of Jews from Romania and Bulgaria. In 1958, shortly after he became pope, he exorcized the offensive prayer-invocation for the 'perfidious Jews' (*'oremus pro perfidis Judaeis'*) from the Good Friday liturgy and replaced it with a more irenic formula – something his predecessor had always refused to do. For the first time, he received a group of more than 100 American Jews, and greeted them with words from the biblical story of Joseph in Egypt: 'I am Joseph, your brother'. One day, entirely spontaneously, he ordered his car to stop outside the synagogue in Rome in order to bless the Jews streaming out of the building. On the night before the pope died, Rome's Chief Rabbi, accompanied by numerous Jewish believers, went to St Peter's Square to join with the Catholics praying there for him.

Historically, however, his most important and far-reaching act was his decision, proclaimed in an announcement on 25 January 1959, to convene a general council of the Catholic Church, some ninety years after the First Vatican Council had been suspended. No one expected this; many believed that the declaration of papal infallibility in 1870 had made future councils superfluous. Begun under Pope John XXIII and brought to an end under his successor Paul VI, the Second Vatican Council (1962–5) corrected Pius XII in nearly all important points – reform of the liturgy, ecumenism, anti-Communism, religious freedom, the 'modern world' – and above all, it corrected the prevailing attitude towards Judaism. Encouraged by Pope John, the bishops regained their self-confidence and now felt that they could act again as a body with an independent apostolic authority.

Only towards the end of the Council, in the face of continued vehement opposition from the traditionally anti-Jewish Curia, did the Council finally adopt the declaration *Nostra aetate*, which dealt with Judaism and the Jews in the context of world religions. For the first time, a council of the Church firmly denied the existence of any 'collective guilt' of the Jewish people, then and now, for the death of Jesus. The declaration stated that God's original people were neither rejected nor accursed. It declared that 'hatred, persecutions, displays of anti-Semitism directed against Jews at any time and by anyone' should be condemned, and extended a promise for 'mutual understanding and respect'. Thus, the Council, in the end, complied with the intentions of John XXIII. This was a remarkable achievement.

Two Successful Paradigm Shifts Initiated by the Second Vatican Council

Despite immense difficulties and obstacles thrown up by sections of the Roman System, the Council made an effort to implement two paradigm shifts:

- The first paradigm shift was the integration of the Reformation paradigm: this meant recognizing the collective Catholic guilt for the sixteenth-century schism and the need for constant reform. Simultaneously, a series of central Protestant concerns were recognized – at least in principle, and in many cases in practice as well. There was a new appreciation of the Bible in worship, in theology, in the life of the Church and in the life of individual believers. Authentic worship services were to be celebrated in the vernacular with the active participation of the people using a reformed Eucharist liturgy that brought out its character as an act of the whole community. The creation of parish and diocesan councils and new offices for theologically trained lay men and women (pastoral assistants) raised the profile of the laity. Regional churches were encouraged to adapt to national and local circumstances, and emphasis was placed on the local churches and the national bishops' conferences. Finally, practices of popular piety were reformed and many pious practices going back to the Middle Ages, the Baroque era and the nineteenth century were eliminated.

- The second paradigm shift was the integration of the modern paradigm: at long last, many positions of the Enlightenment were adopted. Freedom of religion and conscience – condemned as late as 1953 by Pius XII – and human rights as a whole were unequivocally affirmed. The Church's share of collective guilt in the matter of anti-Semitism was admitted, and, in a positive about-turn, the Church's relationship with Judaism as the root of Christianity was redefined. A fresh, constructive approach to Islam and other world religions was also initiated. The possibility of salvation 'outside the Church' for non-Christians, even of atheists and agnostics, acting according to their conscience, was now clearly admitted. The Council adopted a new, fundamentally positive attitude towards progress and modernity – both so long repudiated – and towards the secular world, science and democracy.

Right from the start, the machinery of the Curia did its best to control the Council; constant wrangling between the conciliar fathers and Curia resulted. Most unfortunately, John XXIII died after the first session; he was 82 years old, but his death was still far too early. Roncalli was replaced by the serious-but-vacillating ('Hamlet') Pope Montini, who took the name Paul VI (1963–78). Despite many liberal tendencies on the surface, he was a man whose career had inclined him more to follow the Curia than to support the Council.

It was clear that the Roman System that had emerged in the eleventh century with the Gregorian reform and accorded supremacy within the Church to the Pope and Curia alone had been shaken up by the Second Vatican Council – much the same had happened at the Council of Constance in the late fifteenth century – but it had not been eliminated. It was tacitly accepted that retention of the absolutist Roman System of rule would be firmly rejected by the Eastern Orthodox churches and reformed churches as well as by many Catholics who considered the matter more deeply. Thus the Curia saw no point to ecumenism.

For the period after Vatican II, the tabooed topics excluded from conciliar discussion proved disastrous. No discussion of clerical celibacy and the marriage of priests was permitted. Equally excluded from discussion were the issues of divorce and remarriage, reform of the appointment of bishops and, above all, reform of the papacy itself. On one and the same day, there were three interventions by influential cardinals in favour of a more sympathetic position on birth control (contraception). The discussion was nipped in the bud by the pope. Together with the issue of confessionally mixed marriage, the matter was referred to a papal commission. This commission later decided against the traditional Roman position, but its findings were rejected in 1968 by the pope himself, and, as related above, the traditional prohibition of contraception was reiterated in Paul VI's encyclical *Humanae vitae*, too late to change the behaviour of the majority of Catholic women.

Restoration Rather than Renewal: Paul VI

Despite substantial concessions to liturgical reform, the process of revitalization and recovery of the Catholic Church and of ecumenical understanding with other Christian churches, which John XXIII and the Council set in motion, ground to a halt under Paul VI. Simultaneously, the hierarchy began to lose credibility, a process that by 2010 was to reach dramatic proportions. In 1967 the typical Roman contradiction between foreign policy and home affairs was already becoming evident: outwardly (where it cost the Church nothing) there was progress, as outlined in Pope Paul's encyclical *Populorum progressio*, but internally (where the Church itself was affected), reaction increasingly prevailed, as demonstrated for example in the celibacy encyclical *Sacerdotalis coelibatus* of the same year. The idea that the celibate life is a charism and, according to the Gospel, should be completely voluntary was once again rejected by Pope Paul VI. And, citing the same Gospel texts, he defended it as a law that suppressed any real freedom.

And so, for the first time since Vatican II, a pope had once again decided – single-handedly, in an authoritarian pre-conciliar manner, and in complete disregard of the solemn resolution of the Council that bishops should act collegially in such important matters – on a question of vital importance for the Church in the many areas where priests were in short supply (parts of Europe, Latin America, Africa and Asia). He made this unilateral decision after having himself forbidden any discussion of the matter in the Council. For the first time since the Council, the episcopate had been openly snubbed, but a storm of protest failed to materialize; only very few bishops in Belgium and Canada raised their voices in favour of collegiality.

It was clear: in spite of the impetus given by the Council, in the post-conciliar period there would be no possibility that the authoritarian institutional and personal power structure within the Church leadership might be significantly altered in the spirit of the Christian message. The pope, the Curia and most bishops continued to behave in a pre-conciliar, authoritarian fashion even when faced with inevitable changes. Little seemed to have been learned from the proceedings of the Council. In Rome, as in other areas of the Church, those who held the positions of ecclesiastical power were far more interested in retaining their power and maintaining their comfortable *status quo* than in any serious renewal of the spirit of the Gospel under the conditions of collegiality.

As before, the Holy Spirit continued to be invoked to justify all sorts of papal and curial decisions, large and small, and with it the apostolic powers supposedly invested in the pope by Christ. How far this could go became evident for all to see when, in 1968, Paul VI precipitated the Church into the crisis of credibility, which has persisted ever since, with his ill-fated encyclical *Humanae vitae* against contraception in all forms. This encyclical represents the first instance in the history of the Church in the twentieth century of a refusal by a broad majority of Catholic laity and clergy to obey the pope on an important issue. From the Roman viewpoint, what the encyclical taught was effectively an 'infallible' doctrine promoted continuously by the 'ordinary' Magisterium of the pope and bishops (according to section 25 of the *Constitution on the Church*). Something similar happened in 1994, when John Paul II, in his apostolic letter *Ordinatio sacerdotalis*, expressly declared the disastrous rejection of women's ordination for all time and all eternity to be an 'infallible' doctrine.

It would be false to suggest that the reactionary U-turn after Vatican II was exclusively the work of Paul VI or of the Curia. Many traditional Catholics were deeply attached to some of the elements of Catholic life that were changed by the Council and were put off by the insensitive and sometimes stupid way the changes had been introduced at local level by bishops and priests who personally neither understood nor believed in them. Many Catholics preferred the comfortable warmth and stability of the fortified Catholic ghetto, compared with exposure to the chill winds and swaying platforms of the modern world. The anti-democratic mentality and fear of liberty among Catholic clergy and laity were not completely extinguished by Vatican II; on the contrary, the fact that the Council's impact coincided with the cultural revolution of the late 1960s reinforced such attitudes. Few conservative Catholics officially joined schismatic groups like Archbishop Lefebvre's Society of St Pius X, but many sympathized with their ideas, and many more joined the vociferous movement within the Church to tame the Council and roll back its innovations or render them harmless. Over the next decades, this grassroots reaction would develop a dynamic of its own that played into the hands of the curial roll-back policy and intimidated the shrinking number of liberal-minded Catholic bishops, priests and lay leaders.

After Paul VI, who, in some respects, was a tolerant pope (for instance in granting dispensations to priests seeking to leave the priesthood and marry), and after Pope John Paul I, who died after only 33 days in office under unexplained circumstances, a completely different kind of pope came to power on 16 October 1978. He was the first non-Italian Pope since Hadrian VI in the sixteenth century, a pope from Poland.

Relapse into a Pre-conciliar Constellation: John Paul II

From the start, John Paul II showed himself to be a man of character, deeply rooted in his Christian faith, an impressive champion of peace, human rights, social justice, and later of inter-religious dialogue. At the same time, he promoted the concept of a strong traditional Church. Endowed with personal charisma, he knew how to satisfy – in an impressive and media-savvy manner – the yearning of a global public for a moral and trustworthy role model, so rare in today's world. Within an incredibly short time he became a media superstar, and for many a living cult figure.

We should not, however, be deceived by the well-organized popular rallies or spectacular religious media events orchestrated by PR experts. In comparison with the seven fat years which coincided with the pontificate of John XXIII and the Second Vatican Council (1958–65), the four-times-seven years of the Wojtyla papacy were lean and sterile. Despite his myriad public addresses, his spectacular gestures and his many costly 'pilgrimages' to places around the world – they ran up millions of dollars of debt for the local churches who had to finance them – under his pontificate little or no real progress in matters of church reform or ecumenical rapprochement took place.

Although not an Italian, John Paul II was very much to the liking of the Curia, since he came from a country where neither the Reformation nor the Enlightenment had produced lasting effects. While still a cardinal, he had been conspicuous for his absence from the sessions of the papal commission on birth control, although, behind the scenes, he was busy pulling strings and writing letters of intrigue. As pope, with his charismatic appeal and with the theatrical talent that he had retained from his youth, he brought to the Vatican what Ronald Reagan brought to the White House: a media-wise great communicator who understood how to use his charm, his athletic image and his symbolic gestures to make even the most conservative teaching or practice seem palatable. The effects of the climate change associated with this pope were soon felt:

- first, by priests seeking to leave the ministry: he quickly ended the compassionate practice of his predecessor in granting dispensations;

- then by the theologians: he supported the witch-hunt against innovators and dissidents, especially against unruly theologians in Europe and North America and against the liberation theologians of Latin America;

- soon after, by the bishops: he forced them into line and appointed closed-minded conservatives as successors to open, liberal-minded prelates;

- and finally, by women: he disciplined progressive congregations of women religious, and 'infallibly' excluded women from ordination.

Despite Wojtyla's public avowals of following the spirit of Vatican II, it became increasingly evident that, from the start, his real intentions had been to slow the momentum of the Council, to halt internal Church reforms, to prevent serious reconciliation with the Eastern churches, the Protestants and the Anglicans, to return to the old reactionary defence strategies, and to nip the dialogue with modernity in the bud. Reining in the practice of collegiality, he returned to the policy of unilateral papal decision-making and one-sided indoctrination of the clergy and laity. On his 'pilgrimage' to Santiago de Compostela in 1982, he announced his programme of re-evangelization, a Christian spiritual reconquest of Europe, but what he really meant was re-Catholicizing and re-Romanizing. His dramatic but diffuse and inconsequential invocations of ecumenism were subliminally aimed at return or conversion to the Roman Catholic Church.

Many people rightly saw here a betrayal of the Council, and this alienated many Catholics worldwide. Instead of the mottos of Vatican II, slogans of a neo-conservative and authoritarian Magisterium, supported by a vociferous reactionary movement among clergy and laity, now set the tone:

- instead of *aggiornamento* in the spirit of the Gospel, traditionalist Catholic doctrine (rigorous moral encyclicals, the neo-traditional 'world catechism');

- instead of collegiality between the pope and the bishops, strict Roman centralism overriding the interests of local churches in matters such as the appointment of bishops and theology professors, and enculturation of the liturgy;

- instead of the '*apertura*', i.e. opening up to the modern world, a growing list of denunciations and indictments, the demonizing of alleged accommodations to non-Catholic and secular ways, and the promotion of traditional forms of piety (Marianism and Papalism);

- instead of dialogue within the Church, intensified inquisitorial discipline of dissenters, denying the rights to freedom of conscience and academic freedom within the Church;

- instead of ecumenism, renewed emphasis on uncritically accepting traditional Roman doctrine, increasingly enveloped in the cloak of the 'infallibility' of the ordinary Magisterium identified with the latest papal pronouncements, and leaving no place for the kind of discussion, begun at the Council, about possible distinctions between the Church of Christ and the Roman Catholic Church, between the doctrinal substance and its historical, linguistic clothing, and between different levels of importance and binding force within a hierarchy of truths.

Even very modest wish-lists like those submitted to Rome, for instance, by the post-conciliar German, Austrian and Swiss national synods – after years of labour by idealistic clerical and lay representatives and at considerable input of time, money and paper – were turned down or ignored by the high-handed Curia, generally with no explanation whatsoever. With increasing resignation, the German-speaking countries threw in the towel and failed to protest. Similarly, when the reform charter of the We are Church movement, with 1.5 million signatures appended, was presented to Rome, it was ignored completely. In the Vatican, the people count for nothing (unless they support the official line!); a priest is worth little more; a bishop has only minimal value; at best a cardinal has weight and is a *persona grata* (as long as he agrees with the pope).

As far as his native country of Poland was concerned, after the collapse of Communism Pope Wojtyla found himself in a tragic situation. Having dreamed of bringing the militant anti-Modernist model of Polish Catholicism to a Western world he saw as decadent and self-indulgent, he had to look on helplessly as the paradigm of Modernity triumphed in his homeland, just as it had done earlier in Catholic Spain and Ireland. Despite his campaign for re-Catholicization, promoted by his spectacular voyages around the world and his numerous appeals for traditional values, what ensued was a process of de-Catholicization, even in Poland. Pope or no pope, Western secularism, individualism and pluralism were spreading everywhere.

Unlike John Paul II and his successor Benedict XVI, together with their numerous neo-conservative followers among the bishops, the clergy and the laity, one need not see this development as being something purely negative or lament it as evidence of cultural decline. The new situation of de-Catholicization has its positive aspects as well. Disencumbered of the distorting accretions accumulated over the centuries, a reformed and renewed Catholic Church will be in a better position to bring the Christian message to today's men and women and in this way realize the goal of re-evangelization without being tied to obsolete paradigms.

'Santo Subito'? Maciel, Miracles and Inflationary Increase of Saints

In 1980, John Paul II visited Germany. At a mass rally in Munich on 26 November, Barbara Engl, a representative of the Association of German Young Catholics, broke with the official protocol forbidding questions being put to the pope, and addressed him directly:

> Holy Father, you have spoken in your sermon about things that concern us greatly. But it is often hard for young people living in the Federal Republic of Germany to understand the Church. They have the impression that the Church is anxious to keep things as they are, that the Church once again stresses the differences between the Christian confessions instead of emphasizing what they have in common, that the Church all too often reacts to young people's questions about friendship, sexuality and partnership with mere prohibitions, that their quest for understanding and their openness to dialogue meets no response. Many are unable to understand why the Church so adamantly insists on celibacy, in spite of the lack of priests. In view of the lack of youth ministers many are asking whether women might not be allowed to play a larger role in the ministry of the Church. (German Press Agency report, 21 November 1980)

This young woman, who would later suffer greatly for her courageous action, was simply expressing what most young Catholics in Germany were thinking: 'We discussed these problems at the annual general meeting of the Association of German Young Catholics,' she added. 'Recently, we dealt with issues of friendship, sex and partnership at such a meeting … It is difficult to discuss such things with some of the clergy, but many youth ministers are on our wavelength.'

The pope reacted with embarrassed silence. He offered no answer, neither then nor later, to these fundamental questions of Catholic religiosity so vital to the younger generation. All that happened was that the officials responsible for such events saw to it that the pope would never again be confronted with uncomfortable questions. Nevertheless, the innumerable papal appearances, pilgrimages and doctrinal statements failed to persuade the majority of Catholics to change their minds on controversial questions and to follow the Roman line.

When, on 6 April 2005, in St Peter's Square, Cardinal Ratzinger celebrated the funeral Mass for the late pope from Poland, supporters of Pope Wojtyla from the neo-conservative *movimenti* unfurled enormous, well-prepared banners with the slogan: *'Santo subito'* – 'Make him a saint immediately' – to the accompaniment of the chanting crowds. Shortly thereafter, the newly elected pope, Joseph Ratzinger, indicated his support of this well-organized canonization campaign, when he announced to the masses in St Peter's Square that he saw John Paul II looking down on them from heaven – something he would never have dared to say as a professor of theology in Germany. Only two months later, Pope Benedict initiated the beatification process, in direct contravention of the canon law prescription for a five-year waiting period, and only a few months later, in December 2005, he took the first step in the beatification process by declaring John Paul II 'venerable' by reason of his 'heroic virtue'. Plans were made to canonize him on 16 October 2010, the 32nd anniversary of his election as pope.

But in that same year, five years after John Paul's death, doubts about the canonization process arose in connection with the sexual abuse crisis that had meanwhile hit the press. Firstly, all too many people remembered how Pope Wojtyla had protected the paedophile Viennese Cardinal Hans Hermann Groër, the successor to the great Cardinal König, even though the Austrian Bishops' Conference was convinced of Groër's guilt (see Chapter 1). The pope had also protected another Austrian friend, Kurt Krenn, the Bishop of St Pölten, who did not step down until he came under great public pressure following reports about homosexual activities by the seminarians and staff of his diocesan seminary. American Catholics were infuriated when the pope named Cardinal Bernard Law as Archpriest of the Basilica Santa Maria Maggiore, one of the four principal churches in Rome, after he had been forced to resign as Archbishop of Boston, Massachusetts for trying to cover up a sexual abuse scandal in his archdiocese. Evidently, John Paul II was ready to forgive his loyal servants every kind of misdemeanour and failing.

Even more shockingly were the scandals surrounding the Mexican priest Marcial Maciel Degollado and the ultra-conservative Legion of Christ (LC), which he founded in 1941. The Legion is a congregation of religious priests and clerics engaged in charitable and educational ministries and bound, until 2007, by a special vow not to speak ill of their superiors and to denounce anyone who violated this injunction. According to the congregation's own official statistics for December 2011, the congregation counts among its members three bishops, 920 priests and more than 2,000 religious, novices, candidates and minor seminarians; it maintains houses in 22 countries and its own university in Rome. In 1959, Maciel founded Regnum Christi, an association of consecrated men and women, mostly lay people, to extend the work of the Legion. According to the latest statistics, it numbers some 70,000 members.

Outwardly, Maciel, who directed both organizations until forced to step down in 2005, conducted himself as a devout

Catholic pledged to special loyalty to the pope and staunchly defending traditional Catholic moral values including clerical celibacy. Behind this façade, however, he lived a well-camouflaged double life. He was addicted to drugs and sexually abused young seminarians, including minors. He had intimate relations with at least three women and fathered at least three children with them.

All this, however, was initially at least unknown to the Polish pope, who was deeply impressed by the Legion's militant defence of papal infallibility and traditional teaching and its organizational and financial talents. He relied on it so thoroughly that in January 1979, only weeks after his election, he chose Mexico as the destination for what would be the first of his many 'pilgrimages'. Three additional visits to Mexico followed in 1990, 1993 and 2002, the first two accompanied by Maciel and all of them shrewdly organized by the Legion as triumphant demonstrations of Catholicism in this officially laicistic nation.

As early as the 1950s, however, rumours had begun circulating about Maciel's secret life. In 1956, he was investigated by the Vatican on charges of morphine abuse, but was eventually cleared and reinstated as director of his institute. In the 1970s, accusations of his homosexual and paedophile activities were sent to Rome, but no action was taken. After his election in 1978, John Paul II made Maciel one of his chief advisors in matters of clerical recruitment and training and appointed him to a variety of high positions. In 1998, nine victims of Maciel's homosexual abuse filed formal charges at the Vatican, but a year later they were informed that the investigation had been closed. Towards the end of his life, the Polish pope allowed himself to be photographed blessing Maciel. And on 15 March

2005, when he was terminally ill, the pope made a point of specially greeting the Legionaries of Christ (nicknamed 'Millionaires of Christ' in the Vatican because of their financial power) from his window overlooking St Peter's Square.

It was only during the Pope's very last days that Cardinal Ratzinger initiated fresh proceedings against Maciel. On 26 May 2005, five weeks after his election as pope, he ordered Maciel to retire as director of his movement. A year later, the Congregation for the Doctrine of the Faith announced that, in view of Maciel's ill health, he would not be subjected to a canonical trial; instead he was directed to withdraw into a life of prayer and penance without exercising any public ministry. He died two years later.

In 2009, Benedict XVI ordered an 'apostolic visitation' of the order that confirmed the accusations of 'objectively immoral behaviour' by Maciel and others, uncovering a 'paedophile network' in the movement. It also became clear that Maciel had misused the movement's sizeable financial resources to buy influence even in the Vatican. The visitators also condemned the aggressive recruitment practices, the authoritarian power-structures and the personality cult that had already led many bishops to forbid the movement in their dioceses for creating a sect-like parallel church outside their control. However, neither the religious community of the Legion of Christ nor its lay extension, the Regnum Christi, were to be disbanded but merely 'reformed'. As one German observer remarked, under John Paul II:

> ... the rustic but combative Legionaries of Christ rose to become one of the most powerful networks within the apparatus of the Curia, alongside the elitist Opus Dei. Both were

wealthy groups happy to assist the pontiff. John Paul II never tired of praising them and their ilk as the 'spring' and 'hope of the Church' – although he was fully aware of Maciel's sexual abuse of children. Wojtyla remained silent and obstructive. (Hanspeter Oschwald, 'Der Freund und Kinderschänder' ['Friend and Child-Abuser'], in *Publik-Forum*, no. 19/2010.)

Meanwhile, a paedophile scandal had come to light in America, where trials of Catholic priests for sexual abuse of minors were being reported in the press. In 1989, the American bishops sent canon lawyers to Rome to seek permission to defrock paedophile priests without a special procedure in Rome; John Paul II refused. When, in the 1990s, the paedophile scandal literally exploded in the USA, soon to be followed by similar scandals in Canada and other countries in Europe and Asia, Pope John Paul could no longer ignore the issue and issued an instruction *Sacramentorum sanctitatis tutela* (2001) that withdrew the handling of such cases from the jurisdiction of the individual bishops and required that they be referred to the Congregation for the Doctrine of Faith, over which Cardinal Ratzinger presided. Many regarded this, however, as a cover-up to prevent action being taken directly by local bishops. In 2002, faced with the ever-increasing scale of the alleged sexual abuse scandal in the Archdiocese of Boston, John Paul II was forced to become personally involved in the issue. However, his meeting with American cardinals in April 2002 did not result in any clear declaration concerning the responsibilities of the pope or bishops. When, at the end of the year, Archbishop Cardinal Bernard Law was forced to resign, the pope appointed him to a sinecure in Rome. In the extended interview with Pope Benedict XVI published in 2010 as a book with the title

Light of the World, the one-time head of the Congregation for the Doctrine of the Faith conceded that the responsible congregations of the Vatican had reacted 'very slowly and belatedly' to the sexual abuse scandal.

In 1999, George Weigel – a highly prominent lay American Catholic conservative publicist and theologian, a member of a variety of conservative think-tanks and a close friend of John Paul II – published a bestselling biography of the Polish pope, *Witness to Hope*, in which he passed over in silence the sexual abuse scandals that had already come into the open. Only in the second edition six years later, after the whole world was discussing them, was Weigel, too, forced to voice criticism of the scandals, attributing them, however, to the *'mysterium iniquitatis'*, the 'mystery of evil'. On 7 January 2011, Jason Berry, who had already written several articles about the development of the scandal, wrote an extended essay in the *National Catholic Reporter* attacking Weigel for 'whitewashing John Paul's culpability'. Michael Walsh, author of the *Oxford Dictionary of Popes*, closed a critical article on John Paul II's planned beatification in *The Tablet* of 22 January 2011 with the remark: '... popes have adopted the ancient imperial tradition of deifying their ancestors'.

This extremely hesitant approach to the problem of sexual abuse, and especially the failure to act in the case of Maciel, is believed by experts to be the reason that doubt was cast in the Vatican on the *'Santo subito'*. All the same, Karol Wojtyla was duly beatified by Benedict XVI on 1 May 2011, although the 'authenticated' healing miracle supposedly performed through the intercession of the Polish pope – a requirement for beatification – is highly controversial. Some doctors, in fact, doubt whether the French nun who claimed to have been inexplicably healed from Parkinson's disease had ever had this disease in the first place. Meanwhile, however, Pope Francis has cleared the way for John Paul II's full canonization by a decree of 13 July 2013 officially certifying a second miracle attributed to his intercession. It is expected that he will be canonized together with Bl. John XXIII before the end of the year.

In striking contrast to the problems surrounding his own beatification, John Paul II, a staunch believer in miracles, himself carried out a colossal number of beatification and canonization processes – no fewer than 1,338 beatifications and 482 canonizations, more than twice as many as all of his predecessors together had carried out in the past 400 years. John Paul II was not especially keen on studying files, but he adored public appearances. He was convinced that these ceremonies would strengthen people's piety and loyalty to the Church, even when, as was often the case, the person in question was virtually unknown outside a particular order or religious community. And he certainly knew what a lucrative business the beatification and canonization processes were for the Vatican – lucrative not only for the Roman tourist industry because of the crowds of additional pilgrims to Rome, but also for the Vatican itself because of the high procedural costs involved. As someone high up in the organization of one religious order told me, the community preferred to forgo a beatification in order to be able to use the several hundred thousand euros it would have cost for better purposes.

On taking office, Pope Benedict XVI slowed down the run-away beatification and canonization operations and downgraded the beatification ceremony: instead of taking place in the Vatican with the pope presiding, it now generally takes place in the location where the person lived and worked, and, as a rule, is presided over by the prefect of the Congregation for the Causes of Saints as the delegate of the pope. But Benedict left the canonization process unchanged and declined any reform of this highly problematic veneration of individual saints. It is well known that serious malpractices have crept into this tradition, especially since Medieval times. From antiquity, canonization was performed by the local bishop or by a provincial synod, as is the practice in the Orthodox churches to this day, but in 1200 the powerful Innocent III definitively reserved all canonizations to the pope, effectively making it an instrument of curial politics. In John Paul's reform of the process in 1983, the number of required miracles was reduced and the office of the 'devil's advocate', who was commissioned to present the strongest possible case against beatification or canonization, was abolished.

Is this really the way to revitalize the sick Church? Increasingly, these events have been used for papal self-promotion, and to further the particular interests of the Church and individual orders. The canonization of the anti-modern pope Pius X in 1954 and the beatification of the infallibility pope Pius IX in 2000 were highly controversial decisions. For many people, the canonization of Padre Pio in 2002 was a scandal (it is now viewed with suspicion because of the manipulation of his alleged stigmata), as was that of the founder of Opus Dei, Josemaría Escrivá, in 2002, whose sanctity is extremely controversial. In spite of all this, not a single voice of warning was ever heard from the bishops.

Why the Bishops Maintain Their Silence

Luckily, in spite of John Paul II's restoration politics, the conciliar and ecumenical movements have continued at the grassroots level in many parishes all over the world, even though they are constantly being obstructed and thwarted from above. The result, however, is a growing alienation, bordering on indifference, between the 'Church from below' and the 'Church from above'. Whether a parish will have a vibrant pastoral life with frequent and creative worship services, will show sensitivity in ecumenical matters, and will demonstrate pastoral concern and social commitment depends, more than ever, on the individual priests and lay leaders, both men and women.

Between Rome and the parishes stand the bishops, and they play a significant role in this crisis. Since Vatican II, the bishops in various countries – many of them much more open to people's needs and hopes than those in the Curia – have found themselves under pressure from both sides: pressure from grassroots expectations and pressure from Roman directives, more often confidential than public. People often wonder why the bishops remain silent on controversial reform issues. Why do they more often reflect the voice of the head office in Rome than that of the majority of the faithful? Why does no one dare publicly to contradict the pope, as St Paul once rebuked St Peter to his face in the midst of the assembly? Why do some bishops after their election voice exactly the opposite opinions to those they held before their appointment? In order to understand all this, we need to understand the internal workings of Roman personnel policies.

Bishops do not fall from heaven, even in Rome; they are created by the Roman Curia. Every cathedral chapter and in

addition various Rome-minded private individuals are regularly requested to send lists of possible episcopal candidates to
Rome or to the papal nuncio in their countries. If one of these
candidates happens to hold a position on a topic that is at odds
with the ideas prevailing in the Curia, he will immediately be
struck off the list as unsuitable. Or, if a selection is imminent,
he will be forced to distance himself publicly and in writing
from his earlier non-conformist position. Apparently this
happened in the case of three cardinals, who abruptly changed
their position a short time before their appointments. For me,
this was a sure sign that they had been previously selected '*ad
maior*' ('for higher things'), on the condition that they conform.
One of them explained publicly that he had never distanced
himself from the birth-control encyclical *Humanae vitae*.
Another suddenly declared himself ready to ban lay theologians from preaching, despite the dearth of priests in his diocese.
The third was suddenly full of praise for the reactionary secret
organization Opus Dei that he had previously abhorred.

All of this means that, long before consecration, a future
bishop will have had his arm twisted and will have been
injected with a massive dose of unconditional submissiveness.
Before actual appointment, the nunciature in his country
re-checks the candidate's orthodoxy with a questionnaire to
ensure that he holds a positive position on the *Humanae vitae*
encyclical, affirms the obligation of celibacy and rejects the
ordination of women. If any of his answers do not ring 'true to
Rome', his candidacy will be stricken.

At his consecration, every bishop must make a public vow
of obedience to the pope, expressed with no restrictions whatsoever: 'Are you resolved to be faithful in your obedience to the
successor of the Apostle Peter?', to which the candidate must

answer: 'I am.' What this promise of loyalty means becomes clear when you look at the oath of allegiance that every bishop must take upon installation in office in his diocese:

> I vow that I will always be faithful to the Catholic Church and to the Pope as its supreme pastor, Vicar of Christ, successor to St Peter the Apostle in the primacy and head of the college of bishops. I will obey the free exercise of the primatial authority of the Pope over the entire Church and diligently support and defend his laws and authority.

It is hardly surprising that this kind of oath of absolute allegiance has sometimes been compared to the oath of allegiance once made by German soldiers of the Third Reich to the Führer: to him they had to swear 'unconditional obedience'. One need not compare the pope to the Nazi Führer to see that what is at stake is the unconditional nature of the oath taken in both cases and the psychological effects such an oath has on those forced to take it.

A Catholic bishop must do his utmost to avoid violating his oath by expressing any contradictory opinions. Here we should recall the words from the Sermon on the Mount against taking oaths: 'But I say to you, Do not swear at all ... Let your word be "Yes, Yes" or "No, No"; anything more than this comes from the evil one' (Matthew 5:34, 37). According to Jesus, the obligation to absolute truthfulness makes oath-taking superfluous. What is more, moral philosophers remind us that even the most solemn oath can never oblige us to violate a moral imperative. When keeping an oath entails approving something immoral, it must be refused. No person should ever be coerced into making an unconditional oath to another person, even if that person holds the highest position in the State or Church. For this reason, in Germany now, having learned from bitter historical experience under the Nazi regime, soldiers do not take an oath or pledge to any person, but only 'to serve the Federal Republic of Germany faithfully, and to bravely defend the law and freedom of the German people'.

Enforced Conformity of the Episcopate

As in every political system, personnel policy has always been vitally important in the Church, since over the long run it can have implications for change. The right to appoint bishops, which was increasingly usurped over time by the Curia, is without doubt the chief instrument of the contemporary Roman roll-back. Equally important is the appointment of cardinals by the pope alone, since they are the electors of the next pope (provided they are under 80 years of age when a pope dies). A further instrument is the promotion of conformist theologians to professorial chairs and their appointment to influential advisory bodies.

The 'Wojtyla system' consisted of naming as bishops priests who were conspicuously loyal to Rome and often personally loyal to the pope himself, and especially those with strong 'Marian' leanings. This was done with no regard for the wishes of the local clergy and without any consultation with, or involvement of, the faithful of a diocese. Appointments of truly outstanding personalities have been the exception rather than the rule. In numerous dioceses, highly qualified priests – often very good auxiliary bishops named under Paul VI – were passed over as being not sufficiently conformist. Right from the start, no one who had drawn attention to himself by holding a dissenting opinion had the slightest chance. Already toeing the Roman line before their consecration, and confirming their continuing conformity at their consecration by taking the solemn vow of obedience to the pope, the bishops feel that their first responsibility is to the pope, not to their congregation. They are obliged to make regular trips to Rome '*ad limina Apostolorum*' to report in person. In this way, the Vatican is kept very well informed about the state of affairs, both positive and negative, in various countries, although it never apologizes for its mistakes.

Because of the appointment of conformist bishops and the widespread disenfranchisement of the local churches since John Paul II, both the bishops and the cardinals present an unprecedentedly uniform front, unwilling to listen to any deviating voices on controversial issues and to take such questions seriously. Demands raised by national and diocesan synods, voiced in petitions for a referendum in the Church with millions of signatures, and public and private petitions by numerous individuals calling for the abolition of compulsory celibacy, a re-evaluation of the role of women, toleration of intercommunion, and the practice of 'brotherly and sisterly friendship among Churches' have all been simply ignored by the bishops. Correspondingly, the influence of the episcopate on public opinion is increasingly on the decline.

In particular the churches of Ireland, Poland, Austria, Germany and the USA have in recent years been shaken by political and sex scandals involving both priests and bishops. Initially, the Vatican and the hierarchy did their best to sweep such scandals under the carpet, but under public pressure it finally had to admit them. This is just one example of the kind of problems the current system of Roman church rule and episcopal appointment entails. Affairs involving collusion with secret service organizations, sexual abuse, child pornography, corruption – to all of these the system has responded by remaining silent, covering up the scandal, or, if there was no other way out, granting half-hearted concessions and only as a last resort taking contrary action.

How to Have a Successful Career *Modo Romano*

This was demonstrated in a most striking fashion by the career of the Swiss theologian Kurt Koch, whom I know personally. He was the fifth of the bishops democratically elected by the cathedral chapter in my home diocese of Basel. In July 2010 he became President of the Pontifical Council for Promoting Christian Unity in the Vatican, taking over from Cardinal Walter Kasper, and in November 2010 he was named a cardinal. As a young theologian, he had courageously addressed a number of critical issues and had published research papers on them, which resulted in Rome's longer-than-usual delay in granting him ecclesiastical authorization to teach at the Theological Faculty in Lucerne. In the end, Bishop Otto Wüst granted him the *missio canonica* on his own without waiting for Roman approval, an action for which he was soundly rebuked by Rome. When I received the Swiss Culture Prize in 1991, Professor Koch delivered an impressive eulogy, culminating in the demand for:

> ... the Catholic rehabilitation within his lifetime of the Christian Hans Küng and his theological work ... For no one, who really knows Hans Küng and has studied his work, can doubt his deep Catholic convictions by which he rightfully tries to live

according to the Gospel within the Roman Catholic Church, notwithstanding the combative tone often taken by his tongue and his pen.

So I was happy when, four years later, in 1995, this man was elected bishop by the Cathedral Chapter of the Diocese of Basel. Unfortunately, the Swiss side imprudently made concessions to the Roman Curia, so that the election was not immediately announced with the usual democratic transparency that had previously been the rule; instead, six whole months elapsed between the election and its public announcement and confirmation by Rome. Opus Dei had raised objections, and this half-year delay provided sufficient time to transform the progressive theologian Kurt Koch into a toady bishop who would toe the Roman line; one can only speculate about the methods used. To the great annoyance of the people and clergy of his diocese, he was not consecrated by his fellow Swiss bishops in his Solothurn cathedral; instead, Pope John Paul II consecrated him personally in St Peter's Basilica in the Vatican. It was an ominous portent.

From the beginning of his episcopate, he vigorously championed Roman positions – he even praised Opus Dei, contrary to previous public statements – and very soon he believed it expedient to disparage publicly respected theologians such as the Old Testament exegete Herbert Haag and myself as being untrustworthy. It was particularly embarrassing to see how Koch, quite early on, aligned himself with Cardinal Ratzinger, and how in 2009 he even defended Benedict XVI's reconciliation with the traditionalist bishops of the Society of St Pius X, including the Holocaust denier Williamson. Along the same lines, Koch defended Benedict's revision of the Good Friday

Prayer to include once again the petition that the Jews should be converted to Christianity. Koch's pedantic attempts to explain this change theologically to the shocked and scandalized Swiss Federation of Jewish Communities did nothing to convince them. The same fate met his long-winded letter to the President of the Federation of Swiss Protestant Churches, Dr Thomas Wipf, defending Roman claims and shifting to the Protestants the blame for the cooling of the ecumenical climate.

Kurt Koch's reversal on the question of homosexuality is equally painful. Six months before his ordination as a priest in 1982, he published a short paper, 'Friendship and the Game of Life: A Meditation to My Friend'. It is a hymn about physical tenderness addressed to a friend, whom he describes in bizarre language as 'the second, social, womb of my life'. Curiously enough, this publication no longer appears in Bishop Koch's official bibliography. But in his carefully researched article 'Der Nächstenlieber' ('The Charitable One') (Das Magazin no. 43/2010), Michael Meier, an expert on church and religious topics for the Zurich daily Tages-Anzeiger, placed Koch's forgotten publication in the context of his personal relationships. In fact, as a young professor Koch had convincingly campaigned against the discrimination against homosexuals in the Church. But this ended as soon as Koch became a bishop. From that time on, he resolutely banned from church office self-confessed homosexual priests and lay theologians.

In spite of his striking about-faces, Koch protested strongly against the charges that he was an ecclesiastical turncoat. Increasingly, it became clear that what he really wanted to do was to rule his diocese autocratically like the bishops of Germany and other countries, who have personal control over the proceeds of church taxes and the almost unlimited power that goes with that control. Thus he found the Swiss system, in which the bishops depend on the individual parishes and cantonal synods which call the financial shots, a nuisance. Armed with the mighty arrogance of his Roman office, Koch inveighed against the Swiss dual system, in which the priests and ministers enjoy full freedom of action, but financial management lies in the hands of elected committees of lay people.

Koch's plans for the pastoral development of his diocese did nothing to remedy the catastrophic state of pastoral care arising from the increasing number of parishes without priests; all they did was to mask the problems by merging parishes. In the end, Bishop Koch completely lost face when he attempted to remove the recalcitrant parish priest of Röschenz in the Basel-Land canton. In defiance of Swiss Federal law, Koch tried to impose his own ecclesiastical power, but to no avail. In September 2007, the Basel-Land cantonal court decided that, by summarily withdrawing the priest's canonical mission, the bishop had violated the priest's right to a due process. Thus the parish was not required to dismiss their priest, as Koch had demanded. It was a heavy blow for the bishop who, from that time on and in his capacity as President of the Swiss Bishops' Conference, had the audacity to question the tried-and-tested Swiss constitutional law on the relationship between Church and State and openly mused about a complete separation of State and Church in Switzerland. Soon thereafter, however, Koch suddenly effected reconciliation with the priest, much to the astonishment of the whole Swiss population. Within the parish, many people were convinced that Rome had offered Koch a high position in Rome on the condition that he would clear up this long-standing messy affair.

In the eyes of the press, by 2006, ten years after he took office, Koch's balance sheet was largely negative, summed up as 'a rift between a bishop and his people'. For three months he was out of action due to health problems; then in July 2010 he announced his resignation as bishop of Basel and acceptance of an appointment to the Roman Curia; curiously, he was already in Rome when he did so. Many priests and lay persons were very happy.

This typically Roman solution was of course conditioned on his aligning himself – much to popular annoyance – even more closely with the opinions and policies of Cardinal Ratzinger, later Pope Benedict. Thus nobody in Switzerland was optimistic about the nomination of the newly created Cardinal to head the curial department charged with promoting Christian unity. How could this former ray of hope, who had so miserably failed as the bishop of his diocese, achieve the long-overdue breakthrough in the ecumenical movement? Would he go beyond uttering polite platitudes about ecumenical Christianity and ecclesiastical public relations to put an end to the mutual excommunications of the churches and help re-establish Eucharistic community? Personally, I would be the first to welcome such serious ecumenical progress with open arms.

A different example, but one revealing the same symptoms, is the case of the theologian David Berger. As a young rising star in right-wing Catholic circles, he was appointed corresponding professor of the Pontifical Academy of Thomas Aquinas located in Rome and editor-in-chief and publisher of the German periodical *Theologisches*, the most important forum for traditionalist Catholics in the German language area. In 2009 the Vatican Congregation for the Doctrine of the Faith named him its regular censor for two theological journals under suspicion. In March 2010, however, suspicions were raised about his nearness to homosexual circles, and, worn down by vicious attacks, he publicly outed himself as a practising homosexual in an article that appeared on 23 April 2010 in the *Frankfurter Rundschau*. In his shattering book *Der heilige Schein: Als schwuler Theologe in der katholischen Kirche* ('*The Holy Illusion: A Gay Theologian in the Catholic Church*' [2012]), Berger described how, after voicing criticism of the pope, he had been blackmailed by conservative Christians because of his homosexuality; this is what led him to break with them and to out himself. Since then, he has been the target of an ongoing aggressive and defamatory campaign from these circles.

The Church is a Façade

It is true that hundreds of thousands attend the papal rallies, where the problems of the Church are brushed under the carpet and no critical questions are permitted. But apart from the many curious onlookers and those who are merely searching for any kind of meaning whatsoever, many of those present at such rallies are young people caught in the nets of the Catholic *movimenti* – for the most part highly conservative movements especially active in southern Europe and Poland. They are in no way representative of today's 'youth' in most countries. Most young people very often choose alternative paths in moral questions, and they have little understanding of the verbal intricacies of the Church's teaching. For most young people, as for most adults, the Catholic Church is a quaint, obsolete institution of yesteryear: backward-looking, with authoritarian structures and a strange morality. Thus, the monster papal rallies have little real enlivening effect on parish life; on the contrary, many Catholics are alienated by the slick, media-savvy, ostentatious papal personality cult that spares no expense to demonstrate militant Catholicism. Nowhere have these demonstrations substantially increased attendance at parish church services.

Immediately after Pope Benedict's spectacularly staged visit to England, the Catholic news weekly *The Tablet* printed on the cover of its 16 October 2010 issue a jigsaw-like colour picture of the pope surrounded by smiling candidates for the priesthood, but in the upper right corner a piece had been broken out and the lead article explained that the last Catholic seminary in the north of England, Ushaw College, was being closed for lack of candidates. In 2010 there were only 26 candidates studying there; in its heyday, in the 1950s, there had been as many as 400 junior and adult seminarians. On the very same day I read about the closure of the 1,000-year-old Benedictine monastery at Weingarten in Upper Swabia; to soothe their grief, Bishop Gebhard Fürst of Rottenburg-Stuttgart celebrated a special Mass with the three remaining monks. And these are just two examples of the innumerable closures of seminaries and monasteries all over the world.

The monstrous triumphant rallies staged for the predecessors of Pope Francis do not demonstrate strength, but instead reveal the extent to which the Church has become largely an external façade for an interior urgently in need of repair. Of course, there are still many parishes that are full of life because they have a good pastor working with a good team of lay workers, and because they have dedicated parishioners who actively participate in parish life. These good pastors are committed to their work not because of backward-looking popes, whom they do not see as shining lights for Christian life in today's world, but rather in spite of such popes, preferring to ignore their moralizing preaching, their pedantic dogmatic teaching and their authoritarian exercise of office. This Church does not live on proclamations from above but is sustained by the impetus from below.

Even the Catholic Church in Germany has for years been 'a church in crisis' (Matthias Drobinski, *Oh Gott, die Kirche. Versuch über das katholische Deutschland* ['O God, the Church: An Investigation into Catholicism in Germany'], 2006):

- despite the fact that it is so well organized, and is, thanks to the state-collected church tax, possibly the richest church in the world;

- despite its elaborate social organization, with charities, hospitals and other welfare institutions, and its giant educational apparatus with its own kindergartens, schools and university-level theological schools, many of them incorporated into state universities;

- despite its local organizations for young people, women, and girl and boy acolytes;

- despite its elected parish councils and diocesan boards;

- despite its active lobbyists in the media and in politics, who give it substantial political influence within the government.

Obviously, the complex, multi-layered crisis in which the Catholic Church currently finds itself does not have any one single cause. It is caught up in the general crisis of modernity and secularization that is engulfing every area of human existence. But many of the Church's problems are home-made, generated from within. Right at the centre lies the crisis of the celibate priesthood and the threatening collapse of organized pastoral care. There is also the crisis of shrinking church membership and dwindling finances. If one looks deeper, however, it is a crisis of authority, credibility and communication. Some people have lost hope that anything can still be salvaged, and thus reform movements have been losing much of their thrust. After so many frustrations, the majority of Catholics have given up all hope of change, even when strong, constructive, persuasive and well-organized opposition to the prevailing Roman System still exists.

Among those dependent on the church hierarchy, all opposition and dissident opinion is systematically suppressed. In 2010, for example, faced with the alarming blunders of the church leadership, the respected TV priest Michael Broch, spiritual director of the Catholic School of Journalism, criticized the ongoing endorsement of the celibacy rule, the antiquated sexual ethics and the siege mentality of the hierarchy, giving vent to his irate anger: 'If this goes on, Pope Benedict will drive the Church to the wall' (*Stuttgarter Nachrichten*, 22 May 2010). For this outburst he had to make an immediate public apology, but the conservative minority of the German Bishops' Conference was not satisfied with that. Supported by Rome, they pushed through Broch's removal from his posts against the wishes of his own diocesan bishop, Gebhard Fürst, who is ironically the bishop in charge of the Church's presence in the media.

The decline of academic theology goes hand in hand with the crisis in the Church and of those in its service. Of course, many conscientious theologians still exist, and, fortunately, many of them are women. But young independent-minded theologians with the stature of the conciliar theologians of the past are few and far between. How can they possibly develop in this climate of suspicion where independent thought and intellectual creativity are so unwelcome and advancement depends on toeing the line? Critical topics are hardly ever addressed, and the voices of dissenting authors are silenced. In many theology departments, intellectual life and staff are wasting away. So it is not surprising that far-sighted bishops talk about an evaporation of belief and an erosion of attachment to the Church.

Let me reiterate the question I posed at the beginning of the book: how can we go on with a Church that is indeed possessed of a unique tradition, but that is only prepared to refurbish its traditional exterior, while allowing, at its core, the dismantling of its tradition on an epochal scale? There are now:

- ever fewer priests and candidates for the priesthood;

- ever fewer baptisms and weddings;

- ever fewer people attending church services and family prayers;

- more and more parishes with empty churches and presbyteries;

- parishes being forcibly merged, against the will of their parishioners, into anonymous 'pastoral units';

- churches being sold, deconsecrated and converted to other uses; and

- educational and charitable institutions being shut down.

Millions of Catholics – and this applies not just to Latin America – have turned to the livelier Pentecostal, Adventist and Mormon churches and other religious groups. The spiritual welfare of Catholics that has been built up over centuries is now being jeopardized by this generation of bishops through a combination of narrow-mindedness, helplessness and inarticulateness. This holds true even for the Church in Poland (which I will deal with in Chapter 6). In this crisis, one is often reminded of the failure of the popes and bishops at the time of the Reformation.

This process of decline is accompanied by a massive confidence and image loss for the institutional church, whereas individual religious leaders, Catholic priests (and Protestant pastors) do much better. Opinion polls rank churches at the lower end of the scale of public trust, often even below the political parties. There are hardly any significant Catholic intellectuals any more, and many Catholics, especially the younger ones, do not consider their Church to be capable of change. In many places, committed Catholics ask themselves how the Church can extract itself from this crisis. Where can it find new strength and new confidence? The only satisfactory answer is that we must resolutely reflect once again on the origins of the Church, as witnessed to in the New Testament.

The New Testament Mission to Rehabilitate the Church Leadership

We have the Apostle Paul to thank for the earliest documents of Christianity. But in modern Rome he is entirely overshadowed by the other chief apostle, St Peter. Ironically, while the New Testament recounts very few historical details about St Peter's personal leadership in the Church, we are very well informed about St Paul's leadership thanks to his epistles. St Paul enjoyed astonishing authority: he is well aware that his religious communities are in many respects immature and often make mistakes. In spite of this, he never behaves towards them in a way that would suggest that they need him, the wise teacher, to lecture them about their freedom, much less to curtail it. On the contrary, he takes their freedom for granted, respects it and struggles with it, so that his communities are not forced to follow him, but do so freely.

Certainly, in cases where Christ and his Gospel are in danger of being repudiated in favour of foreign doctrine, Paul resorts to the threat of condemnation and expulsion. But he never punishes a whole community, even in the case of serious deviations, in the way he disciplines individuals, e.g. by temporary exclusion for their own good. As far as he can, Paul at all times steps back from exercising his apostolic power: instead of commanding his communities, he exhorts them; instead of issuing prohibitions, he appeals to personal judgement and responsibility; instead of using compulsion, he attempts to persuade; instead of the imperative, he uses the hortative; he speaks of 'we' instead of 'you'; he speaks words of forgiveness rather than of punishment, and instead of repressing their freedom he challenges his communities to live in Christian freedom.

St Paul never abuses his power by implementing a system where one person dominates another. On the contrary, in matters of church discipline he avoids any kind of authoritative decree even when it would have been within his competence. In questions of morality unrelated to the Lord and his Word he prefers to give his communities full freedom and does not place a noose around their necks. Even where he feels that a decision is clear-cut he avoids unilateral measures, and involves the community in the process of decision-making. Even in matters where he has the power to make an incisive intervention he still holds back, earnestly begging his community not to compel him to use his power. Even when he has a perfect right to intervene he is unwilling to take advantage of it.

St Paul never presents himself to his communities as their overlord, nor indeed as a priest with hierarchical power. An apostle is not the Lord: Jesus alone is the Lord, and it is the Lord who sets the standards for his churches and for St Paul himself. He refuses to treat his followers as children; instead he addresses them as 'brothers' (and sisters); he is their servant in patience, candour and love. It is because he wants to be a faithful servant of the Lord, not simply out of good manners or courtesy, that he is always ready to refrain from exercising his power. In this way he uses his power constructively, not destructively.

At the centre of Paul's understanding of the Church is Jesus Christ and his Gospel, not a pope. All officials in the Church must comply unconditionally with this Gospel. This democratic view of the Church held by St Paul is reflected generally throughout the New Testament, and it prevailed in the Church throughout the first millennium. It calls for a unity in diversity with different languages and cultures, different liturgies and theologies, and different styles of leadership. Even today, on the level of the universal Church, such unity in diversity can still be seen, despite its being severely compromised by the workings of the Roman System. A truly and realistically 'Catholic' vision of the Church, which is quite different from the Roman illusion of unity in uniformity, takes very seriously both the spatial/geographical and the temporal/historical dimensions of Catholicity: it takes account not only of patristic and Medieval Christianity, but also of the preceding early Jewish form of Christianity, and the subsequent forms of Reformation and modern post-Enlightenment Christianity.

Naturally, the Church today must maintain its own identity and remain a place of specifically religious community. It should never succumb to the dictates of a radicalized Enlightenment, or lose its essence in a melting-pot of reductive secularization. Of course, it should use sophisticated communication initiatives, marketing and image campaigns, and economic strategies to integrate itself fully into modern society and adapt itself accordingly, without compromising its specifically Christian identity, but it should not try to preserve its identity by clinging to obsolete traditions, formulations and configurations that have become problematical with the years. Instead, it should strive to re-establish its fully 'Catholic' identity defined by faith in Jesus Christ, the one and only Lord of the Church, and it should strive to live out this faith in the day-to-day practical following of Christ. It is precisely this following of Christ which is the form of succession that St Peter was concerned about, and it should be the form of succession that the pope today should be concerned about, if his claims to be the successor of St Peter are to have any substance.

Three Petrine Promises – Three Papal Temptations

The real St Peter would hardly recognize himself in the image of the papacy created over the centuries. This is true not simply because he was never a prince among apostles and because, until the end of his life, he remained a humble fisherman – after Easter, a fisher of people – who wanted only to follow in the footsteps of his Lord. But it is also true because, according to all the Gospels, he had a second, dark side that again and again reveals to us the mistaken, deficient, failing, but still utterly human Peter. To support a Petrine office in the church, the three biblical promises of St Peter's pre-eminence are easily cited: 'you are Peter, and on this rock I will build my church, and the gates of Hades will not prevail against it' (Matthew 16:18); '... I have prayed for you that your own faith may not fail; and you, when once you have turned back, strengthen your brothers' (Luke 22:32); 'Feed my sheep' (John 21:17).

But each of these passages was counterbalanced by the shocking addition of a stark contrast, whose hard, sombre tone almost overshadows the bright overtones of the promises. The same Gospels recount three grave failings on Peter's part that correspond to the three lofty promises. Any pope who lays claim to the Petrine promises must also attend to the three Petrine failings that constitute three paramount papal temptations. And if the promises are displayed in huge black letters on a golden background in the frieze encircling the centre of St Peter's Basilica, then, by the same token, the contrasting sentences should be added to the same frieze in golden letters on a black background, to make sure that they not be forgotten.

- *The first temptation* – in Matthew's Gospel, the promise in 16:18 ff. is followed by Peter's failing in 16:22 ff. When Jesus told his disciples that he was to suffer and die, Peter took him aside and reprimanded him, claiming to know better than Jesus what would happen; Peter foresaw a triumphalist path that would bypass the cross. It is precisely these know-it-all claims of papal strategies of power and might that are at once so very human and so sharply in contrast to what God intends. This is the pious version of the *ideologia satanae*, the ideology of Satan the tempter. Whenever a pope presumes to think that he alone is thinking God's thoughts, whenever he strays – perhaps even without realizing it – from the profession of faith in Matthew 16:16 ('You are the Messiah, the Son of the living God') to the shameful misconception of 16:22 ('God forbid it, Lord! This must never happen to you'), and takes the all-too-human course instead of God's path, then the Lord turns his back on him and speaks the stinging words: 'Get behind me, Satan! You are a stumbling-block to me; for you are setting your mind not on divine things but on human things' (16:23).

- *The second temptation* – In Luke's Gospel, Jesus first warns Peter that he will fail, before he promises him that, after he does penance, he will strengthen his brethren (Luke 22:32), but when Peter protests his unfailing loyalty Jesus rebukes him with an explicit description of how Peter will deny him three times (Luke 22:34). Special status and special talent entail special responsibility, but this does not exclude temptations and failures. Once again, the devil appears in this context, claiming power over Jesus' disciples to shake them like wheat in a sieve. The faith of Peter theoretically should not falter, but it often does so in practice. Whenever a pope self-confidently believes that his commitment can be taken for granted and that his faith is steady as a rock, whenever he no longer recognizes how much he depends on prayer, and how much his faith and fidelity need to be continually renewed (pious platitudes and protestations here are not enough!), whenever he self-confidently overvalues himself and no longer places his whole faith in the Lord – it is then that the cock crows, signalling the moment of denial. At that moment he effectively no longer acknowledges his Lord, and becomes capable of denying his Lord not just once, but three times, indeed many times: 'I tell you, Peter, the cock will not crow this day, until you have denied three times that you know me.'

- *The third temptation* – According to the Gospel of John in chapter 21, when the Lord was about to commission him, Peter was evidently jealously concerned about the role that John, the beloved disciple, would play alongside him (John 21:20). In John 21:15–17, the Lord three times questions Peter, who had previously three times denied him: 'Simon, son of John, do you love me?' Only after Peter's insistent protestations of his love does Jesus express the threefold commission: 'Feed my lambs'; 'Tend my sheep'; 'Feed my sheep'. And Jesus concludes with the prophecy that '... someone else will fasten a belt around you and take you where you do not wish to go'. Immediately thereafter, according to John 21:20–22, Jesus further warns Peter not to concern himself with God's plans for his fellow disciple

John. Exercising leadership in the Church, according to this passage, is based on the condition of following Jesus in love even where one does not want to go, and without jealous concern about God's intentions for one's fellow disciples. But a pope who is concerned mainly about others being closer to Jesus will get the same answer that Peter got to his jealous question concerning John: 'What is that to you? Follow me!' There are things that are no business of the pope's. Whenever a pope does not focus on his own tasks, whenever he wants to concern himself with everything, whenever he does not see that there are people and things that he cannot judge, whenever he forgets that there are special relationships with Jesus that bypass him and his papal office, whenever he fails to accept that there are other ways to serve the Lord than his own, then he must listen to those hard words of Jesus that remind him to recognize the limits of his office: 'What is that to you? Follow me.'

The magnitude of the temptations corresponds to the magnitude of the commission. Without doubt, the burden of responsibility on Peter's shoulders will be immense if he really wants to be the rock, the key-bearer, the shepherd in the service of the whole Church. In Luther's time, Pope Leo X is reported to have said that the times had passed when it was possible to enjoy the papal office as a God-given privilege. He was referring to the Renaissance pastimes of hunting and banqueting and other even-more-questionable amusements. Today, Leo's prophetic observation applies to the current anachronistic enjoyment of ostentatious liturgical ceremonies performed in opulent vestments and elaborately staged to promote a personality cult at grandiose mass rallies. Given all the grief and tribulation involved in true service to the Church, all the misunderstandings and personal failings, how often will faith falter (cf. Luke 22:32), how often will love fail (cf. John 21:17), how often will the hope of prevailing against the gates of Hell fade (cf. Matthew 16:18)?

However, the long list of papal failings and the sharp criticism of the Roman System outlined in these chapters is not meant to be the last word on the matter. Here we need to ask the question: would there be something lacking to the Catholic Church, and perhaps to all of Christianity, if the Petrine office were to disappear or be abolished? The answer is an unqualified 'yes'. Unquestionably, there is something great about the Petrine ministry, provided, as I keep insisting, it is understood in the light of the Holy Scripture and is practised soberly and unsentimentally, as it should be, namely as a service to the universal Church. The full biblical concept of a ministry of service exceeds by far the legal categories of the First Vatican Council of 1870. Let me reiterate:

- This primacy of service is more than an honorific primacy (*primatus honoris*) with only limited opportunities to exert influence.

- This primacy of service is more than a judicial primacy (*primatus iurisdictionis*), when that is understood in terms of power and authority – that is a grave misunderstanding, and if taken literally it would mean denying or passing over in silence precisely what is essential to this office. Petrine ministry, correctly described in the biblical sense, is a primacy of service, a pastoral primacy.

- This primacy of service can rightly expect a great deal from the brothers and sisters it is meant to serve – much more, in fact, than it so often unhelpfully receives from sycophantic hangers-on. It has no need for servile submission, unquestioning devotion or sentimental idolization. On the contrary, it has a right to authentic prayerful support, loyal cooperation and constructive criticism, following the example of St Paul who confronted St Peter and rebuked him publically for his vacillating leadership.

In the next chapter, in a spirit of loyal cooperation and constructive criticism, I will consider some concrete steps that could be taken to help the Catholic Church out of its sickbed. I will propose a hopeful programme of treatment. Can it be fulfilled, at least in part?

CHAPTER 6

ECUMENICAL THERAPY

Prescriptions for Reform

Osteoporosis of the Church System?

'But the Church is not a democracy!' This is the standard reply to grassroots demands for reform. In New Testament terms, however, the Church is not a dictatorship – not even a spiritual one. In fact, it has much more in common with democracy (government by all believers) than with monarchy (government by a single ruler) or theocracy (government by a religious caste). While the New Testament strictly avoided giving either royal or sacred titles to office-holders within the Church, it quite freely applied such titles to all believers collectively, describing them as 'a chosen race, a royal priesthood, a holy nation, God's own people' (1 Peter 2:9), and as being made 'a kingdom and priests serving our God, and they will reign on earth' (Revelation 5:10).

Right from the start, there were numerous offices in the Christian community, often described as 'charisms' or 'callings'. Such offices could be either permanent or temporary. First and foremost among the permanent office-holders were the apostles. In the Gospels the apostles are generally identified with the 'Twelve'. i.e. those first disciples whom Jesus had called at the beginning of his public life. They formed the original inner circle of his disciples and after Jesus' resurrection they formed the collegiate leadership of the Jerusalem Church. But from other New Testament writings, particularly the epistles of St Paul, we learn that the term was also applied to St Paul himself, and to others who were charged with founding and leading churches. Alongside these apostles, prophets, teachers, evangelists and pastors are also mentioned as exercising leadership in the churches. Whatever the names and precise functions, all of these permanent offices were essentially pastoral ministries intended to serve the Church by providing guidance and leadership. It was this servant character of church leadership that gave the office-holders (bishops, priests, others) their special authority. Thus the pastoral ministers do not constitute a ruling class in the Church enjoying a unilateral right to lord it over the faithful who owe them unilateral obedience. The pastoral leaders do not exercise a ruling *dominium*, but instead a *ministerium*, a ministry of service. They do not represent a power structure, but rather a special kind of structure defined by their serving role in the community – a 'servant structure'.

Continuing the medical analogy, this servant structure can be likened to a skeleton which holds up the body of the Church, supporting all the other organs in the body, and keeping the Church together and upright. It is naturally a very bad situation when this supporting structure becomes ill, suffering from a disease such as osteoporosis (Greek: *ostéon* = 'bones'; *póros* = 'opening, pore'), i.e. bone atrophy. In this disease, the bones appear externally intact and strong, but, painlessly and often unnoticeably, the internal bone substance and structure deteriorate over a period of time, reducing the bones' density and making them brittle. Usually the condition is only discovered by accident, often too late, when a bone breaks.

Is this a plausible analogy that can be applied to a social body like the Church? Is it an appropriate way of describing the attrition and weakening of the Catholic Church's infrastructure, which, if it is not arrested in time, could lead to paralysis and ultimate collapse? Political systems, in any case, are not brought down solely by external influences; they can also be eroded from within. Could this also happen to the Catholic Church?

Authoritarian Systems Can Implode

'Might not the same thing happen to the Vatican and the Catholic Church that happened to the Kremlin and the Communist Party of the Soviet Union?' Recently this question was put to me by an astute Catholic observer of current affairs in Italy. One well recalls the pictures of elderly Soviet Politburo members still waving proudly at the impressive Red Square parades of military forces, party soldiers and youth groups marching by in endless ranks, while, at the same time, the apparently unassailable Soviet system was doomed to collapse from the inside. The threat came not so much from external foes, against which the formidable array of Soviet tanks, missiles and aircraft was effectively deployed, but from internal decay, corruption and attrition. In the language of physics, the Soviet demise was not so much an explosion as an implosion; a sudden collapse of a hollow body as a result of growing internal social pressure on the ruling Communist Party.

In the opinion of my interlocutor, this is a process that could also happen with astonishing rapidity within the Catholic

Church generally, as the rapid collapse of the formerly dominant, majority Catholicism in Ireland, Spain, Belgium and even Italy shows. Another example is the critical developments in Germany in recent years, where the jubilant headline from Germany's leading tabloid, 'We Are Pope!', celebrating Ratzinger's election was followed, only a few months later, by the headlines 'We Are Not Pope!' and 'We Are an Embarrassment!' According to a survey by the magazine *Der Spiegel* published on 6/7 July 2010, only 35 per cent of Germans considered Pope Benedict to be a good representation of Germany, whereas the same question asked about the former German Federal Chancellor Helmut Schmidt clocked up a figure of 83 per cent.

Against the idea of the Catholic Church's being swept away by history, I argued that one cannot compare the 2,000-year-old Christian faith with the less than 70-year-old Soviet ideology, or the 2,000-year-old institutional Church with the 70-year-old totalitarian Soviet system. The Kremlin itself reflects this chequered history. Byzantium followed ancient Rome as the 'second Rome', and Moscow followed as the 'third Rome'; the second Rome was destroyed by Turkish Muslim conquest in 1453, the third Rome by the October Revolution of 1917, and its successor, the ensuing Communist empire, ended with the fall of the Iron Curtain in 1989. Yet the 'first Rome' is now, once again, raising its old claims to supremacy over the whole Church.

Have not all three 'Romes' deceived themselves about the real balance of power? The Patriarchate of Moscow now sets its hopes on a restoration of the Russian Orthodox Church. The Ecumenical Patriarchate of Constantinople dreams of uniting all Eastern Orthodox churches under its leadership.

The Vatican dreams of re-Christianizing the Western, increasingly secular world, re-Romanizing the Protestant and Anglican churches, and restoring the monolithic pre-conciliar Roman Catholic Church. Can such dreams come true?

Probably not! The wish to bring Eastern Orthodoxy under the authority of the Roman pontiff and the infallibility of the pope, based on affinities in structures and attitudes, will in any case remain a Roman illusion. Equally illusory is the Roman belief that Protestantism and Anglicanism will disintegrate as their fragmentation escalates, their spirituality evaporates, and they threaten to wither away, however much such processes of erosion need to be taken seriously. Finally, the third Roman illusion: the belief that centralization and bureaucratization can modernize the Church and intensify its claims to power by setting up an alternative Roman Catholic world in opposition to the modern secular world, and by arresting the growing alienation between the Roman hierarchy and the Catholic people with improved PR tricks and sanctions against dissenters.

Even in a Catholic country like Poland, the church that developed remarkable resilience under National Socialism and Communism is threatened with implosion. Since the fall of Communism, the church in Poland has shown ominous signs of erosion that have become even more visible since the death of the Polish pope. Just before Christmas in 2010, the highly regarded Dominican Fr Ludwik Wisniewski, who had been very active in the popular social protest movements of the 1970s, sent to the papal nuncio in Warsaw a letter of complaint about the oppressive conditions within Polish Catholicism. He simultaneously sent a copy of his letter, summarizing his critique in seven propositions, to the liberal newspaper *Gazeta*

Wyborcza. As Adam Krzeminski, journalist for the weekly Warsaw newspaper *Polityka*, wrote in the *Neue Zürcher Zeitung* on 6 January 2011:

> The findings of this Dominican are devastating. Five years after the death of John Paul II, the papal 'super'-father of Poland, the Polish church has virtually disappeared in a fog of vain triumphalism. Twenty years after the victory over Communism, the Polish church still appears on the outside to be powerful, impressive, gaily coloured. In reality, it is more like an over-inflated balloon. The Spanish spectre of rampant secularization of society, combined with the massive departure of the younger generation, could soon reach Poland as well.

Wisniewski's findings about Poland confirm my own analysis:

> It is the conservative bishops who are to blame for this miserable state of affairs in the Church. Entrenched behind walls of stupid conservatism, they authorized the quasi-pagan, hate-filled activities of nationalistic, Catholic fundamentalist groups who abuse the cross as a totem for their own political beliefs.

Wisniewski, too, saw the weakness of the Church as emanating primarily from the episcopate:

> The 'Achilles' heel' of the Polish church and its bishops' conference is their inability to cope with a democratic society. Pluralism can be an opportunity, but only when people who hold different attitudes and values communicate with each other. The choice of bishops during the last twenty years, i.e.

under the reign of the Polish pope, was so astonishing because those appointed were so often 'not of this world'; they had good connections in Rome but little or no contact with their own congregations, and were completely antipathetic to any kind of cooperation.

According to Wisniewski, the country is in the middle of a social revolution. Young Poles travel abroad in thousands. Many of them lose their orientation, and cannot be reached by unctuous phrases, by the constant condemnation of the rotten Western world and its conspiracy to annihilate Christianity. In reality, the Polish Church has no need for 'super-fathers' like Cardinal Wyszynski in the years after 1945 and the Polish pope after 1978; what it needs are people of the church who are prepared to change their language and reach out to the younger generation.

Let me add a minor comment here: instead of the bishops travelling to Rome, together with thousands of Polish Catholics, to attend the problematic beatification of Karol Wojtyla, it would have been better to take up the suggestion of the Dominican Wisniewski to form six working groups in which the bishops would discuss the situation of the Church in modern-day Poland with laymen and -women.

Every single diagnosis in this book has shown that the condition of this ecclesial patient is serious. Radical therapy is urgently required if we want to ensure that the Church will remain viable in the future. What is required is not just discussions to pacify the faithful but decisive measures of church reform. The demands voiced in this chapter are not simply my own private ideas – they are reforms that have been demanded for years, decades, sometimes even for centuries, but have always been postponed. They contain many bitter and painful medicines necessary to effect a cure. But (bearing the osteoporosis in mind) they also include therapies involving more exercise, more fresh air and more sunlight.

As I did in my programmatic book addressed to the soon-to-meet Second Vatican Council (1960), I am now, 50 years later, setting forth a list of needed reforms: perhaps it too will require a council to realize them. In any case, many of these reforms will take a generation or more to accomplish; others, however, are so urgent that they can and should be implemented immediately. On all of these issues, there is an urgent need for action – at least in the long term, often in the medium term, but for the most part in the short term. The Church will only recover and regain its strength when its leadership finally faces up to these issues and follows words with deeds. What actions are required then? To answer that question, we must look at the nature of the Church and its functions.

The Norm for Church Reform Is Not Any Canon Law Fabricated by the Church, but the Historical Jesus Christ as Testified to in the Bible

Put in a nutshell, the Church can best be defined as the community of believers in Christ: the community of persons who are committed to Jesus Christ and to his cause and who actively bear witness to him as the hope for the world. The Church's credibility depends on preaching the Christian message first of all to itself and only then to others. To do this, the Church must not only preach Jesus' demands; it must also live them. Thus, the Church's entire credibility depends on being faithful to Jesus Christ. None of today's churches – the Roman Catholic

Church included – is of itself automatically and in every way identical with the Church of Jesus Christ. An individual church is only identical with the Church of Christ to the extent that it keeps faith with Jesus Christ in word and deed.

All reforms have to be measured against the central benchmark of the Church, against the historical Jesus as we come face to face with him in the New Testament: the Christ of the Christians, inimitably present in the outlines of his Gospel, his behaviour and his destiny, notwithstanding all attempts at critical deconstruction. He must be brought to people of today in contemporary language, not in antiquated, dogmatic terms incomprehensible to lay people. That is the only way in which Jesus can enter into our lives as a living presence and become a standard for us to follow.

It is inconceivable that if Jesus, on whom Christianity is based, were to come again, as in Dostoyevsky's story (see Chapter 1, p. 59), he would hold, in many of today's controversial issues, all of the positions taken by the Vatican and often by the leadership of other churches as well. It is inconceivable, for instance:

- that he who warned the Pharisees against placing unbearable burdens on people's backs would today brand all artificial forms of contraception as deadly sins erosive to authentic sexuality and equate them simply with abortion and infanticide;

- that he who invited outcasts to his table would today ban permanently all remarried divorcees from his Eucharistic banquet;

- that he who was always accompanied by women who cared for him and supported him, and who chose married men to be his apostles, would today forbid ordained men to marry and forbid women to be ordained, at the cost of depriving communities of their pastors and curates and withholding from them regular celebrations of the Eucharist;

- that he who protected adulterers and sinners would today mete out such harsh verdicts in matters requiring delicate and discriminating judgement, such as premarital sex, homosexuality and abortion.

Equally, I cannot believe that in the area of ecumenical relations, if Jesus were to come again today, he would support Rome:

- in making the choice of a marriage partner belonging to a different Christian denomination a serious obstacle to entering marriage or an obstacle to being accepted into the pastoral ministry as a lay Catholic theologian (or to ordination, as in many Protestant churches);

- in contesting the validity of the ordination of Protestant clergy and of Protestant celebrations of the Eucharist;

- in refusing Eucharistic hospitality to non-Catholic Christians, prohibiting joint celebrations of Holy Communion, forbidding joint construction of churches and parish centres and opposing ecumenical religious teaching in schools;

- in using coercive measures such as 'notifications', censures and withdrawal of teaching licences to bring into line professors of theology, pastors, student chaplains and religious education teachers, and even journalists, politicians and youth leaders, instead of endeavouring to persuade them with convincing reasons;

- in denying that those who are neither Jews nor Christians can recognize the true God and find their way to him. Jesus treated people of other faiths very differently from many of his contemporaries, who prided themselves on their orthodoxy and righteousness. He respected persons of other faiths as people, and respected their dignity. Born of a Hebrew mother, he rejoiced to discover the faith of the Syro-Phoenician woman and of a Roman officer. He gave a friendly welcome to Greeks who sought him out, and he provocatively portrayed the 'heretical' Samaritan as an example of charity to his Jewish compatriots.

If we bear the Jesus of the Gospels in mind, then it is easy to recognize the reforms of basic attitudes that are urgently needed:

- The Church as a whole should not take the form of an apparatus of power; it is not a hierarchically structured religious corporation that seeks its own profit and constantly hinders internal dialogue and democracy; it should be a people of God, the body of Christ and a global and local spiritual community.

- Church offices should not take the form of a 'well-ordered battle formation' (*'acies bene ordinata'*) or a 'holy lordship' (*'hierarchia'*), but should see themselves as offering service (*'diaconia'*) to the people of God.

- The pope should not act as a demi-god and spiritual autocrat, nor as a military commander or as corporate chief executive, but instead he should see himself as nothing more than the leading bishop of the Catholic Church, bound by collegial links to all the other churches and exercising his pastoral primacy within the collegiality of the whole episcopate and in the service of the whole ecumenical movement.

The consequences of these reforms of basic attitudes – all of them founded on the Bible – will be worked out in detail in the following sections of this chapter.

The Church Should Concentrate on Its Core Functions and at the Same Time Face Up to Its Social Responsibilities

If the Church wants to make a full recovery, it needs primarily, both globally and locally, to concentrate on its core or basic functions:

- It should communicate the Christian message in language as it is spoken today, without either biblical archaisms or antiquated, no-longer-intelligible dogmatics; at the same time, it should avoid trendy theological jargon. It should use clear, concise, adequately differentiated and gripping terms.

- Baptism, the sign of belief in Christ common to all Christians, forbids one denomination from claiming to be the only way to salvation or discriminating against and excommunicating other Christian denominations on the basis of unessential doctrinal differences.

- The Eucharist or Holy Communion should be celebrated as a meal of commemoration, thanksgiving and fellowship, a sign of unity in the spirit of Jesus and the early Christian community, without regard to the differences in status, education, gender and theology of those who take part.

If the Church wants to regain people's trust as a Church of service, it must provide pastoral liturgies – from baptism to confirmation, from the celebration of communion to funerals – in a form that that is understandable and appealing to all who participate.

But if the Church wants to make a full recovery, it must at the same time, both globally and locally, face up to its social responsibilities:

- It should not withdraw into itself as a reclusive coterie of 'true Christians' or those true to Rome, focused exclusively on itself or on its clerical leadership.

- It should not become a politicized, partisan, right-wing or left-wing Church that, in the interests of its secular allies, moralizes and meddles in all manner of questions.

Although individual Christians can and often should take a public stand on contemporary issues, the Church as a community of faith and its representatives should take such public stands on controversial social issues only when the Gospel of Jesus Christ himself and the fundamental human rights and human responsibilities based on the Gospel are unequivocally in jeopardy or make an intervention mandatory; when this is not the case, it is better to show tolerance and patience and allow the matter to be settled by the slow process of consensus-building.

Of course, the Church should courageously and intelligently take a public stand for Christian values in today's pluralistic secular society, but this should always be done in the context of the values shared by all human beings. The specifically Christian ethos can only be credibly presented within the framework of a human or global ethic that represents the common moral standards and attitudes of the different religions and philosophies; it can never stand in contradiction to true human values.

In view of the complexity of most social issues, as a rule the Gospel can only provide general orientation regarding the fundamental principles that should govern actions in a particular context; thus it is generally impossible to fabricate ready-made, off-the-shelf solutions. Put in other terms, the Church should concentrate on formulating objectives rather than pronouncing partisan political prescriptions; it should concentrate on outlining basic legitimate options, rather than dealing out specific moral recipes, and it should aim at offering orientation for a better future, rather than attempting to endorse the *status quo* or insist on returning to a *status quo ante*.

The Pope Must Strive to Maintain
Community with the Church

Anyone who lays claim to the Petrine office must, by virtue of his belief in Christ, be a 'rock' of Church unity, not a boulder blocking the way to a new unity, as Pope Paul VI himself admitted with shame. It was the popes who bore the main responsibility for the great East–West schism (see Chapter 2, p. 97 ff.) and for the split following the Reformation (see Chapter 3, p. 135 ff.). Paul VI tried to overcome the schism between the Western and Eastern Churches, but he was reluctant to give up the presumptuous Roman claims dating from the Gregorian reforms of the eleventh century. Some people have suggested that Pope John Paul I, who died in mysterious circumstances after 33 days in office, might have gone a step further. Certainly, both his successors, the restoration popes John Paul II and Benedict XVI, achieved nothing concrete in support of the reuniting of Christendom, despite their many fine words and a few impressive gestures. The ecumenical declarations and intentions of the Second Vatican Council have been implemented only to a small extent.

On the contrary, many Catholics discovered with growing consternation and unease that, in many areas, Benedict XVI moved further and further away from the Council (see Chapter 1, p. 12 ff.). His missed or botched opportunities to improve relations with Jews, Muslims and the indigenous people of South America were not the only disconcerting marks of his papacy; much more serious were the setbacks in achieving a better understanding with Protestants and Orthodox Christians. Particularly significant were the often scarcely noticed decisions of a factual nature and in personnel politics that indicated that Pope Benedict, who had been most zealous in seeking a rapprochement with the four schismatic bishops of the Society of St Pius X, notorious for its anti-Council, anti-Semitic and anti-Modern attitudes, was moving further and further away from the Second Vatican Council, and thus away from the community of the faithful.

The gradual disavowal of Vatican II found its symbolic expression in Pope Benedict's new/old love of ostentation and ornate Baroque vestments, in sharp contrast to Pope Paul VI's preference for simple and modern styles of dress and furnishings. During the Council, on 11 November 1964, Paul VI solemnly divested himself for all time of the papal tiara, that Medieval triple crown that was at once a symbol of ecclesiastical and secular power. And after the Council, on 21 June 1968, he issued a *motu proprio, Pontificalia Insignia,* aimed at simplifying and restricting the use of pontifical insignia by prelates without episcopal consecration; needless to say, this was hardly appreciated by the many Vatican *monsignori.*

Pope Benedict made concessions to the reactionaries in the Vatican and attempted to carry out a reform of the reform by reverting to the past. Perhaps he thought he could compensate for the loss of the papacy's moral radiance due to the many scandals by restoring its old pomp and glory? It is well known that Joseph Ratzinger has an innate affinity with the Baroque and nostalgia for the old liturgy. Nevertheless, many people were surprised that this apparently simple and modest man would soon draw attention to himself as pope by his clothing choices. Together with his famous tailor-made red shoes of the finest leather, he enjoyed wearing the *mozzetta,* the red velvet cape trimmed with ermine and bordered with silk that dates from the thirteenth century. He retrieved the jewelled mitre worn by Pius IX at the opening of Vatican I from the Vatican's storerooms, together with the ornately carved princely throne of Pius' successor Leo XIII and a heavy golden papal staff.

Many in the Vatican rejoiced that with the appointment of the new Master of Pontifical Liturgical Celebrations, Mgr Guido Marini, pre-conciliar traditions were reintroduced: six enormous candles were placed on the papal altar and two mitre-wearing cardinal deacons now assisted at a solemn papal Mass. All this was designed to make clear that it was not just an ordinary bishop who is celebrating the liturgy, but a Roman monarch.

One could smile about Benedict's penchant for splendid robes and towering bejewelled mitres, were it not that such ridiculous old-fashioned pomp encouraged imitation by the bishops. Worse still, the German pope's affinity for outmoded forms was not just a traditionalist whim, it was also a programme: thus he made a point of using the cope and mitre of the autocratic Pope Pius IX to celebrate the liturgy and in 2008 he not only brought out the vestments of the notoriously anti-Protestant Borghese Pope Paul V to celebrate the Ash Wednesday liturgy, but also, in the same year, commissioned a set of 30 new liturgical vestments for concelebrations at high feast days, following a design copied from the robes of the Medici Pope Leo X (1513–21), the very same pope who had arrogantly condemned Luther and tragically misunderstood the significance of the Reformation (see 'Vested with symbolism', Keith F. Pecklers, *The Tablet*, 8 March 2008). One can only shake one's head in disbelief over such demonstrations of tactlessness directed against Protestants, and of bad taste directed against reform-minded Catholics. In this kind of papal liturgy, Jesus' simple Last Supper is hardly recognizable.

Much worse than Benedict's fashion escapades and his reactionary liturgical changes (for example, his insistence that communion be administered to the tongue again instead of by hand) were the consistent appointments to bishoprics and key positions in the Curia of people aloof from or even hostile to the Council. One of the more recent examples was the appointment in October 2010 of Archbishop Mauro Piacenza as prefect for the crucially important Congregation for the Clergy, in which Piacenza had previously served as secretary. Archbishop Piacenza was the chief architect behind the Year of the Priest 2009/2010, which proved to be a total flop, not least because of the disclosures about paedophile scandals. He was also the author of the odd recommendation that the nineteenth-century Curé d'Ars could serve as a role model for priests in the twenty-first century. Piacenza is adamantly opposed to any discussion about compulsory celibacy; he also opposes the use of the vernacular in the liturgy and the celebration of the Eucharist facing the people. In the *Osservatore Romano*, he formally called for a 'reform of the reform' and he was a leading proponent of Benedict XVI's 'hermeneutic of continuity', essentially a hermeneutic of pre-conciliar nostalgia designed to blunt and roll back all the changes initiated by the Council. This fitted in well with the special esteem accorded to the apologetic German church historian Professor Walter Brandmüller, who, in addition to numerous other honours, was made a cardinal in 2010 and singled out to celebrate the first traditionalist Mass in St Peter's at the *Cathedra-Petri* high altar on 15 May 2011.

Long before Pope Benedict's resignation in February 2013, people within and without the Church were calling for him to step down, not only on account of his overall reactionary course but specifically because as prefect of the Congregation for the Doctrine of the Faith and later as pope he was the one principally responsible for the cover-up of the sex abuse scandals. Whether such demands played a role in his decision to resign is a moot question. In any case, his pontificate teaches us a very important lesson: a pope who sets himself apart from and over and against a substantial segment of the Church runs the risk of alienating himself from the people of God. As the great Spanish Jesuit Baroque theologian Francisco Suarez pointed out in his classic tract on schism (*Disputatio XII de schismate*, sectio I), a schism can occur not only when a part of the Church separates itself from the pope, but also when the pope separates himself from the rest of the body of the Church: 'the pope can become a schismatic if he does not firmly will to maintain union and the bond with the whole body of the Church' ('... *posset Papa esse schismaticus, si nollet tenere cum toto Ecclesiae corpore unionem et coniunctionem quam debet ...*').

To put it more positively, the pope has a duty to maintain inner community with the whole Church. He must cultivate solidarity not only with his staunch supporters but also with his critics, who today make up a significant majority in many countries. His duty obliges him not to retreat into a sheltered, comfortable Vatican refuge as Ratzinger did while in office, so that even senior members of his Curia saw him as an 'autistic', self-centred, egoistical, unsociable scholar, who preferred to celebrate the traditional liturgy and write the books he has always wanted to write while neglecting the day-to-day management of the Church and doing nothing to resolve its pent-up accumulation of serious problems.

Dealing effectively with these problems is crucial to ensuring the public recognition on which the Petrine office so heavily depends. It is not the bare title, nor the right, nor the line of succession as such that counts; it is the actions and the practice, the service actually rendered. When we look at John XXIII's great ecumenical initiatives for the Catholic Church, Christianity and the world, we see how little interest people had in his chain of succession or in the proofs of the historical legitimacy of his office. People were impressed by what they saw, namely someone who, in spite of all the human limitations and weaknesses of the church leadership, was really acting like a 'rock', someone who was intent upon giving Christianity a new cohesion and support (Matthew 16:18: 'On this rock I will build my Church'). Here was someone whose strong faith enabled him to strengthen and encourage others (Luke 22:32: 'strengthen your brothers'). Here was someone who, in terms of the powerful biblical metaphor, wished, like his Lord, to care for his flock with an unselfish love (John 21:15–17: 'Feed my sheep'). By itself, of course, the enthusiasm for John XXIII did not result in mass conversions to Catholicism; but people gained a new respect for the Catholic Church because they instinctively perceived that Pope John's conduct and spirit were rooted in and legitimized by the Gospel of Jesus Christ.

Thus at the beginning of the pontificate of Pope Francis I the Roman Catholic Church stands at a crossroads. Will he be a truly ecumenical pope in the tradition of John XXIII or will he follow the pattern of Benedict XVI, changing perhaps the outward style, but pursuing in essence the same policy of restoration and re-isolation? The answer to that question will depend very much on how he goes about the reform of the Roman Curia, which until now has proven itself to be the principal obstacle to serious church reform and to ecumenical understanding.

The Roman Curia Should Not Be Destroyed, But It Should Be Reformed in Accordance with the Gospel

The great Roman senator Cato the elder used to conclude every speech he made in the *Curia*, the Roman Senate, with the sentence: '*Ceterum censeo Carthaginem esse delendam*' ('Furthermore, I think Carthage must be destroyed'). One need not apply this sentence to the papal Curia literally; but I would join with many others in proposing: '*Ceterum censeo Romanam curiam esse reformandam*' ('Furthermore, I think the Roman Curia must be reformed').

A papal 'Roman' Curia, in the present sense of the term, only came into being in the eleventh century, as a consequence of the centralized church administration in the Latin West imposed from above by the Gregorian reforms. In our day and age, what is needed is not the elimination of the Curia but its radical reform according to the demands of the Gospel. These were formulated by St Francis of Assisi (see Chapter 3, pp. 127–28) as:

- *Evangelical humility:* non-biblical honorific titles that are appropriate only to God or to Christ ('*Sanctissimus Dominus*' – 'His Holiness', '*Beatissimus Pater*' – 'Holy Father', 'Head of the Church') or titles to which all Christians or at least all bishops are entitled ('Vicar of Christ', etc.) should be abandoned. Referring to the pope as '*Pontifex Maximus*', the honorific of the heathen high priest, or other similar terms, is, at least, open to misunderstanding. Suitable titles would be: 'Roman Bishop', 'Servant of the Servants of God', perhaps 'Spiritual

Shepherd'. Special caution should be exercised when using the words 'apostolic' and 'holy' in relation to people and institutions.

- *Evangelical simplicity:* this does not mean an unrealistic and romantic notion of poverty as an end in itself, but it does mean the renunciation of pomp and opulence. Clothing, attendants, court ceremony, guards of honour, and especially liturgical services should be modest. There is little justification for papal legions of honour or Roman court titles in a Church committed to serving others.

- *Evangelical brother- and sisterhood:* Rome must eschew absolutistic government, imperial styles of speaking and issuing decrees, and all forms of secret proceedings. There should be no more lonely decisions without the participation of the rest of the Church, no decisions taken without collegial consultation with the episcopate. The Synod of Bishops should not be merely an advisory body whose resolutions are pre-formulated by the Curia; instead it should enjoy freedom of discussion and should partake in decision-making, if possible, complemented by a council of laypersons. The influence of papal nuncios within the episcopal conferences should be limited, likewise their influence on the appointment of bishops. Already Vatican II had sharply criticized their role as informants to the Curia.

- *Evangelical freedom:* the autonomy of the individual churches and their bishops should be encouraged in accordance with the principles of subsidiarity. The over-inflated curial power apparatus can be slimmed down and cut back when Rome no longer insists on dealing with local issues that can best be handled at home. In the long run, the entire Church should be involved in the election of the pope through the Synod of Bishops with lay representation.

Of course, I am well aware that these maximum demands have been formulated within a long-term perspective. It remains to be seen what can be achieved in the short term, or at least in the medium term. A lesson can be learned from the history of the surviving secular monarchies in modern times. To ensure its survival, the status of the British monarchy has had to undergo a major overhaul in the course of the eighteenth to twentieth centuries. Surely it is not too much to expect the pope, together with his Curia, to undergo similar radical changes in order to create a contemporary Catholic common-wealth out of the relics of the Medieval Roman empire. From a Christian viewpoint these demands should be nothing less than self-evident.

Competent Expert Staff Appointments Instead of Cronyism

The power structures in the Vatican must become transparent and open. To see who holds the power in the Vatican, one need only glance at the yearly *Annuario Pontificio* (the 2012 edition, which appeared in March 2013, has some 2,500 pages) to see the complexity of the curial structure, with the Secretariat of State as the central hub, with numerous congregations (the equivalent of ministries in a state), tribunals, pontifical councils, bureaus and commissions. Listed there, under the pope and his cardinals, is the whole global hierarchy including the ancient Eastern patriarchates, and the archdioceses and dioceses, ordinariates, vicariates and prefectures which so often function as the prolonged arms of the Vatican.

The superficially modernized administrative apparatus of the Vatican tends to obscure the fact that in essence the Vatican is still the royal court of an absolute ruler with Medieval and Baroque trappings. It includes countless 'courtiers' of various ranks distinguished by colourful costumes and pompous titles, from reverends and monsignors to excellencies and eminences; it is a celibate, male courtly society with its own very special etiquette and atmosphere. The higher one rises and the closer one comes to the ruler's inner circle, the more this depends on royal patronage, rather than on competence and character: it is the ruler and his cronies who determine who is *persona grata* or *non grata*. But even the lower Vatican echelons are a hotbed of cronyism, i.e. the practice of appointing friends to high-level posts regardless of their suitability.

This is confirmed by recently published documents on WikiLeaks. According to a report by Ulrich Schwarz in *Spiegel online* on 11 December 2010, the 729 dispatches by American diplomats to the US State Department attest to the difficulties of trying to figure out how this strange Vatican court functioned. According to a dispatch from 2009, the Church is 'highly hierarchical' and yet chaotic. Generally, 'only a handful of experts are aware of upcoming decisions', the report continued, and even then they normally simply acquiesce in whatever the man at the top decides. Hardly anyone ever dares to criticize the pope or to deliver bad news to him. Independent advisers are rare. The Vatican's innermost circle is made up almost exclusively of Italians, and their influence was considerably strengthened by the appointment of new cardinals in 2010. They communicate among themselves in a barely comprehensible curial jargon and have no understanding of modern media or information technologies. The Cardinal Secretary of State does not even speak English, and is generally considered to be a 'yes-man'.

Everywhere, at the top of this curial power apparatus, one finds the cardinals. The Latin word *cardinalis*, from *cardo*, meaning 'pivot' or 'hinge', was used very early in the sense of 'assigned to' and later acquired the meaning of 'principal' or 'pre-eminent'. Originally it was applied to the principal deacons of the city's charitable districts, then to the principal priests of the city parishes, and soon thereafter to the bishops of Rome's suburban dioceses. Already by the eighth century the cardinals formed a privileged class within the Roman clergy, playing special roles in the papal administration and liturgy, but they did not gain church-wide significance until the Gregorian reform, when they became a kind of permanent synod enjoying the sole privilege of electing the pope (since 1059) and sharing in papal government now reaching out to the whole Church. Individual cardinals were entrusted with high administrative, financial and judicial offices and were sent as legates to act in the pope's name in foreign nations. In the Middle Ages, they came to rank over all other bishops and archbishops and enjoyed equality with emperors and kings, whom they addressed as 'brothers'.

The cardinalate – unlike the office of a bishop, which is conferred by consecration and in earlier ages depended on local election – has always been bestowed solely at the will of the pope ('The Roman pontiff freely selects men to be promoted as cardinals', Canon 351, §1). In the language of the Curia, even today they are described as 'creatures of the pope', because they do not obtain their coveted red hat through any sacramental act, but only by papal favour. The pope refers to the bishops as his 'brothers' but he calls the cardinals his 'sons'. Although as a group, they once served as 'chief advisers to the pope', today, in practice, even the curial cardinals, with the exception of a select few constituting the inner circle, are seldom in a position to communicate with the pope directly. Apart from electing the pope, they hardly ever convene for collegial consultation: Pope Ratzinger made a feeble attempt to revive the practice at the beginning of his pontificate but soon gave up. Even the so-called 'consistory' for the election of new cardinals is largely a formality, since the candidates have already been chosen in advance. Here, too, Benedict XVI tried but failed to institute a change. After all, he who always has the final say can hardly expect any real opposition.

The consistory on 19 November 2010 was typical. All the cardinals were summoned, like seminarians, to attend a retreat for reflection and prayer, but no provision was made for frank and serious discussions about the problems of the Church. Instead they were lectured by top papal advisers on issues such as the reconciliation of traditionalist Anglicans, the *Dominus Jesus* declaration limiting ecumenism, the dangers of secularism in Europe, and lastly the sexual abuse scandals. As usual, Roman indoctrination replaced free discussion. Commenting in advance on the coming consistory, Eugene Cullen Kennedy, a well-known psychologist–theologian from Loyola University in Chicago, remarked:

If the cardinals really spend their time on self-reflection and prayer, they will have no time to express personal concern about what is not just 'an agenda topic' [the sexual abuse scandals], but is really a grave wound that remains undiagnosed, largely untreated, and clearly unhealed. Leaving this topic to the end of the day without any opportunity for serious discussion by men who share the solemn obligation to explore and deal with this subject may make them docile seminarians, but it does something far worse to Catholics in general and to the sexual abuse victims in particular. It shows that these princes of the Church, reduced to the status of mere seminarians, cannot pray and reflect at the same time. It also reveals how, on one and the same day, they can … simultaneously scandalize and abuse Catholics all over the world. (*National Catholic Reporter*, 12 November 2010)

Also dependent on the patronage of the ecclesiastical monarch are the papal court bishops, whose number and influence have increased radically following a misguided decision by John XXIII. Members of the Curia had persuaded him, automatically and without closer examination, to promote the heads of all the important curial departments, the so-called 'secretaries' of the congregations, to the rank of archbishops and to consecrate them accordingly, thus sacralizing their power – previously, they were for the most part simple priests or honorary prelates enjoying the various grades of the title 'monsignor'. As consecrated archbishops, they now enjoy the same official status as territorial archbishops and a higher status than ordinary diocesan bishops. In this way, the weight of the curial faction has been strengthened within both the Council and the Church.

The Vatican bureaucracy, which of course contains more than a few truly competent employees, could easily shrink to half its size, if – in keeping with the principle of subsidiarity – it were freed of unnecessary tasks and if more competent people were appointed to key positions. Currently, there is a serious lack of well-qualified clerical candidates. Here the general shortage of priests takes its toll; fewer and fewer dioceses are willing and able to send their best people to Rome to study or to work in the Curia. Like the diocesan seminaries in many regions, the papal universities and colleges in Rome increasingly lack both qualified staff and students. Even the Collegium Germanicum in Rome, where I myself spent seven valuable years of study, and which used to be known as the 'breeding ground of the German episcopate', has shrunk radically. In the academic year 2009/10, there were only 63 alumni compared with 120 in previous years. And the nationalities represented have shifted considerably. Previously, the alumni came principally from German-speaking countries, but now at least half are from former 'Eastern' countries. In 2009/10 there were only four new students from Germany, and none at all from Austria or Switzerland. But these vocation problems do not just affect the dioceses; they also apply to the classical religious orders.

Thus large segments of the Roman Curia are now staffed by people from the often fundamentalist *movimenti*, which have experienced a tremendous upsurge since the Polish pontiff took office, and their influence in the Roman Curia is steadily increasing. Here, the credit must go to the journalist and author Hanspeter Oschwald, a Vatican reporter with more than 40 years' experience, who has analysed this impenetrable network of the new *movimenti* that controlled the Vatican under Benedict XVI (See *Im Namen des Heiligen Vaters. Wie fundamentalistische Mächte den Vatikan steuern*, 2010). Basing his findings on a variety of factors, Oschwald has identified (p. 157 ff.) a hierarchy of these movements and distinguished two main groups, ranking the individual movements within each group according to the degree of their influence:

- The first group exercised greater power within the curial apparatus. it consisted of:

    1. Opus Dei;

    2. the Legionaries of Christ;

    3. Comunione e Liberazione;

    4. the Neocatechumenal Way;

    5. the Focolarini; and

    6. the Sant' Egidio Community.

- The second group had more direct influence on the pope himself. It consisted of:

    1. the pope's secretary Georg Gänswein and Cardinal Secretary Tarcisio Bertone;

    2. the Catholic Integrated Community (through personal and private connections);

    3. Opus Dei; and

    4. Catholic traditionalists (through the pope's sympathies with their way of thinking).

But these movements do not always pull in the same direction. Thus based on the self-definitions of the respective organizations, Oschwald distinguishes three groups:

1. the reactionaries, which include Opus Dei and the Legionaries of Christ, both founded in Spanish countries, together with the traditionalists of various colours;

2. communities which look back to the teachings and practice of the early Christian Church, among whom the Neocatechumenal Way, the Focolarini and the Integrated Community (Munich) predominate; and

3. the political heavyweights, among them the Comunione e Liberazione movement and the Sant' Egidio Community.

Some readers may be bewildered by the multitude of names, but the names are less bewildering than the whole situation that has developed within the Roman Curia. There is a shortage of competent people, but no shortage of careerists. Careerism in the Curia, the ruthless pursuit of success and of a fast-track rise, was publicly denounced by Cardinal Joseph Ratzinger while himself a member of the Curia, but he could have been a lot more explicit in referring to what since the Middle Ages continues to be one of the characteristics of the curial system, namely nepotism, i.e. the preferential treatment of relatives and cliques with accompanying greed, corruption and cover-ups. Writing in 1999 at the age of 72 under the pseudonym 'I Millenari', the late Mgr Luigi Marinelli, for many years a member of the Congregation for the Oriental Churches, published a shocking exposé under the title *Via col vento in Vaticano* ('*Gone with the Wind in the Vatican*'), claiming to have collaborated with nine or ten co-authors. In just three weeks the Italian edition sold 100,000 copies. For his courage, Marinelli received the 2003 Herbert Haag Prize 'For Freedom in the Church'. The book describes the Roman System as a system rotten to the core, whose day-to-day administration is in urgent need of radical reform and whose financial system even more urgently needs radical reform.

Glasnost and *Perestroika* (Openness and Restructuring) for the Church Finances

Ever since the creation of the Roman Curia in the eleventh century, the popes have had problems with money. The Cluniac reforms placed hundreds of monasteries under the direct authority of the Holy See, creating large streams of income and huge estates all over Europe. Like other Roman bishops, the great Innocent III was constantly creating new sources of revenue, even going so far as to require every participant in the Fourth Lateran Council to present him with a farewell gift. The new papal residence and curial administration in Avignon during the Great Schism required vast sums of money, and led to the creation of an ingenious system of fees and charges, which has survived in part to this day. The scheme of Leo X, a scion of the great Medici banking family, to finance the building of St Peter's Basilica by the sale of indulgences was the immediate provocation for Martin Luther's theses.

In modern times, there has been no shortage of financial scandals (and modest financial reforms) in the Roman Curia. Toward the end of the nineteenth century, Pope Leo XIII established the Commission for the Works of Charity to work in close collaboration with the secular Banco di Roma, thus enabling the Vatican to invest in the stock exchanges of London, Paris and Berlin. In 1942, under Pope Pius XII, this institution was transformed into the IOR (*Istituto per le Opere di Religione* = 'Institute for the Works of Religion'), commonly known as the Vatican Bank. Although it is located within the Vatican State and its head is directly responsible to a commission of cardinals and thus to the pope, it is not officially either a Vatican State bank or a part of the Curia; it does not manage the assets of the Holy See, and, until recently, it was not supervised by any official Vatican control agency, although its profits, 55 million euros in 2010, go to the pope. Legally, it is a private banking institute, exempt from taxation and from public auditing control, serving private as well as institutional investors such as religious orders. Currently it looks after some 33,000 accounts, many of them anonymous, with deposits amounting to over 6 billion euros. It is alleged to have supported right-wing, anti-Communist activities around the world and even to have helped to spirit away Nazi gold during and after the War. Its structure, combined with utmost secrecy and confidentiality, has made it an easy instrument for financial manipulations and the topic of numerous conspiracy theories with various degrees of credibility (see *Spiegel online*, 2 July 2012).

The latest series of financial scandals involving the IOR began under Paul VI, and since then more and more scandals have been coming to light. The first wave of exposés involved three main criminals about whom much has been written. They were:

- the American Mgr Paul Marcinkus, a career curialist who was a close friend of both Montini and Wojtyla and a titular archbishop. He became the head of the IOR in 1971 and allowed his friends to use the institute to transfer Mafia and other undercover funds illegally to a variety of destinations. In the course of the exploding financial scandals involving the Vatican Bank, he was forced to step down in 1989.

- the Sicilian Mafia banker and money launderer Michele Sindona, a friend of Montini and Andreotti and a close adviser to Marcinkus. He was named financial advisor to the Vatican in 1968. Soon after World War II, he began building up a financial empire that controlled a large number of businesses and banks around the world, including the American Franklin National Bank, which collapsed due to fraud and mismanagement in 1974, costing the Vatican Bank some 30 million dollars. Sindona's efforts to save the rest of his banking empire continued until 1980, when he was sent to jail in the USA and two years later extradited to Italy, where he was sentenced to 25 years in prison in 1982 and died two years later.

- Roberto Calvi, chairman of the Banco Ambrosiano from 1975 onwards until it went bankrupt in 1982. It was Italy's largest private bank and the Vatican Bank was its largest stockholder. Calvi used the Vatican Bank to siphon off millions of US dollars for various purposes including Mafia money laundering; the Banco Ambrosiano went bankrupt in 1982 after the discovery of losses estimated at between 700 million and 3 billion US dollars.

The Vatican protected Archbishop Marcinkus from arrest by the Italian judiciary. After being sheltered in the Vatican for seven years, he was quietly spirited off to the USA to enjoy a peaceful retirement until his death in 2006; the Mafia banker Sindona died in 1984 in an Italian prison after drinking a poisoned cup of espresso, a death that was either murder or suicide; 'God's banker' Calvi was found hanging under London's Blackfriars Bridge in 1982. Calvi's death triggered the first Italian investigation into the Vatican's finances in the same year. As a consequence, the pope appointed a three-man lay commission to investigate the Vatican Bank, but the investigation shed little light on the matter. In 1984, the Vatican, as the Banco Ambrosiano's principal shareholder, agreed to make a voluntary payment of 240 million dollars to the bank's creditors, without, of course, admitting any guilt. Instead of attending to the affair, Cardinal Joseph Ratzinger, at the centre of power in the Vatican since his appointment in 1981 as head of the Congregation for the Doctrine of the Faith, preferred to concentrate on the fight against Latin American liberation theology, which among other things was particularly critical of collusion between the hierarchy and capitalism. Ratzinger masterminded the proceedings against the highly respected Brazilian theologian Leonardo Boff and others.

In his bestseller *In God's Name*, published in 1984, David A. Yallop described the tangled machinations of the Vatican in detail. He was unable, however, to prove any link to the sudden and mysterious death of Pope John Paul I, a pope who was not exactly well disposed towards the IOR and who died after only 33 days in office; neither was he able to clarify the role of the seven-times Italian Prime Minister Giulio Andreotti with close ties to the Vatican and the Italian Catholic hierarchy, who repeatedly managed to evade the Italian judiciary in spite of a number of accusations of Mafia dealings. The Vatican, usually so quick to mete out moral judgements, did not utter a single critical remark about either the Andreotti affair or the later Berlusconi affair.

A new situation arose in 2009, when more than 4,000 original documents were published – accounting records, letters, minutes of supervisory board meetings, figures, accounts, balance sheets – from the secret archive of the conscientious Mgr Renato Dardozzi (1922–2003), who had worked in the Papal Secretariat of State for the IOR and was therefore privy to all the Vatican's financial secrets. During his lifetime he kept his oath of confidentiality, but in his last will, he wrote: 'These documents should be published so that everyone may discover what has happened here.' The documents were hidden for safety at a farm in Tessin, and after Dardozzi's death they were registered in Italy and photocopied. In 2009, on the behest of the executors of his will, the most important of these documents were published with commentary by the journalist Gianluigi Nuzzi under the title *Vaticano S.p.A.*, ('Vatican Ltd'), with the subtitle 'From a secret archive – the truth about the church's financial and political scandals'. Since then, we have known in detail about the cover-up strategies, the streams of bribes, and the secret accounts belonging to senior Italian politicians, especially Andreotti, and other prominent individuals. Within just a few months, the book, which came out in May 2009, had sold 250,000 copies in Italy.

The Dardozzi papers document not only the shady financial activities of the Vatican Bank in the Marcinkus era, which included bunkering and laundering funds from illegal Mafia operations, expediting bribes to corrupt Christian-Democratic politicians and aiding tax-dodging businessmen. They also show how such activities went on behind the back of Marcinkus's successor after 1990, Mgr Angelo Caloia, whose uphill efforts to clean up the bank's shady activities were repeatedly thwarted by covert activities on the part of his subordinates, by false friends and by Vatican intrigue, with the result that he ultimately resigned in 2009 (see the articles by Sandro Magister in *L'Espresso*, 18 June 2004 and 27 January 2011). In that same year, behind Caloia's back and that of his successor, it would seem, a financial pipeline to Germany had been created that continued to transfer millions of euros out of Italy every day via IOR accounts with J.P. Morgan branches in Milan and Frankfurt. By the time the scheme exploded in 2011, over a billion euros are estimated to have flowed to Frankfurt in this way (*Spiegel online*, 2 July 2012). Not surprisingly, in the eyes of the international finance world, the Vatican Bank was compared to the obscure offshore organizations that serve as tax havens and money-launderers in the Caribbean and elsewhere.

Drastic changes in the Vatican resulted. As well as Angelo Caloia's replacement by the layman Ettore Gotti Tedeschi, the post of prelate in the IOR – a position that had been at the heart of the unscrupulous financial operations – was abolished, and the incumbent (the former Private Secretary to the Cardinal Secretary of State Sodano) was appointed nuncio and sent to Africa. In his social encyclical *Caritas in veritate*, Benedict XVI even ventured to condemn in a general way socially damaging financial activities.

These events were to have political and legal ramifications. On 29 November 2009, in the hope of improving the reputation of the IOR, its new head, Gotti Tedeschi, signed an agreement on behalf of the Vatican with the European Community, committing it to adhere to current EU regulations on the prevention of money-laundering:

> The Vatican City State shall undertake to adopt all appropriate measures, either by direct implementation or equivalent actions, to enforce the EU regulations to prevent money-laundering and to prevent fraud and counterfeiting of cash and non-cash forms of payment. Furthermore, it commits itself to implement all of the European Community's regulations for the banking and financial sectors, if and when a banking sector shall be created in the Vatican City State. (Nuzzi, p. 26 ff.)

The agreement came into force on 1 January 2010. In October 2010, however, a report began circulating through the media that left the Vatican 'perplexed and astonished': Roman prosecutors were once again investigating the Vatican Bank for alleged money laundering. Investigating an IOR middleman, the Italian authorities had discovered that 23 million euros of undeclared funds were supposed to be moved from the Vatican into the account of an Italian bank and from there some 20 million were to be passed on to the J.P. Morgan Bank in Frankfurt, the rest going to another Italian bank. Before the deal could be completed, the funds were seized by the Roman state's attorney's office. Legal proceedings were initiated against the new President of the IOR, Gotti Tedeschi, and against the General Director Paolo Cipriani, who were called in for questioning. The previously so often abused Vatican immunity ('We are a sovereign state!') no longer applied. Gotti Tedeschi was forced to step down from his office following a vote of no confidence. However, in July 2013, Italian prosecutors dropped charges against him, but two of his subordinates, PC and MT, continue to be under investigation and were forced to step down after a new scandal involving a senior Vatican accountant, MNS, and an alleged attempt to transfer millions of euros from Stitz to Italy.

Dogged by legal proceedings in Italy and with the threat of EU sanctions hanging over the Church, Pope Benedict and senior staff in the Curia decided to make a new effort to reform the Vatican finances. This was exactly 30 years since Cardinal Joseph Ratzinger had entered the inner circle of curial power, and he had already been pope for more than five years – more than enough time to have taken action earlier. But now, suddenly, there was a great rush. On 30 December 2010, the pope created a financial five-man supervisory body, the Financial Information Authority, under Cardinal Attilio Nicora, long-time administrator of the papal assets. At the same time he enacted new, stringent laws for all organs of the Curia (including the Congregation for the Evangelization of Peoples, which with its extensive real estate holdings had also been the subject of legal proceedings). The aim of these papal actions was the 'prevention of and fight against illegal activities in the financial and monetary sectors'. With these measures, the Vatican also secured the release of the impounded euros. Soon thereafter, however, Cardinal Bertone, the Vatican Secretary of State, weakened the force of the papal transparency decree by placing the supervision of the Vatican Bank under his own control. Cardinal Nicora, designated head of the new financial control authority, protested in a letter: 'we are taking a step backward and will remain a tax-haven' (*Spiegel online*, 2 July 2012). On 2 July 2012, the pope named Ernst von Freyberg to be the new head of the bank after a vacancy of almost a year. In the same year, an independent audit by Europe's anti-money laundering agency found that the Vatican Bank had made significant progress in achieving greater transparency, but that much still needed to be done (*ABC News online*, 15 February 2013).

What is at stake is not the 'design faults' of the Vatican Bank and the curial offices dealing with finances; the issue is rather the fundamental lack of transparency within the Roman system overall. The whole affair of the Vatican Bank demonstrates how incapable the popes (to whom Vatican I had ascribed full and supreme jurisdiction over all churches and all individual Christians) have proven themselves to be in maintaining order within their own immediate surroundings and their own financial institutions.

The Vatican largely survives on the financial contributions of the faithful and on taxes and charges to the dioceses, and the Vatican Bank administers billions of euros of savings from religious orders, church institutions and dioceses all over the world, with the profits accruing to the pope. In view of its completely opaque financial conduct, the Catholic Church's headquarters needs to fulfil the same demands that Mikhail Gorbachev in 1985 formulated as a reform programme for the Kremlin:

- *Glasnost* (Russian: 'openness'): the Vatican should endeavour to be transparent in its financial dealings, and inform the public openly and honestly.

- *Perestroika* (Russian: 'restructuring'): the Vatican should commit itself to a restructuring of the Vatican's finances and a 'reconfiguration or reorientation' of its financial policies. Is that asking too much?

These, in effect, were the demands also made by the European Union in the agreement concluded with the Vatican on 29 November 2009, which came into force in 2010.

The members of the Catholic Church could well demand something similar from the Church headquarters in Rome. Until recently, the Vatican's elaborate and costly system of taxes and fees has largely been kept secret. Everything – from honorary titles through marriage proceedings to canonization processes – has its price in the Vatican. The Vatican does not publish a detailed budget, only an annual consolidated financial statement, which contains few details. The statement for 2011 (reported on the Vatican Information Service's website *NEWS.VA* on 5 July 2012) does not give the total revenues for 2011, but only indicates that the year closed with a deficit of *c.* 14.9 million euros, a sharp contrast to the 12.6 million euro surplus of the previous year. The Vatican spokesman attributed this deficit principally to losses on the Vatican's financial investments. Of the specific revenues listed, canonical taxes imposed on ecclesiastical circumscriptions and religious institutes amounted to over 32 million US dollars; the Vatican Bank contributed 49 million euros. Contrary to popular opinion, the 'Peter's Pence' – a worldwide special collection taken up annually on the Sunday closest to the feast of St Peter and Paul – is intended for the pope's charitable projects and thus is not officially part of the Vatican budget; it brought in 69.7 million US dollars. Also outside the Vatican budget in the narrow sense is the budget of the Governorate of the Vatican State, which registered a large surplus thanks to record income from the Vatican museums amounting to 91.3 million euros.

Conspicuously absent from the public report is the revenues from fees and direct gifts to the Vatican, and especially income from the Vatican's financial investments, which according to Father Lombardi, the Vatican spokesman, was down from previous years. But such statistics are hardly satisfying, and the public, Catholics in particular, want to know the exact sums paid annually to the Roman Curia in the form of taxes, fees and 'free' contributions, in particular by the Catholic Churches of Germany and the USA – both of them main sponsors of the Vatican, although, in practice, they are often little appreciated or respected by the Curia. Clarity and transparency regarding the monies given by the faithful are therefore urgently needed. 'What I say to you in the dark,' I am tempted to quote, 'tell in the light; and what you hear whispered, proclaim from the housetops' (Matthew 10:27).

The use of Church taxes in German bishoprics is much more transparent, especially in dioceses such as Rottenburg-Stuttgart, where the pastoral council, consisting of clerical and lay representatives, is involved in decisions regarding the budget. In the cantons of Switzerland the church taxation system is even more democratic and more in line with the church structure of the New Testament. The taxes, amounting to several hundred million francs each year, are collected and allotted locally and do not automatically flow into the central coffers of the bishops as they do in Germany. According to the Swiss system, the local parish decides on the amount of taxes due, and a certain percentage is then passed on to the diocese.

Recently a problem has arisen in Germany with respect to a growing number of people who leave the church by making a formal declaration at the civil registry office, intending to leave the church as a statutory body under public law – for instance, because they are unwilling to pay the church tax – but continuing to consider themselves to be members of the Catholic community of faith; these individuals are often willing to make voluntary financial contributions. Instead of automatically excommunicating these people, the German Bishops' Conference has now been instructed by Rome to check carefully in each case whether that person has turned away from the Catholic faith, or simply intends to leave the Church as a statutory body under public law. In the latter case, they can still take advantage of church services even though they are not paying church taxes. To achieve clarity in the matter, the emeritus Freiburg canon law professor, Hartmut Zapp, declared in 2007 before the civil registry office his intention to leave the Catholic Church of Germany as a statutory body, while remaining a member of the Catholic Church as a religious community. The Freiburg Archdiocese then sued the civil registry office to declare Zapp's act of conditioned exit to be invalid. The case went through a series of hearings, eventually landing before the supreme Federal Administration Court in Leipzig, which ruled on 26 September 2012 in favour of the Church's argument that one cannot leave a religious community as a statutory body while remaining a member of the community of faith (see the critical report in *Spiegel online*, 27 September 2012.) Anticipating such a decision, the German bishops' conference, with Roman approval, had already ruled several days before that any Catholic who leaves the Church as a statutory body, whatever his or her reasons, is guilty of a 'grave transgression against the ecclesial community' and 'in the eyes of the Church is no longer a Catholic', although he is no longer formally excommunicated as was previously the case. For this reason, such a person shall be 'invited' by letter to a 'discussion' with his local pastor about his motives and the consequences of his action. Among these consequences is exclusion from reception of the sacraments and from exercising any ecclesial offices or functions – in short, a back-door excommunication, despite a Vatican declaration in 2006 that a merely formal act of leaving the Church before a civil authority does not automatically mean a lapse from faith that must be punished with excommunication (*Spiegel online*, 20 September 2012).

Abolish the Inquisition, Don't Just Reform It

Among the most terrible pages of the Church's history are those filled with the sinister term 'inquisition', a term the Catholic Church itself created to name its tribunals for the systematic legal persecution of heretics and other miscreants ('*inquisitio haereticae pravitatis*'). It was a creation of the Middle Ages, officially established in 1184, and reflected the barbarous legal standards of the time. Thus it enjoyed not only the support of the secular authorities but also that of the general populace, who relished the spectacular executions by burning at the stake. Not surprisingly, the term 'inquisition' has come to be seen as a characteristic element of Roman Catholicism, although inquisitorial procedures and executions of dissenters were likewise practised by secular authorities and some Reformation churches well into the modern age.

The history of the Inquisition is a chequered one. It began with the establishment, by papal order, of diocesan tribunals to seek out heretics and to punish them with ecclesiastical sanctions like excommunication. Innocent III issued regulations for the 'inquisitorial process' used to determine a person's guilt; in some respects this was an improvement on previous legal practice, both ecclesiastical and secular, and was soon adopted by worldly courts as well. Accusations alone no longer sufficed; material proofs and rational argument were admitted; and special weight was placed on obtaining a confession from the miscreant. But joining the roles of accuser and judge in the same person and insisting on a confession by the accused opened the door to horrendous abuse. In 1224, Emperor Frederick declared it the duty of the State to root out heresy and established punishment by burning at the stake or at least cutting out the tongue for those found guilty by the ecclesiastical courts. Convinced that the measures against heretics were not effective enough, Pope Gregory IX, a nephew of Innocent III, withdrew the matter from the episcopal tribunals and appointed travelling papal inquisitors, principally from the mendicant orders, to seek out persons guilty of heresy, witchcraft and other crimes and after establishing their guilt to hand them over to the secular authorities for punishment. Secret denunciations were encouraged. Even social contact with a suspected heretic sufficed as grounds for persecution. Not appearing before a tribunal was taken as a sign of guilt, but anyone who appeared was immediately incarcerated until his innocence was proven. To prevent the spread of heresy, lay people were forbidden to discuss their beliefs either privately or publicly. In 1252, Pope Innocent IV authorized the inquisitors to use torture to elicit confessions. Although bloodshed, mutilation and death were officially prohibited, the unimaginable torments suffered by the often innocent victims could sometimes lead indirectly to death or permanent injury. Once a person was convicted and sentenced, they were handed over to the secular authorities who executed the sentence. Since conviction also entailed loss of property, the Inquisition proved a lucrative revenue source for the civil community, the local ecclesiastical authority and not least the inquisitor himself.

The Church's use of torture is often excused on the grounds that until the eighteenth century both judicial torture to gain testimony – often in even more hideous forms than those officially allowed by the Church – and torture as a form of punishment were commonly practised throughout Europe, by the state as well as by Protestant state churches. In fact, it was not until the Enlightenment that these barbarous practices gradually went out of use and were officially abolished in one country after the other over the course of the late eighteenth and early nineteenth centuries. It was officially abolished by the pope in his territories in 1816. Nevertheless, Catholic theologians were hardly in the forefront of its critics, and, until recently, they have spent more effort in defending or at least excusing its use than in showing that it violates basic Christian and human values.

Scholars distinguish between the loosely organized Medieval Inquisition and the centrally organized modern Inquisition. The first modern Inquisition was the Spanish Inquisition, established in 1478 and operating independently of the papal Inquisition in all territories under Spanish control, including the Netherlands, until it was abolished in 1834. A similar Portuguese Inquisition was established in 1536 and continued until 1821. In 1542, the 'modern' Roman Inquisition was established as a curial institution with dependent tribunals throughout Italy and in a few other places in Europe. Unlike the Medieval papal institution, it was not only a tribunal but also a bureaucratic organization responsible for censorship. This institution continues to exist to this day, although under different names, namely from 1904 until 1965 the abbreviated form '*Sanctum Officium*' ('Holy Office') and since 1965 the innocuous title 'Congregation for the Doctrine of the Faith'. Although it no longer uses physical torture, it now practises more subtle forms of psychological torture, and its proceedings continue to be secret, which was one of the reasons why the Vatican was not permitted to join the 1950 European Convention on Human Rights, which demands compliance with certain minimal human rights.

Although in 1997, under Cardinal Ratzinger, the congregation published for the first time – a concession wrung from it as a result of the infallibility dispute – its *Regulations for Doctrinal Examinations*, the proceedings continue to be conducted in secrecy. Moreover, provision is made for an extraordinary procedure bypassing the normal rules in urgent cases. In an ordinary trial, the accused does not know either who the informants were or which experts were appointed to examine his writings or to defend him. The prosecutor and the judge are essentially one and the same person. Only after the accused has been condemned is he given an opportunity to answer in writing the charges brought against him; if he desires, he can also meet with representatives of the tribunal. In preparing his written defence and in presenting his case at such a meeting, he can be seconded by an expert of his choice. No cross-examination of witnesses or experts, however, is allowed, and he is not given access to the records of the proceedings to judge their fairness. No provision is made for appeal to an independent court, since the decision of the Congregation has already been approved by the pope. If the accused is convicted of heresy, apostasy or schism, he is automatically sentenced to excommunication.

Because the congregation operates on the assumption that it is in full possession of the truth and alone authorized to decide what is truth, the aim of such proceedings is not the discovery of truth in a process of dialogue, but simply unconditional submission to Roman views, in short: 'obedience' in accordance with the phrase, still in use today: *'humiliter se subiecit'*, 'he has humbly submitted'. This kind of obedience needs to be learned early on. Thus, according to Canon 245 §2, seminarians 'are so to be formed that, imbued with love of the Church of Christ, they are bound by humble and filial charity to the Roman Pontiff, the successor of Peter ...'. This corresponds to the concluding paragraph of the oath of allegiance required of every bishop before taking office:

> Moreover, adhere with religious submission of will and intellect to the teachings which either the Roman Pontiff or the college of bishops enunciate when they exercise the authentic Magisterium even if they proclaim those teachings by an act that is not definitive.

The power of the head of the Congregation for the Doctrine of the Faith is still formidable, and is especially feared by bishops and theologians. The whole of the curial machine is at his disposal. It is easy for him to contact directly every one of the papal nuncios all over the world to induce them to intervene at bishops' conferences, with governments, or even to take action against individuals. In addition, he can direct each one of around 5,000 bishops all over the world to initiate proceedings against one of the theologians, priests or members of a religious order working within his territory. All this happens noiselessly and completely unobserved by the public, often expressly '*sub secreto pontificio*', i.e. the highest level of papal secrecy. This was how the numerous cases of clergy sexual abuse were kept under wraps for so long.

Even in its modernized form, the Inquisition makes a mockery of the Gospel, just as it makes a mockery of the modern sense of justice expressed in the various declarations on human rights. It is not enough merely to reform the Inquisition as Paul VI attempted to do; it must be abolished, purely and simply. What is needed is a 'Congregation of Love', responsible not for supervising the loyalty of local churches and individual theologians but instead for monitoring the actions of the Roman Curia to ensure that they conform to the spirit of Christian love.

Eliminate All Forms of Repression in the Church

Abolishing the Inquisition is not enough: it is only one of many forms of Roman repression and oppression. 'Repression' refers to all forms of subjugation of human beings to a system and its representatives which restrict their legitimate freedom to think and act. Obviously, every religious community has the need and the right to lay down standards for its members. But Catholics rightly complain about the restrictions and obstructions imposed on them by the application of spiritual, and often political, legal and financial pressure by representatives of the Church. Instead of freedom in the spirit of the Gospel, they experience being treated like naughty children in need of discipline. Church representatives, on the other hand, are keen to play down the repressive element. They acclaim the atmosphere of brotherhood and loving concern that allegedly prevails in the Church; they insist that theological research and teaching are free as long as they remain loyal; and they vehemently deny that ecumenism has been thwarted or stalled. However, they chose to ignore both the frequent alliances between conservative curial offices and bishops, and reactionary political, cultural and social forces and movements.

Of course, I do not want to paint everything black, but on the other hand there are no grounds for painting a particularly rosy picture. Not only 'critical' theologians, but also numerous ordinary Catholics have no sympathy with:

- the methods still used by the official Church to discriminate against and discredit those church members or groups who hold views on doctrine, morality, discipline and politics differing from those of the pope or prominent cardinals and bishops in Rome and elsewhere;

- the defamation of socially committed Christians – bishops, ministers, theologians and lay people – in Africa and particularly in Latin America, where attempts are made to silence them by discrediting them as Marxists and Communists;

- the defamation of women, including nuns (e.g. the recent Roman 'visitation' in the USA), who campaign against the discrimination against women in the Church and against the ban on women's ordination;

- the defamation of moral theologians all over the world who stand up for the moral maturity of modern-day Christians, and who take more sympathetic and differentiated positions on burning ethical questions.

How many loyal Catholic men and women have suffered under the repressive measures of this Roman Catholic Church in recent times? Some cases are well known; many more remain unknown. When I think only of the many such cases that have been reported to me personally, both in writing and orally, by people who have suffered during the 45 years of the Wojtyla–Ratzinger regime, I would need hundreds of pages to document the warnings, threats, subpoenas and disciplinary measures taken: arbitrary transfers, dismissals, impositions of silence, withdrawal of teaching and preaching licences and suspensions from priestly office.

The *National Catholic Reporter* (the reputable mouthpiece of critical Catholics in the USA) published a special report, 'Theology Censure', on 28 September 2007. It included a long list of 'targets', not to say 'victims', during '28 years of papal discipline' going back to the last days of Paul VI. The list, it claimed, was 'not exhaustive' but 'substantially representative'; it included such famous names as the French Dominican moral theologian Jacques Pohier, the Belgian Dominican professor of dogmatics Edward Schillebeeckx, the German Jesuit professor of dogmatics Karl Rahner, the American moral theologian Charles Curran and, significantly, only one conservative theologian, the schismatic traditionalist Archbishop Marcel Lefebvre.

Also on the NCR list were:

- people known for their social engagement, such as the American Archbishop of Seattle Raymond Hunthausen, the French Bishop of Evreux, Jacques Gaillot, and the liberation theologians Ernesto Cardenal (Nicaragua), Leonardo Boff (Brazil) and Jon Sobrino (El Salvador);

- advocates of an 'inculturated' theology such as Tissa Balasuriya (Sri Lanka), Jacques Dupuis SJ (Gregorian University, Rome) and Anthony de Mello SJ (India); and

- people engaged in the ministry to homosexuals such as the American priest Robert Nugent and the American Sister Jeannine Gramick, as well as the Catholic layman Dr John McNeill, who studied homosexuality.

American nuns such as Mary Agnes Mansour, Elisabeth Morancy and Arlene Violet (Sisters of Mercy) were forced to choose between their important social and political positions and their vows as religious, with the result that they left their communities. The American nuns Barbara Ferraro and Patricia Hussey (Sisters of Notre Dame de Namur) and the Brazilian Ivone Gebara were penalized for criticizing Rome's position on abortion. The American Dominican priest Matthew Fox was expelled from the order for his teachings on original sin, sexuality and 'pantheism', and an American Jesuit, Roger Haight, was forbidden, on account of his defiant Christology, to write and teach on theology, even at non-Catholic universities; because he complied, he was not forced out of his order. And so the list goes on.

I can only repeat: if the Catholic Church wants to survive, and not to shrink even further, it must cease suppressing its most creative spirits and returning to an anti-modern, siege attitude. It must once again welcome the spirit of that freedom to which Christ has liberated us. This is what John XXIII had in mind when he spoke of opening the windows of the Church: fresh air and sunshine are excellent remedies against osteoporosis.

Canon Law Needs to Be Completely Remodelled, Not Just Improved

Canon law is the next item on the therapy agenda. It developed in the eleventh century and quickly became identified with papal law, so that ecclesiastical jurisprudence became the most important ideological structure supporting the Roman System. Only with its help was the Medieval and Counter-Reformation papacy able to enforce its claims (see Chapter 3). But even in its modern garb, this basically Medieval and Counter-Reformation paradigm of church law is in conflict with the outlines of the New Testament constitution of the Church, despite the attempt of Vatican I (1870) to give it sacral legitimacy and despite the attempts after Vatican II (1962–5) to restore its authority with authoritarian/inquisitorial methods and the new/old *Codex Iuris Canonici* (*Code of Canon Law*) (1983). This paradigm of the Church and of canon law likewise stands in complete contradiction to the ideals of modern democracy and to those of the people of God, even when it is supported by a populist personality cult and uncollegial, undemocratic personnel politics aimed at maintaining and extending Roman power.

We should remember that Pope John XXIII, unhappy with the *Codex Iuris Canonici* of 1917, had already proposed a reform of the canon law in 1959, at the same time as he announced his intention of calling a council. This did not please the Curia, and when the reform commission was constituted in 1963, even before the end of the Council the Curia took control. The Council had expected fundamental reforms, but the new *Codex* with its 1,782 canons that Pope John Paul II solemnly promulgated in January 1983, after 16 years of work, did not achieve what the Council was aiming for, but rather what the Curia wanted, despite the numerous citations of conciliar documents. Of course, this new *Codex* did bring some improvements in terms of form and content, but behind the structure and the terminology, which adopted certain terms and ideas of the Council, little of the substance reflected the spirit of the Council: for the most part it took over unchanged the canons of the earlier code. The title of an article written by the respected German canonist Knut Walf aptly sums up the result: 'The New Canon Law – The Same Old System. Preconciliar Spirit in Postconciliar Formulation' (see the anthology *The Church in Anguish – Has the Vatican Betrayed Vatican II?*, 1987, edited by Leonard J. Swindler and myself).

Although the new codes *de facto* incorporate certain key terms used by the Council, e.g. the Church as a '*communio*' and church office as a '*munus*', i.e. as a service, not a '*potestas*' or power, and also includes a number of concrete conciliar decisions, it often betrays the underlying intentions and spirit of the Council.

Changes that Betray the Spirit of the Council

- The new *Codex* emphasizes the primacy of the pope even more strongly than its predecessor: in addition to all of his other titles, the pope is now officially given the new title 'Vicar of Christ' (Canon 331).

- By contrast, the ecumenical council is downgraded. No longer is it treated in a chapter of its own, and in Canon 337 §1 it is no longer clearly assigned 'supreme power' over the universal Church, on the basis of a decree of the

Council of Constance that was still cited in Canon 228 of the 1917 *Codex*.

- At the same time, the collegiality of the bishops and the authority of the Synod of Bishops is made to depend on the pope as 'head' of the college of bishops, so that without his authorization the college of bishops is incapable of acting (Canon 336).

- The authority of bishops' conferences to make decisions is likewise limited: decisions on issues with further-reaching consequences must be approved by the Holy See. Before each meeting, the papal envoys (nuncios) must be given a copy of the agenda, and afterwards the minutes of the meeting, so that they can closely monitor all proceedings. The Holy See can also request that the nuncio be invited not just to the first session, but to all subsequent meetings. This is a clear example of institutionalized Roman mistrust.

- Additional changes of traditional legislation cut back the power of the bishop in his diocese in favour of papal authority.

- The pope is empowered to create 'personal prelatures' for organizations like Opus Dei. These are quasi-dioceses with their own bishop or superior and both clerical and lay members. They answer directly to the pope and are authorized to operate independently of the jurisdiction of the local bishop, though they must seek his permission to establish a foundation in his diocese and should inform him of their activities. That this can lead to tensions, if not divisions, is obvious.

- The pope is empowered to appoint at will a coadjutor bishop, i.e. a second bishop with equal governing rights alongside the incumbent, who then automatically enjoys the right of succession. In this way, the pope can push aside an incumbent bishop without officially dethroning him and can circumvent the rights of the cathedral chapter to elect his successor.

Measures like this, together with the right of the pope to name bishops, where this right is not limited by a concordat, and the subtle measure by which the Curia is able to control the bishops, reduce the conciliar idea of episcopal collegiality to empty words.

Omissions That Betray the Spirit of the Council

- Lay people, their rights and responsibilities are frequently mentioned, but there is no legislation governing lay people permanently employed by the Church; they are not granted even the merest shadow of a power of 'jurisdiction. No reference is made to important ecclesiastical offices like pastoral assistants (men or women). On the contrary, in an official instruction of the Pontifical Council for the Interpretation of Legislative Texts dated 15 August 1997, they are explicitly denied authority to direct, coordinate, moderate or govern a parish (Art. 4 §1 b), to preside over a parish council (Art. 5 §3), to participate in the diocesan presbyteral council (Art 5 §1), or to exercise more than a consultative vote in the diocesan or parochial pastoral councils and financial councils in which they are allowed to participate (Art. 5 §2).

- No provisions for the laicization of clerics were included in the *Codex*, although the revision commission had already developed simpler and quicker procedures that Pope Paul VI liberally made use of in granting dispensations to priests desiring to leave. But this displeased his Polish successor – not least because of the many requests for dispensations from Poland – and on 14 October 1980 he notified the bishops and heads of religious orders, through a secret letter of the Congregation for the Doctrine of the Faith, that a laicization procedure would not automatically result in a dispensation from the obligation of celibacy; on the contrary, such dispensations would in the future be granted only under extraordinary circumstances. The effect of this decree was only to exacerbate the problem of celibacy and to encourage the cover-up of violations of the celibacy obligation.

- The same John Paul II was personally responsible for the rejection of the detailed provisions for the creation of a system of ecclesiastical administrative courts, which had been included in the 1980 draft of the new *Codex*. The 1983 *Codex* (Can. 1732–9) allows only a humble appeal to the author of a decision deemed unfair to reconsider his decision or, if this fails, to make a similar appeal to the author's superior. Thus administrative acts are effectively exempted from control; the often arbitrary actions of the Curia or individual bishops cannot be reviewed or punished by independent courts.

I can only agree with Knut Walf's verdict, expressed in his article cited above: 'Because of its retrogressive adaptation, it [the new *Codex*] can offer no help and direction for the course of the Church in its near or farther future.' If this book of law was already antiquated when it came into force, then a real and fundamental reform of canon law is still to be carried out. A real reform of canon law, then, must take the following points into account:

- The reform must be based on a fundamental examination of the nature and function of law in the Church.

- The norm for concrete reforms should not be continuity with particular historical legal traditions, in particular those of the Curia, but rather the standards of the Gospel and the sense of justice and the legal standards of our own day and age.

- Legislation that found its way into Latin canon law on the basis of Medieval forgeries, e.g. the rules governing the convocation, presidency and papal approval of ecumenical councils, and those governing the election of bishops, must be examined individually, and only retained when they are proven necessary from a pastoral point of view.

- '*Salus animarum suprema lex*' ('The salvation of souls must always be the supreme law of the Church') is an old maxim still to be found in the new *Codex*, albeit buried in the very last canon (Can. 1752) dealing with the transfer of pastors. Among the 442 canons here at the end of the *Codex* devoted to criminal trials and punishment are 13 particularly unedifying canons dealing with the procedures required for dismissing or transferring priests. Significantly, however, not a single canon makes provision for dispensation from the obligation of celibacy.

Allow Priests and Bishops to Marry

The celibacy issue is the next item on the agenda of urgent therapy. It is true that Jesus and Paul lived exemplary celibate lives dedicated to serving people, but they never denied individuals the full freedom of choice in this matter; Peter and the other apostles were married while they served the Church. According to the Gospel, celibacy must be a freely chosen vocation or charism and cannot be mandatory. There is only one place where Jesus talks of celibacy, and there he clearly means voluntary celibacy: 'Not everyone can accept this teaching, but only those to whom it is given ... Let anyone accept this who can.' He does not say that one must make himself a eunuch 'for the sake of the kingdom of heaven' (Matthew 19:11–12). It is also testified that Jesus visited the house of Peter and healed his sick mother-in-law (Matthew 8:14). Paul expressly contradicted those who believed that 'it is well for a man not to touch a woman', stating that 'because of cases of sexual immorality, each man should have his own wife and each woman her own husband' (1 Corinthians 7:1–2). And in the first epistle to Timothy he wrote: '... a bishop must be above reproach, married only once ...' (1 Timothy 3:2). He explicitly does not say a bishop should be unmarried!

This was accepted for many centuries for bishops and priests and, at least for priests, continues to be the rule in the Orthodox churches and even in most of the Eastern churches united with

Rome, despite vigorous Roman efforts in the past to suppress or restrict it, usually at the behest of local Latin bishops. The obligation of celibacy contravenes the Gospel and the ancient Catholic tradition. It is also in contravention of the *Declaration of Human Rights*, according to which every human being has the right to marry.

Of course, many priests live a celibate life without great problems, and many might well find that the heavy burdens of their work would leave them too little time for a partner or family. On the other hand, in practice, compulsory celibacy often leads to intolerable situations: many priests long desperately for love and security and take refuge in secret relationships that in many cases become more or less open secrets. And if children result from such a relationship, they too must be kept secret, with devastating lifelong consequences for all those involved. Celibacy often makes priests embittered or otherworldly and edgy or neurotic in their dealings with women, who, in the worst case, are viewed only as carnal objects or as sexual temptations. This is one of the reasons why many ordained men who have been forced into or taken refuge from their own anxieties in a celibate way of life are so reluctant to welcome the ordination of women and to accept working with them on an equal, collegial footing in the Church's governing and decision-making bodies. This is yet another reason why compulsory celibacy should be replaced by freely chosen celibacy for those called to that life, and why the Church should accept the married life as having its proper place in holy orders and perhaps even in monastic communities, where, as in certain contemporary Protestant religious communities, married members are accepted with the consent of their spouses. According to a recent poll, 87 per cent of Germans hold the view that the ban on marriage is no longer appropriate for priests today (*ARD Deutschlandtrend*, 19 March 2010). A similar poll in Italy showed that 65.9 per cent favoured a change (*UPI.com*, 17 May 2010). A recent Irish poll found that two-thirds of Irish Catholics believe priests should be allowed to marry, and thousands of British Catholics presented a statement asking for married priests and discussion of women priests to the Bishops' Conference of England and Wales.

A correlation between the sexual abuse of young people by the clergy and the obligation of celibacy has always been strenuously denied, but one cannot ignore the connections: the compulsorily celibate and single-sex Church was able to deny women all Church offices, but it was not able to deny human beings their sexuality and so it had to accept the risk of paedophilia, as the Catholic religious sociologist Franz-Xaver Kaufmann argues. Numerous psychotherapists and psychoanalysts have confirmed that although the rule of celibacy forces priests to abstain from all sexual activity, their urges remain as strong as ever, and there is the constant danger that these will be repressed and relegated to a taboo world where they will be compensated for by other actions outside of marriage. The celibate lifestyle, and particularly the kind of socialization that leads to this lifestyle (frequently all-male boarding school, followed by seminary) takes place in a world of celibate men and can easily foster paedophile tendencies. Various studies have shown that inhibited psychosexual development is far more frequent in celibate people than in the average population. Such deficiencies in psychological development and deviant sexual tendencies, however, often do not manifest themselves until after ordination. The Catholic Church systematically draws a veil over any undesirable sexual developments or behaviour. What we need is a new, positive attitude, not only towards sexuality, but especially towards women.

Open Up All Church Offices to Women

For a long time now, women have refused to accept the way the Church treats them, from the ban on women and girls acting as altar servers (this ban has now been lifted) to the ordination of women and the rules on artificial birth control. These days, women are no longer willing to be treated as merely subject to commands, prohibitions, rules and roles imposed on them by men. Just as in the family and in society in general, now in the Church more and more women are demanding the equal opportunities and rights due to them. Many, particularly young women, have reluctantly turned their backs on the Church, have left religious communities, or have forged their own individual theological and spiritual paths. Those who stay increasingly reject the constraints and work for a different Church. The most important criteria for church office should no longer be male gender and opportunistic, conformist affirmation of the *status quo*. We need to take account of the different skills, callings and charisms that can contribute to the development of a community based on a real partnership of men and women in the Church.

A reintroduction of the diaconate for women would be a welcome first step. But this measure is not enough in itself. Unless women are granted permission to enter the presbyterate (priesthood) at the same time as they are granted permission to become deacons, there will be still be no real equal opportunity, and the ordination of women will only be delayed. The practice in many Catholic parishes of allowing women to assist at liturgical functions (as altar servers or readers, distributors of the Eucharist, preachers, etc.) can be an important step towards the full integration of women in the running of the Church, but these steps are not a reason for ceasing to demand the full ordination of women.

Despite the papal 'infallible' declaration mentioned earlier, there are no serious theological reasons why women should not be admitted to the priesthood. The exclusively male composition of the quorum of Jesus' twelve apostles has to be understood in the context of the socio-cultural situation existing at that time. None of the traditional reasons for the exclusion of women – e.g. a woman having brought sin to the world; the woman being created in second place after the man; the woman not being created in the image of God like the man; the woman not being a full member of the Church and the menstruation taboo – can be ascribed to Jesus; they testify only to a deep-seated theological denigration of women. In his epistles, the Apostle Paul explicitly refers to women as *synergoi*, literally, 'co-workers' (Philippians 4:3). He mentions several women respectfully by name, above all Junias, whom he describes as 'prominent among the apostles' (Romans 16:7).

In view of the leading roles of women in the early Church on the one hand, and, on the other hand, the presence, now taken for granted, of highly capable women in business, science, culture, government and society, the admission of women to the priesthood should no longer be postponed. Jesus and the early Church were ahead of their time in holding women in high esteem; by contrast, the Catholic Church today lags far behind the times, and behind other Christian churches where female pastors and bishops have fulfilled their roles very successfully. The ecclesial services of these women are shown the same respect as those offered by men in the same positions, and the roles of these women are completely different from the subservient positions and functions of the increasingly numerous women of the *movimenti* who now work in the Roman Curia.

That active opposition and even disobedience can sometimes lead to positive results is shown by the case of female altar servers. Some years ago Rome attempted to ban them. But this provoked great outrage among both the people and the clergy, and most parishes simply retained their female altar servers. At first, the practice was silently tolerated by Rome, but eventually it was officially permitted. In August 2010, at a conference of altar servers in Rome, the female altar servers outnumbered the male altar servers by 60 per cent to 40 per cent. And, on 7 August 2010, an article in the *Osservatore Romano* expressly praised this development as an important breakthrough, because now women could no longer be seen as 'impure', and a 'profound inequality' could thus be eliminated. How long do we have to wait until Rome accepts that the same arguments also apply to the ordination of women? A great deal depends on the recruitment and deployment of bishops.

Include Clergy and Lay People in the Election of Bishops Again

In early Christian times, bishops were elected by both the clergy and the people. Thus, both Ambrose of Milan and Augustine of Hippo, perhaps the all-time greatest bishops of the Western Church, were elected directly by the people. '*Nos eligimus eum*' ('We elect him') was the phrase used by people in Latin parishes to acclaim their bishop. Neighbouring bishops – but not the bishop of Rome – played an important role in the elections: according to a ruling of the First Council of Nicaea, the right of confirmation and ordination belonged not to the bishop of Rome but to the metropolitan of the respective Church province.

In the Middle Ages, the right to appoint bishops frequently passed to the princes, and then in the eleventh century, in connection with the Gregorian reforms, to the cathedral chapters. But soon the popes began to undermine the rights of the chapters by issuing so-called 'reservations', allowing the pope himself to directly appoint a bishop, initially only in individual cases, then for whole dioceses, and finally, from the fourteenth century onwards, universally.

Thus, the electoral rights of the cathedral chapters were gradually suppressed entirely or reduced – with a few notable exceptions, such as the Swiss dioceses of Basel, Chur and St Gall and the Czech-Moravian diocese of Olomouc – to minimal rights to propose candidates or to elect one person from a list of candidates dictated by Rome. Similarly, the remaining rights of the State to influence the choice of a bishop by presenting or approving candidates prior to nomination or subsequently confirming, or at least not vetoing, the nomination have been systematically eliminated with few remaining exceptions. In effect, the participation of the local church in episcopal election was eliminated and the way was clear for the universal appointment of bishops by the pope alone – more exactly by the Curia, since it is the Curia that processes the appointments and presents the candidates to the pope. This papal right was formalized in the 1917 *Codex*, decreed unilaterally by Rome without any participation of the episcopate or the Church at large.

We need to return to the venerable tradition of bishops being elected by a representative organ of the diocese, e.g. by the diocesan pastoral council or at least by the presbyteral council supplemented by lay people. The election could then be confirmed by the pope (on this tradition, see G. Hartmann, *Wählt die Bischöfe: Ein Vorschlag zur Güte* (*'Elect the Bishops: A Conciliatory Proposal'* [2010]).

No More Restrictions on Joint Celebrations of the Eucharist by Catholic and Protestant Christians

After so many consensus documents have been produced by official and unofficial ecumenical commissions, the time has come for the Catholic Church, which after all bears the chief responsibility for the Reformation schism, to recognize the validity of Protestant ministers and of the Protestant Eucharist. In practice, this is already done covertly in many parishes.

As long ago as 1971, at the Ecumenical Pentecost Assembly in Augsburg, where thousands spontaneously celebrated the Eucharist together, a formal request, backed by a huge majority, was made to allow ecumenical groups and interdenominational couples to celebrate the Eucharist together, and to allow any Christian who wished to receive Holy Communion to receive it in any Christian church.

Forty years later, we are still no further on! Why do people still react – often on both sides of the confessional divide – in such a narrow-minded, distrustful and fearful way? Why are they so anxious about orthodoxy? Why, in spite of the many fine words, was there no ecumenical follow-up after the

Wurzburg Synod (1971–5) or indeed after the various papal visits when similar demands were raised?

Out of fear of spontaneous ecumenical Eucharistic sharing, the German hierarchy postponed any further ecumenical conventions until 2003. For the Berlin convention of that year, the hierarchy again explicitly forbade giving communion to Protestants at Catholic liturgies and blackmailed the Protestant authorities into renouncing their standard practice of inviting Christians of all denominations to communion.

As early as 1982, a consensus statement was approved in Lima, Peru, with the title *Baptism, Eucharist, Ministry*. It had been compiled by the Faith and Order Plenary Commission of the World Council of Churches, together with official representatives of the Catholic Church. This document makes clear that the theological differences that led to the Church schism in the sixteenth century are no longer insurmountable. Already the Second Vatican Council had resolved two of the most acrimonious issues of that time: the use of the vernacular and chalice communion for the laity. And who today, apart from a handful of die-hard controversialists, still takes seriously the ancient controversies about the Mass as a propitiatory sacrifice or the use of the term 'transubstantiation' to describe the manner in which Christ becomes present in the gifts of bread and wine? Even the issue of treating respectfully the remnants of bread and wine after the Eucharistic celebration is hardly sufficient grounds to deny the validity of the Protestant celebration as such.

As to the trickier question of who can celebrate the Eucharist, fewer and fewer Catholics insist that it can only be celebrated by individuals ordained by bishops in unquestioned apostolic succession, and no Protestants claim that anybody can celebrate it at his or her own pleasure without ecclesial recognition in some form. On the other hand, it is clear from the New Testament that in addition to the calling of ministers by other ministers, there also existed the possibility of receiving a calling from those who had not been set apart in this way: the Acts of the Apostles speaks of the laying on of hands by prophets and teachers as well as by apostles. And finally there existed the possibility of spontaneously receiving a charismatic calling to exercise leadership in the community (1 Corinthians 12:28; 16:15) and even to preside over the community worship services (Romans 12:8). In the post-apostolic Church, it was the first of these routes to the ministry that, for understandable reasons, came to prevail, with the result that one came to speak of 'apostolic succession' by the laying on of hands.

In 1973, a joint study group of the ecumenical institutes of the German universities produced a detailed memorandum entitled *Reform und Anerkennung kirchlicher Ämter* ('Reform and Recognition of Church Offices', Mainz, 1973) which called on the Catholic Church to recognize, in principle, the existence of alternative paths to ministry. This would mean no more objections to recognizing Protestant ministers or to sharing in the celebration of the Eucharist. Groups or parishes that are already practising this without official permission have the New Testament behind them. A similar study reaching the same conclusions appeared in 2003, this time drawn up in cooperation between the ecumenical institutes of Tübingen, Strasbourg and Bensheim, under the programmatic title *Abendmahlsgemeinschaft ist möglich: Thesen zur eucharistischen Gastfreundschaft* ('*Eucharistic Communion Is Possible: Theses on Eucharistic Hospitality*', Frankfurt/M. 2003).

Truthful Ecumenical Understanding and Collaboration, with No Excuses and No Secrets

The Church is expected to speak the truth: 'Let your word be "Yes, Yes" or "No, No"; anything more than this comes from the evil one' (Matthew 5:37). The *pro forma* 'Yes' to ecumenism must not be distorted into a virtual 'No'. More and more people refuse to tolerate the indolent, constantly repeated excuses made by Catholic churchmen (women, significantly, have little or no say in the matter) in Rome and in the various countries around the world to explain lack of progress in this area. But there is equally no excuse for the Protestants, who chime in with such excuses in the interest of maintaining Protestant identity. Typical excuses are that:

- the time is not yet ripe for ecumenical understanding, for the lifting of excommunications, for the establishment of communion, for hospitable or joint celebration of the Eucharist – as if all the discussions and consensus papers of the last decades are meaningless;

- many more commissions and synods are needed to prepare for such a step – as if all of the agreements achieved in the last decades are meaningless;

- we need to pray more before such a step – as if the prayers of the faithful over the last decades have no influence on the actions of the Church;

- we need to suffer more patiently with the Church and its divisions – as if the suffering that the Church schism has brought, and still brings, to humanity as a whole, to

Christian people and their parishes, and to married couples and their families do not cry out to heaven.

The spirit that speaks through such excuses is not the oft-invoked Holy Spirit, but an all-too-human spirit that divides, defers and delays. For the Holy Spirit liberates the Church from its self-righteousness, purges it of its hypocrisy, melts the stubbornness of its theologians and hierarchs, and dispels fear with a love that transcends all boundaries and builds bridges of trust.

Of course, speaking the truth does not mean neglecting to examine and discriminate. Regarding prophetic utterances, Paul wrote to the community in Thessaloniki, 'test everything; hold fast to what is good' (1 Thessalonians 5:21). These words apply in our day to the pronouncements of the modern prophets, in particular to the scientists and other experts. They too should be heard in the Church, but not uncritically accepted, and they should be thoroughly examined to make sure they are true and good for humankind and faithful to the Gospel.

This applies, for instance, to the hotly debated issues of medical ethics, for example pre-implantation genetic diagnosis (PGD), in which embryos created in a test-tube outside the mother's body are screened for genetic diseases and disposed of when judged unfit. Clearly, this method can be abused, but the ethical axiom: '*Abusus non tollit usum*' – 'wrong use does not preclude proper use' also applies here. The blanket ban on PGD imposed by church leaders rests on questionable arguments.

Of the hundreds of thousands of Catholics who leave the Church every year, not a few take this step because they are unable to follow the Church's rigorous teaching on contraception, artificial insemination and PGD. They are fed up with hearing only accusations, delivered in arrogant and moralizing tones by the same celibate churchmen who often have few scruples about committing or at least covering up sexual abuse. High-sounding charges of 'meddling with God's work of creation', of an 'opening of the floodgates' to moral depravity, of setting oneself up as 'lord over other human beings' are mere empty rhetoric.

The rigid position currently taken by Rome that a human person comes into existence at the moment of biological conception, i.e. when an ovum unites with a sperm cell prior to implantation, passes itself off as unanimous Catholic tradition held from all antiquity. In reality the matter is much more complicated. In previous ages there was no universal agreement about when an individual, spiritual human being comes into existence. Thomas Aquinas, for instance, following the biology of his day, thought that animation was a gradual process ('*animatio successiva*') in which, corresponding to the state of embryonic development, first a vegetative soul ('*anima*' or life) came into being, then a sensitive or animal soul, and only later, when the embryo had sufficiently developed, an '*anima intellectualis*' or rational soul. Without the *anima intellectualis*, i.e. rational soul, there can be no human person: '*persona non invenitur nisi in rationali natura*' – 'a person is only found in a rational nature' (*Summa Theologiae III*, q.6, a.4 ad 3, cf. I q.29 1 co, following a definition of Boethius).

This remained traditional Catholic teaching until well into the nineteenth century. But, it might be argued, in view of the state of scientific knowledge prevalent at the time, is this not far too schematic a view of the creation of human life? Undoubtedly this is the case, yet it corresponds far better to the biological facts than the contention that a human person is created at the moment of fusion between the egg cell and the sperm, and that by using PGD, an abortion or even the morning-after pill a human being is killed, or even (maliciously) murdered. To use a perhaps banal example, if someone steals an acorn (in other words, an oak '*in potentia*') from my garden, it doesn't mean they have chopped down an oak tree.

A closer look at Roman Catholic practice reveals the inconsistencies of the present teaching and confirms the classical position. Spontaneous miscarriages or stillbirths, unlike infants, were never given a church burial. The logical conclusion of treating every fertilized egg cell as a human person would be to give church burial to every miscarriage, however early, indeed to every menstrual flow and every artificially inseminated ovum. Even if that were possible, it would hardly make sense.

Finally, we must ask the question; since when has Catholic theology focused so much on the beginnings of human life? A historical study of this question is long overdue. However, there can be little doubt that the definition of the dogma of the 'immaculate conception' under Pius IX in 1854 had much to do with it.

A feast of the conception of Mary (not yet the 'immaculate' conception) arose in the British Isles between the eighth and the eleventh centuries and gradually spread to the continent in the twelfth century. It was only in the twelfth century that the idea originated that the flesh of Mary needed no purification because it had been sanctified already 'before' her conception. Even St Bernard ridiculed such a notion, as did most of the other theologians of the thirteenth century, including Thomas Aquinas, who argued that she could hardly be said to be redeemed if she had not in some way previously been 'tainted' by original sin. It was the great Franciscan theologian Duns Scotus (*c.* 1266–1308), commonly known as 'Doctor Subtilis', who hit upon the idea that Mary could have been protected from original sin by an advance redemption that took effect at the moment of her conception, and this was the version of the doctrine that gradually gained ascendancy, despite the prolonged opposition of the Thomists. Thus there is nothing in the Bible or the Catholic tradition of the first millennium about a '*conceptio immaculata*' as defined in the strange dogma of 1854 supposing a manifold miracle, namely that Mary, from the moment of her virginal conception, i.e. without a union of the ovum with a male sperm cell, was preserved from any taint of original sin and nevertheless redeemed by Christ. How this could be possible is a mystery not only for modern embryology but also for modern evolutionary theory.

With many other medical ethicians, I see a need to make careful distinctions on this issue: human life indeed begins with conception, and therefore a special reverence for this life is called for, and neither fertilized eggs nor later stages of embryonic and foetal development should be treated carelessly; according to a decision by the German Federal Constitutional Court, it should be accorded human dignity. But this initial stage of life does not necessarily constitute a *human person*, and this is where the ethical criteria relating to abortion and stem-cell research must be applied very carefully. With many medical experts, philosophers and other theologians, I believe that personhood demands a certain degree of brain formation; the first appearance of a rudimentary nervous system hardly suffices. Having said this, I would like to advise discretion and restraint, to avoid reverting to the old battle lines – the Church against science – which serve the interests neither of scientists nor of Church members. It would be helpful if the Church's teaching, when dealing with controversial questions that are hotly debated among Catholics, would seek constructive solutions and ecumenical understanding, instead of polarizing and aggravating the situation. Unfortunately this has hardly been the case up to now.

Compulsory Therapy?

When I asked an acquaintance of mine, a doctor in Switzerland, to read a preliminary version of this book, his most important criticism was that a final chapter was needed on the question of possible compulsory therapy for the ailing Church. A committed Catholic and a staunch democrat, he asked me to 'formulate in precise detail what indispensable therapeutic measures can and should be imposed as compulsory emergency treatment on the persistently obstinate patient, the Roman System'. 'Without such enforced measures,' he observed, 'Rome will simply ignore this book, like all the others, and carry on business as usual. You yourself have already had an appalling experience with the open letter to the bishops which triggered no response whatsoever. The same could well happen with this magnificent book.'

Some Catholics might be shocked by the term 'compulsory treatment', others will undoubtedly agree with the complaint. But what are we to understand by compulsory treatment in the context of the *Church*?

Compulsory treatment means that in certain medical circumstances, precisely defined by law, treatment can be imposed on a patient – not, of course, in the case of someone in full control of his or her mental faculties and able to recognize the gravity of the situation, who then makes a deliberate decision to refuse treatment for a life-threatening organic disease. Such a patient has the right to refuse treatment, and no one can force him or her to accept treatment, even if the refusal may lead to accelerated death.

A different situation prevails when the sick person (particularly one with a psychiatric condition) is unable to recognize the existence or gravity of his or her condition and is thus threatened by physical or mental neglect and deterioration. When the patient's comprehension of the situation is impaired, it is justifiable to undertake emergency measures to save his or her life, and to protect others, even if this means the patient's being deprived of his or her liberty by enforced hospitalization. Compulsory treatment is also permissible when parents (for instance Jehovah's Witnesses) refuse a blood transfusion for their dangerously ill child on the grounds of their religious convictions. Treatment can then be carried out against the will of the parents to save the child.

What does this mean for the analogy of the Church as a patient without insight into the gravity of her condition? Of course, no one claims that the members of the hierarchy who are currently refusing dialogue and who are putting obstacles in the way of reform are all pathological cases, although some of them, like the infallibility pope Pius IX, may well have been psychopaths. But, rather, the system in which they have become trapped by their religious socialization and their 'curialization' is psychopathic. Those who have become routine-bound in this way are no longer capable of perceiving how badly the Church is suffering under the system they represent. The Church, however, does not belong to the hierarchy as if they were the sole owners of a corporation; it belongs to Christ, who has entrusted its leadership to them. The Bible uses the term 'hardness of heart' (Mark 3:5 and 10:5; Ephesians 4:18) to describe this condition. Thus, they must be forced to accept treatment in order to save themselves and the Church. But how?

Modern history shows that two models of compulsory treatment have been used to bring about radical changes in absolutist monarchies:

- Violent revolution was the path taken by the French and Russian Revolutions. But a bloody coup is out of the question in a Church based on the non-violent Jesus, to say nothing of the fact that, in violent revolution, one form of tyranny is often replaced by another, because no real change of mentality takes place.

- Political evolution was the path taken in England and other European countries, despite occasional violent upheavals, by which absolute monarchy was gradually transformed into constitutional monarchy. Parliamentary institutions empowered the people, over the course of centuries, to overcome feudal and absolutist forms of sovereignty in favour of a government responsible to a parliament composed of representatives of the people freely elected by all mature citizens. In the Roman Catholic Church, however, there is as yet no globally elected body representing even the clergy, much less the people, that could serve as the equivalent of a parliament.

What then? Should the individual believer, priest or bishop simply be left to his own devices in this absolutist Church? Are we doomed to a losing battle? No! Even within this system the individual has a variety of different options for offering resistance, and more and more people are becoming aware of them and their possible therapeutic effects on the Church:

- The individual can leave the Church: hundreds of thousands have been doing so over the last few years, not just because of unwillingness to pay church taxes, but because of the many scandals and injustices within the Church, including the general stagnation of reforms and, particularly, the recent sexual abuse scandals.

- The individual can refuse to contribute to the Church financially or to pay statutory church taxes, even if doing so means having to leave the Church formally as an institution of public law. (See above.) Parishes can refuse to pass on to the bishop the proceeds of collections, although this can be done with impunity only in Switzerland, where the parish itself decides the level and apportionment of church taxes. Withholding money has always been an important method of pressuring for reform.

- The individual can convert to another church: many Catholic priests who wanted to get married have taken up posts in the Orthodox, Old Catholic, Anglican, Lutheran and Methodist churches which have liturgical traditions resembling Catholic practice. Many lay people simply join these and other Protestant churches as a consequence of their frustrations and disappointments as Catholics.

- The individual can simply refuse to join the Church or to participate in its life, if he or she was baptized into it as a child. The church rolls are full of 'paper Catholics' who have never set foot in a Catholic church, at least not since their childhood.

Or:

- The individual can become actively involved in reforming his or her own parish, and in supporting the pastor in efforts to reform the parish. He or she can join movements – local, diocesan, national, international – working for reform not only of the pastoral practice and structures of the Church but also for reform in theology. Without theological reform, practical reforms will only cure symptoms. This is the option that I have chosen for myself.

What then are the methods that can be used by those who are committed to administering compulsory treatment to a Church caught in this authoritarian–absolutist system? Four decades ago, I began reflecting on how one could use therapy – as I would call it now – 'against resignation in the Church'. In 1972, 33 prominent theologians from all over the world signed a declaration under that name. Among them were Alfons Auer (Tübingen), Gregory Baum (Toronto), Franz Böckle (Bonn), Norbert Greinacher (Tübingen), Herbert Haag (Tübingen), Otto Karrer (Lucerne), Walter Kasper (Tübingen), Ferdinand Klostermann (Vienna), Richard McBrien (Boston), Johann Baptist Metz (Munster), Stephan Pfürtner (Fribourg) and Edward Schillebeeckx (Nijmegen). Acting together in this way, individuals are anything but impotent: on the contrary, they can and should exercise power, i.e. pressure, not domination, in matters both great and small.

Thus five therapeutic actions suggest themselves:

1. Use the power of speech; do not remain silent out of opportunism, despondency or shallowness. Every single Catholic, whether in an official position or not, whether man or woman, has the right, and often the duty, to say what he or she thinks about the Church and its leadership, to take actions deemed necessary, and to put forward suggestions for improvement.

2. Use the power of action; take individual action. The more people in the Church who not only complain and grumble about Rome and the bishops but also begin to take action themselves, the more they help the church community overcome the oppressive Roman Catholic system. Many improvements in local churches and in the Church as a whole have been set in motion through the initiative of individuals. And more than ever in modern society, individuals have the possibility of influencing church life in a positive way, for instance via the media and the internet. Individuals can press in various ways for better church services, for better sermons, for more contemporary pastoral care, for structural changes, for ecumenical cooperation, and for Christian social involvement.

3. Use the power of the community; take joint action. Individuals should not just act on their own; wherever possible they should act with the support of others: their friends, the parish council, the priests' council, lay Catholic associations, independent coalitions, organized reform

movements, priests' associations and solidarity groups. Collaboration between various groups should not be hampered by sectarian isolationism; instead it should be intensified for the sake of the shared goal. In particular, it is important that groups of reform-minded priests maintain contact with the many married priests without a ministry with a view to bringing them back into the full pastoral service of the Church.

4. Use the power of opposition to push through interim solutions. Discussions alone bring little; often you must show by actions how serious you are about your demands. You can do this with good conscience. Putting pressure on the hierarchy in the spirit of Christian brotherhood can be legitimate where the office-holders do not live up to their mandate. Use of the vernacular throughout the liturgy, the changes relating to mixed marriages, the affirmations of tolerance, democracy and human rights, and so much else in the history of the Church have only been achieved by constant, faithful pressure from below.

In practice, this means that wherever a measure undertaken by the hierarchy is manifestly not in keeping with the Gospel, opposition is permissible, and can even be advisable. Take, for example, the previously mentioned successful civil disobedience by German parishes against the Roman ban on female altar servers. Another example is the private Donum-Vitae initiative, set up to provide counselling to women facing the choice of abortion after the German Catholic Bishops, under pressure from Rome, withdrew from the public counselling service. Still another example is the fact that, in a number of dioceses, lay people (both men and women) are allowed to preach, despite explicit prohibition by Rome. In Räschenz, in my own home diocese of Basel, the local parish took its case to the civil court to retain a pastor unlawfully dismissed by the bishop.

Whenever a call for action put to the church leadership is simply shelved or unreasonably delayed, there are various clever yet moderate ways of creating provisional or alternative solutions while safeguarding Church unity. This was done, for example, by the Bishop of Basel, Otto Wüst, when he, on his own authority and without permission from Rome, granted the young theologian Kurt Koch, now a curial cardinal, the needed ecclesiastical teaching licence to assume the professorship to which he had been legitimately appointed. Actions of this type are now being discussed and carried out by the We are Church movement that began in the German-speaking countries and has now spread worldwide. And as to the unbiblical and inhumane law of celibacy, any priest who after deep reflection wants to marry should no longer secretly resign from office; instead, he should inform his parish in good time. If the parish wants him to stay, it should use all legitimate means to ensure that the priest involved is not forced to leave his parish.

5. Rely on the power of hope: don't give up. In all attempts to save or renew the Church, the greatest temptation, often used as a convenient excuse, is to say that nothing will avail, that we will never make any progress, and that the best thing to do is simply leave. Where there is no hope, there will never be any action. Particularly during the recent phase of stagnation and restoration, it has been vital

to keep up hope, to persevere calmly, and be tenacious. There are signs of hope on the horizon. The abuse scandal has shaken up even many bishops; and more and more questions are being asked about the exercise of power, about rigid dogmatism, and about repressive attitudes to sexuality.

In his 2011 New Year's address, Gebhard Fürst, the Bishop of Rottenburg-Stuttgart, gave expression to such hopes when he clearly stated, 'We need a process of purification and renewal in the Catholic Church in Germany.' Yet many in the audience asked themselves how seriously he meant this, when in the same breath he insisted on such renewal being carried out in the context of the 'universal Church', which in practice means 'Rome', and when he felt obliged once again to stress the 'precious value' of compulsory celibacy instead of calling for its abolition. Exactly 40 years before, the Wurzburg Synod of the West German dioceses, which convened in January 1971, had put the celibacy question on its agenda, and despite a decision of the German Bishops' Conference in April 1972 declaring that the synod could make no decisions in the matter it included in its closing documents a strong recommendation that 'the issue of a celibate priesthood be reconsidered from the principal point of view of concern for salvation' (*Beschluss: Dienste und Ämter*, 5.4.6). Participating in this synod were 58 bishops, 88 priests, 30 members of religious orders and 141 lay people with equal voting rights. But because of Roman intransigence and the lethargy of the bishops, nothing came of any of the resolutions of that synod. Commenting on this sad state of affairs 40 years later, Wolfgang Seibel SJ wrote in *Stimmen der Zeit*: 'It is most regrettable that this kind of joint decision-making did not serve as a model ... Today's church leadership has drawn a veil over this venerable piece of church tradition.'

It is true that we must reckon with a longer timeframe to see the implementation of some areas of needed reform: but that also applies to civil society as well. Several years ago, when I was giving a lecture in the USA, an elderly gentleman handed me an encouraging note. On it he listed four groups of people who, until only a few decades ago, had been for the most part prevented from playing any significant role in the larger American society dominated by the WASPs (White Anglo-Saxon Protestants); these groups were Jews, blacks, Catholics and women. Although their full equality has yet to be achieved, no one can deny that their position in American society has changed fundamentally for the better. In the Catholic Church we need to work energetically and resolutely to promote similar long-term transformation.

A Prospect for Convalescence

With this sixth chapter proposing concrete therapeutic measures, I hope that I have fulfilled what I promised at the beginning of this book. Just as I wrote my book *The Council, Reform and Reunion* (1960) in response to the dramatic situation of the Catholic Church before the Second Vatican Council, now 50 years later, I have written *Ist die Kirche noch zu retten?* (2011), which here in 2013, in this 'Year of Faith', appears in a revised and expanded English version with an eye on the dramatic situation currently confronting the Church. On the basis of a careful, historical and systematic diagnosis presented in Chapters 1 to 5, I have now in Chapter 6 attempted to put forward a detailed, comprehensive rescue plan for the gravely ill Church.

Thus, I am hoping for a convalescence (from the Latin: *convalescere* – *com* [intensive form of *cum*] + *valescere* ['to grow strong']), a reinvigoration, a cure, a recovery of our moribund Church. I have recommended therapies, surgery and medication that will lead to convalescence. Some things I have described in harsh, though never intentionally derogatory, terms. I have tried to be explicit without being denunciatory. As a 'therapist', I have spoken so bluntly only because I love the Church and am deeply concerned about its welfare. So I hope that those in authority in the Church (locally and globally) will take this diagnosis seriously and courageously begin the process of implementing the necessary rescue measures.

What then should be done in the immediate short term?

- In the parishes, everyone, especially the members of parish councils, should openly discuss the questions that concern them, without fear or constraint, and, after adequate discussion, they should dare to make decisions and take concrete action.

- Reform movements such as We are Church, Initiative: Church from Below (IKvu), Catholics for a Changing Church and Call to Action should take up this comprehensive agenda for reform that confirms their own proposals, providing historical and theological justification and putting them into a wider context. They are in a position to disseminate these ideas internationally.

- Nationwide lay Catholic organizations such as the Central Committee of German Catholics and the various national associations of Catholic priests and religious men and women should courageously and insistently demand that concrete steps of rehabilitation and renewal be taken by their national episcopal conferences.

- Prominent Catholic lay people should use their authority and influence, as individuals or as groups, publicly to demand concrete reforms from the bishops and from Rome. In January 2011, eight prominent German Catholic political leaders set an example for the world by joining in a bipartisan appeal to the bishops finally to take the matter into their own hands and to relax the celibacy obligation. They were: Norbert Lammert (President of the Bundestag); Annette Schavan (Federal Minister of Education); Bernhard Vogel, Erwin Teufel and Dieter Althaus (former minister presidents of German federal states); and Friedrich Kronenberg (long-term Secretary General of the ZdK [Central Committee of German Catholics]).

- The bishops should begin listening to their consciences instead of to Rome and should summon up the courage to present realistic, well-informed and well-reasoned statements of their personal opinions on reform within their own dioceses and within the Church in general.

- The bishops' conferences of leading countries such as France, Germany, Great Britain and the USA should cease waiting for Rome and begin to take concrete actions on their own and to exert their influence, not only on other bishops' conferences, but also on Rome itself, in order to lead the ailing Church out of its current crisis and to embark on a course of renewal and reform in the spirit of the Second Vatican Council.

- The new pope needs to recognize the fundamental problems posed by the Roman System and to understand and appreciate the unrest and frustration caused by the course of stagnation and restoration taken by his predecessors. Only when he does this can he take the lead in the process of healing the Church. Soon after taking office, he convoked a commission of eight cardinals from around the world to advise him on reform, but it remains to be seen whether this commission will be free of curial tutelage and will produce a programme of radical reform to replace the current programme of retrenchment and restoration.

- A new ecumenical council will eventually be needed to realize such a reform programme with sufficiently broad support and adequate depth. Thus, we can hope that Pope Francis or one of his successors will follow the example of Pope John XXIII by convoking such a council. To achieve its goal, however, it must not be a rubber-stamp assembly like the current episcopal synods, convened for a few days in Rome to give their approval to statements prepared in advance by the Roman Curia. The new ecumenical council must be free of curial domination and manipulation. It will need time for adequate preparation by representative regional commissions of theologians and lay people. It will need to be large enough and broad enough to be truly representative of the whole Catholic Church, but small enough to be manageable and workable – the worldwide episcopate is now too large to meet in a single workable assembly. That means that such a council will have to be composed of freely elected, not papal-appointed, representatives of the national bishops' conferences, as well as elected representatives of the lower clergy, the religious orders and the laity. Like the Second Vatican Council, it will need the critical support of qualified experts (*periti*) and observers representative of the other Christian denominations, of the other world religions and of the secular world at large.

Will Pope Francis or his successors find the inspiration and courage to rise to this challenge?

CONCLUSION:
THE VISION REMAINS

In this book, I have once again – this time at a very advanced stage of life – set forth in summary fashion my vision of a Church which could fulfil the hope of millions of Christians and non-Christians alike. It is a vision based on my experience over decades of careful study, and my experience of struggling and of suffering for it. It is a vision of how the Church could not only be saved and survive but also flourish once again.

Three characteristics mark this vision of the Church:

1. *Christian radicalness:* the basis for all these proposals for church reform is neither pandering to the current 'zeitgeist', nor mere sociological and pragmatic considerations; all are based on the original Christian message itself. This, indeed, is where all demands for church reform must have their roots. At the same time, they need to be supported by a historical understanding of the great Catholic tradition in order to distinguish between particular time-bound expressions and the abiding kernel of the Christian message. Only then can proposals for

reform be effectively formulated to meet the needs and hopes of people of today.

2. *Constancy:* without timid faltering or wavering, without considering whether a proposal is politically opportune or not, without making concessions to prevailing court theologies, I have attempted here to present a concept which incorporates the basic ideas of the Second Vatican Council; it is a concept which has been systematically thought through for many decades and which has been repeatedly tested with a view to practical implementation.

While I cannot and will not hide my growing impatience over the prevailing efforts to block and roll back the programme of the Council, all of these demands for reform stem neither from reckless enthusiasm nor from a hypercritical extremism: I have attempted to formulate them realistically and constructively with a view to what is already possible within the Church.

3. *Coherence:* the reforms called for here are not isolated and separate; they form part of a consistent, overall concept that gives them their coherence. Until basic issues are addressed, detailed issues like clerical celibacy, women's ordination or lay participation in decision-making have little hope of realization. Such concrete demands are not arbitrary details but part of a coherent ecclesiological blueprint which, focused on the Gospel, lays the foundations for a concrete path to change the increasingly stifling paradigm which has ruled the Catholic Church for over a millennium. Such a paradigm change was inaugurated by Vatican II, pursuing a path away from the Middle Ages, away from the Counter-Reformation and

away from anti-Modernism in the direction of a Post-Modernity that avoids the mistakes of its predecessors.

Long ago, I summarized my vision of how the Church could be saved in four contrastingly formulated propositions that apply not only to the Roman Catholic Church but also to all of the churches where similar problems prevail. Over the past decades, the overall view expressed in these theses has been repeatedly confirmed, and I see no reason to depart from it now:

1. A Church which continually looks back to the Middle Ages or to the time of the Reformation and is uncritically enamoured of the Enlightenment and classical Modernity can hardly be saved; but a Church oriented towards its Christian origins, while concentrating on the urgent tasks of our time, can indeed survive and flourish again.

2. A Church paternalistically committed to a stereotypical idea of women, to the use of exclusively masculine language, and to pre-defined gender roles can hardly be saved; but a Church based on partnership, combining office and charism and accepting the participation of women in all ecclesial offices, can indeed survive and flourish again.

3. A Church addicted to an ideologically narrow, denominationalist exclusivity and to an illegitimate exercise of usurped authority, refusing to recognize the need for cooperation and communion, can hardly be saved; but an ecumenically open Church, which not only mouths ecumenical phrases, but also practises ecumenical

deeds in matters such as recognizing ministries and removing the questionable excommunications of the past, and which goes on to give tangible expression to its ecumenical commitment by celebrating together the Lord's Eucharist, can indeed survive and flourish.

4. A Eurocentric Church, that maintains claims to imperial domination of other cultural expressions of Christianity by subjecting them to the oversight of a Vatican bureaucracy as the ultimate spiritual authority, can hardly be saved; but a tolerant universal Church:

- which is willing to respect the ever-increasing diversity of possibilities for expressing the one abiding truth;

- which is willing to learn from other religions and from people with no religion;

- which is willing to share its authority with national, regional and local churches following the principle of subsidiarity that allows the higher instance to intervene only when the lower fails;

- and in this way regains the respect of people – of Christians and non-Christians alike –

such a Church can indeed survive and flourish!

At the beginning of this book, I spoke about Pope Innocent III, who was pope at the time of St Francis of Assisi and was the most powerful pope of the Middle Ages. Aged only 37 when he was elected, he was a born ruler – a theologian educated in Paris, a shrewd lawyer, a clever speaker, a capable administrator and a sophisticated diplomat. The revolution from the top initiated by Gregory VII in the eleventh century, known as the Gregorian Reform, was completed by Innocent. Since his pontificate, the pope (unlike in the first millennium, and never in the apostolic churches of the East) has acted as the absolute ruler, law-giver and judge of Christianity.

Francis of Assisi, in contrast, represented the alternative to the Roman System. And even today his basic Christian concerns remain questions for the Catholic Church in general and in particular for a pope who has called himself Francis, explicitly linking this to the man from Assisi:

> The man of the poor. The man of peace. The man who loved and cared for creation – and in this moment we don't have such a great relationship with the creator. The man who gives us this spirit of peace, the poor man who wanted a poor Church. (Vatican press conference, 16 March 2013)

What does it mean for a pope today if he bravely takes the name of Francis? Of course, the character of Francis of Assisi must not be idealized – he could be single-minded and eccentric, and he had his weaknesses too. He is not the absolute standard. But it is above all his three early basic Christian concerns of *paupertas* ('poverty'), *umilitas* ('humility') and *simplicitas* ('simplicity') which must be taken seriously, even if they need not be literally implemented but rather translated into modern times by pope and Church. This probably explains why no previous pope has dared to take the name Francis: the expectations seem to be too high.

- *Poverty*: a Church in the spirit of Innocent III means a Church of wealth, pomp and circumstance, acquisitiveness

335

and financial scandal. In contrast, a Church in the spirit of Francis means a Church of transparent financial policies and modest frugality; a Church which concerns itself above all with those who are poor, weak and marginalized; a Church which does not pile up wealth and capital but instead actively fights poverty and which offers its staff exemplary conditions of employment.

- *Humility:* a Church in the spirit of Pope Innocent means a Church of power and domination, bureaucracy and discrimination, repression and Inquisition. In contrast, a Church in the spirit of Francis means a Church of humanity, dialogue, brother- and sisterhood, and hospitality for those who do not conform to prevailing norms; it means the unpretentious service of its leaders and social solidarity, a community which does not exclude new religious forces and ideas from the Church but rather allows them to flourish.

- *Simplicity:* a Church in the spirit of Pope Innocent means a Church of dogmatic immovability, moralistic censure and legal hedging, a Church where everything is regulated by canon law, a Church of all-knowing scholasticism and of fear. In contrast, a Church in the spirit of Francis of Assisi means a Church of Good News and of joy, a theology based purely on the Gospel, a Church which listens to people instead of indoctrinating them from on high, a Church that does not only teach but constantly learns anew.

While no reasonable person will expect that all reforms can be effected by one man overnight, a shift would be possible within five years: this was shown by the Lorraine Pope Leo IX (1049–54) who prepared Gregory VII's reforms, and in the twentieth century by the Italian John XXIII (1958–63) who called the Second Vatican Council. But, today, the direction should be made clear again: not a restoration to pre-Council times as there was under Pope John Paul II and Benedict XVI, but instead considered, planned and well-communicated steps to reform along the lines of the Second Vatican Council.

But won't reform of the Church meet with serious opposition? Doubtless, Pope Francis will awaken powerful hostility, above all in the powerhouse of the Roman Curia – opposition which is difficult to withstand. Those in power in the Vatican are not likely to abandon the power that has been accumulated since the Middle Ages.

Francis of Assisi also experienced the force of such curial pressures. He, who wanted to free himself of everything by living in poverty, clung more and more closely to 'Holy Mother Church'. Rather than be in confrontation with the hierarchy, he wanted to be obedient to Pope and Curia, living in imitation of Jesus: in a life of poverty, in lay preaching. He and his followers even had themselves tonsured in order to enter the clerical state. In fact, this made preaching easier, but on the other hand it encouraged the clericalization of the young community which included more and more priests. So it is not surprising that the Franciscan community became increasingly integrated into the Roman System. Francis's last years were overshadowed by the tensions between the original ideals of Jesus' followers and the adaptation of his community to the existing type of monastic life.

Barely two decades after Francis's death, the rapidly spreading Franciscan movement in Italy seemed to be almost completely domesticated by the Roman Church so that it quickly became a normal order at the service of papal politics, and even a tool of the Inquisition. If, then, it was possible that Francis of Assisi and his followers were finally domesticated by the Roman System, then obviously it cannot be out of the question that Pope Francis could also be trapped in the Roman System which he is supposed to be reforming. Pope Francis: a paradox? Is it possible that a Pope and a Francis – obviously opposites – can ever be reconciled? Only by an evangelically minded reforming Pope.

To conclude, I have a final question: what is to be done if our expectations of reform are dashed? The time is past when pope and bishops could rely on the obedience of the faithful. A certain mysticism of obedience was introduced by the eleventh-century Gregorian Reform: obeying God means obeying the Church and that means obeying the Pope and *vice versa*. Since that time, it has been drummed into Catholics that the obedience of all Christians to the Pope is a cardinal virtue; commanding and enforcing obedience – by whatever means – has become the Roman style. But the Medieval equation of 'obedience to God = to the Church = to the Pope' patently contradicts the word of Peter and the other apostles before the High Council in Jerusalem: 'we must obey God rather than any human authority' (Acts 5:29).

Can we save the Catholic Church? As long as we continue to believe that this is truly the Church of Christ in which the Spirit of God continues to work despite all human failings and obstacles, there is no reason to doubt that we can and will save it and that the Church will not only survive its present mortal crisis, but that, sooner or later, we will once again become what Christ founded us to be.

EDITOR'S NOTE

Paradigm and Paradigm Shifts in the History of Christianity

The notion of historical paradigms of church life and the analysis of what happens when in the history of the Church a new paradigm arises to threaten the prevailing pattern of church life is one of Hans Küng's most important contributions to the study of church history and indeed to religious studies generally.

In his book *Christianity: Its Essence and History* (1995), Küng devoted more than 1,000 pages to describing and analysing the history of Christianity as a succession of six typical models or patterns of faith and church life, which, in the course of the centuries, came to divide Christianity and give rise to the rival churches and denominations that we know today. Listed in chronological order, he identified the following six models. (The initial 'P' here stands for 'Paradigm', a technical term to be explained below.)

- *P I*. The apocalyptic, primitive Christian model of the earliest days of the Church, as reflected in the New Testament and other documents of the first and early second centuries.

- *P II.* The Hellenistic model of the Church that took form especially in the East during the patristic period from the second to the sixth centuries; from this pattern, in growing isolation and alienation from the Western Church, today's Orthodox churches eventually emerged.

- *P III.* The Medieval Latin Catholic model, which had already begun to take form in the Western Church in the early centuries but only later, in increasing alienation from the Eastern Church and increasing concentration on the papal office, achieved its definitive character in the eleventh to fifteenth centuries; from this Medieval pattern the Roman Catholic Church emerged as we know it today.

- *P IV.* The Protestant Reformation model born in the sixteenth century; from this pattern the modern Lutheran, Reformed, Anglican and other evangelical churches emerged, especially in northern Europe and in North America. In southern Europe, by contrast, a distinctive Counter-Reformation model of Roman Catholicism emerged.

- *P V.* The Enlightenment model, which took shape over the course of the seventeenth to the nineteenth centuries and is marked by a progressive secularization of civil life, the replacement of autocratic and aristocratic regimes by liberal democracy and a generally optimistic view of the achievements of human reason and science. Within the churches, the Enlightenment gave rise to a split between liberal and conservative movements, with the result that anti-Modernist counter-models emerged, often allied with anti-democratic and anti-liberal social and political movements bent on defending or restoring former autocratic power structures and lost privileges.

- *P VI.* As the twentieth century moves into the twenty-first century, a new Postmodern, ecumenical model is beginning to emerge in response to contemporary challenges. This pattern holds out hope of overcoming the divisions and enmities of the past and of bringing forth forms of Christian life and church structure suited to the modern age.

To describe these typical models of Christian existence and cognitive as well as institutional organization, Küng took up and modified the sociological concepts of 'paradigm' and 'paradigm shift' that Thomas S. Kuhn, a historian of modern science, had proposed some years earlier in *The Structure of Scientific Revolutions* (1962). Kuhn used these notions to explain why the history of science is not a story of continuous progress, as commonly believed, but rather a tale of occasional more or less abrupt revolutions that put an end to relatively long stable periods marked by a prevailing scientific consensus. As long as such a consensus prevails, it allows for progressive development of ideas and practices within its conceptual framework, but it tends to resist any new discoveries or ideas that challenge that framework. To describe such a prevailing consensus, Kuhn used the term 'paradigm', defining it, as 'an entire constellation of beliefs, values, techniques, and so on shared by the members of a given community' (Kuhn, p. 175). Tracing the prehistory of the term 'paradigm' back to eighteenth-century usage, Stefan Toulmin, in his book *Human Understanding: The Collective Use and Evaluation of Concepts*

(1972) pointed out how Ludwig Wittgenstein, before Kuhn, had used the notion to explain how philosophical models or patterns of thought serve as 'moulds' or 'brackets' guiding one's thinking in pre-established and sometimes unsuitable paths. The critical point here is that a paradigm shapes the way people within it see the world and unconsciously blindfolds them to contrary evidence. Kuhn thus pointed out that, when new scientific discoveries or theories are proposed that cannot be fitted into the prevailing paradigm, and especially when they call the very foundations of that paradigm into question, the scientific community, as a rule, tends to resist them. Often it takes a generation or more before the new ideas catch on, since accepting them requires a radical mentality shift within the scientific community. As his prime example of such a scientific revolution, Kuhn pointed to the so-called 'Copernican Revolution', which initially was resisted not only by theologians and philosophers but even more so by contemporary natural scientists. It took almost a century before the heliocentric model of the universe proposed by Copernicus, popularized by Galileo and substantially modified by Kepler eventually replaced the older geocentric model inherited from the ancient Greeks.

Studying Kuhn's ideas and the discussion surrounding them, Küng quickly realized that analogous phenomena can be found in the history of the Christian Church: there too one finds relatively long periods of more or less continuous development within a prevailing model of faith and church life. Now and then, however, one sees more or less dramatic shifts in the way the faith and the church are perceived and practised. Such shifts can take place gradually, especially when one segment of the Church develops in cultural isolation from the other, as in the transition from the Hellenistic patristic model to the Medieval Latin model, or they can take place abruptly as at the time of the Reformation in the Western Church, when Luther and the other reformers radically called into question the theological foundations of the Medieval model. Typical of such shifts is the incomprehension with which the adherents of the former model react to the arguments presented by the advocates of change.

When church history is seen as a succession of paradigms, it quickly becomes clear that neither the traditional Roman Catholic notion of continuous positive development nor the prevailing Protestant or Enlightenment models of progressive de-evolution and decay do justice to the complexities of church history. When the Church is not reduced to a single denomination, e.g. the Roman Catholic Church, and then identified with the currently prevailing form taken by that denomination, church history, in the broader 'Catholic' sense, reveals a sequence of relatively long periods of progressive development within a generally prevailing consensus on essential issues that, despite obvious differences, is at least analogous to what Kuhn had described as a 'scientific paradigm'. Thus, a theological and ecclesial paradigm consists of a constellation of typical ways in which members of the Church think and act, both individually and collectively, and is marked by typical theological and institutional structures and by typical ways of relating to society as a whole, to the state, to the economy, to the arts, etc. In themselves, such paradigms tend to be relatively stable, often prevailing over centuries, even though in the course of time they may develop a variety of more specific manifestations within the overall prevailing pattern. To describe such developments within a prevailing 'macro-paradigm', Küng uses the terms 'meso-' and 'micro-paradigm'.

Now and then, however, epoch-making discoveries, newly emerging intellectual or socioeconomic structures or new patterns of behaviour can destabilize a prevailing paradigm by calling its foundations into question. This can happen slowly in the course of a prolonged evolutionary process, as was the case in the slow emergence of the Medieval Latin paradigm of Roman Catholicism, or it can occur suddenly and dramatically, as in the case of the Protestant Reformation. Such 'paradigm shifts' change the way people understand the Gospel message and the way they see the Church and its structures; they also change the way people relate to the world around them. Very often, such paradigm shifts also involve significant changes in the institutional structures of the Church itself.

In contrast to scientific revolutions or paradigm shifts, in a religion like Christianity the new paradigm often fails to gain universal acceptance; instead it is often embraced only by one segment of the Church, while the remainder continue to hold fast to the older paradigm, modifying it to produce a counter-paradigm. When this happens, the Church becomes divided; a schism takes place, with each side accusing the other of betraying the Gospel.

For the ecumenical effort to overcome these divisions, it is imperative to take into account the distinctive underlying paradigms that form the thinking of those within them. As long as one thinks only in terms of his own paradigm, dialogue with those who live within a different paradigm is extremely difficult if not impossible. On the other hand, when one takes account of the underlying paradigms it becomes easier to distinguish between what is essential and what is not and to recognize fundamental constants uniting the churches despite surface differences. Furthermore, since all of these paradigms are derived from and normed by the original New Testament pattern of church life and structure, focusing on the paradigms not only makes constructive dialogue possible, but also provides guidelines for the kind of constructive church reform that is the presupposition for bringing the churches together again.

BIBLIOGRAPHY AND FURTHER READING

Books by Hans Küng

Rechtfertigung. Die Lehre Karl Barths und eine katholische Besinnung, Johannes/Benziger 1957; Serie Piper 674, München 1986/*Justification. The Doctrine of Karl Barth and a Catholic Reflection*, (org. 1965), Westminster John Knox Press (40th Ann. Ed.) 2004.

Konzil und Wiedervereinigung. Erneuerung als Ruf in die Einheit, Herder 1960/*The Council, Reform and Reunion*. London: Sheed & Ward 1961.

Strukturen der Kirche, Herder 1962; Serie Piper 762, München 1987/*Structures of the Church*. New York: Thomas Nelson & Sons 1964; paperback edition with a new preface: New York: Crossroad, 1982.

Die Kirche, Herder 1967; Serie Piper 161, München 1977/*The Church*. London: Burns & Oates 1967; paperback, London: Search Press, 1971.

Unfehlbar? Eine Anfrage, Benziger 1970; Ullstein-Taschenbuch 34512, Frankfurt/M.-Berlin-Wien 1980; *Erweiterte Neuausgabe: Unfehlbar? Eine unerledigte Anfrage*, Serie Piper 1016, München 1989, mit einem aktuellen Vorwort von Herbert Haag/*Infallible?*

An Inquiry. London: Collins 1971; paperback, London: Fontana Library 1972; new expanded edition with a preface by Herbert Haag: *Infallible? An Unresolved Inquiry*. London: SCM 1994.

Fehlbar? Eine Bilanz, Benziger 1973/Not available as an English translation.

Christ sein, Piper 1974; Serie Piper 1736, München 1993/*On Being a Christian*. New York: Doubleday 1976, also London: Collins 1977; paperback: London: Continuum 2008; new edition, London: SCM 1991.

Theologie im Aufbruch. Eine ökumenische Grundlegung, Piper, München 1987/*Theology for a Third Millennium: An Ecumenical View*, London: Collins 1981.

Die Hoffnung bewahren. Schriften zur Reform der Kirche, Benziger 1990; Serie Piper 1467, München 1994/*Reforming the Church Today: Keeping Hope Alive*. Edinburgh: T & T Clarke 1990.

Das Christentum. Wesen und Geschichte, Piper 1994; Serie Piper 2940, München 1999/*Christianity: Its Essence and History*. London: SCM Press 1995.

Kleine Geschichte der katholischen Kirche, Berliner Taschenbuch Verlag 2001/*The Catholic Church. A Short History*. London: Weidenfeld & Nicolson 2001.

Die Frau im Christentum, Piper 2001/*Women in Christianity*. London, New York: Continuum 2001.

Erkämpfte Freiheit. Erinnerungen, Piper 2002, Serie Piper 4135, München 2008/*My Struggle for Freedom: Memoirs I*. New York, London: Continuum 2003.

Umstrittene Wahrheit. Erinnerungen, Piper 2007; Serie Piper 5387, München 2009/*Disputed Truth: Memoirs II*. New York, London: Continuum 2008.

Was ich glaube, Piper 2009; Serie Piper 6390, München 2010/*What I Believe*. New York, London: Continuum 2010.

Books by Other Authors

Berger, David. *Der heilige schein: Als schwuler Theologe in der katholischen Kirche* ('The Holy Illusion: A Gay Theologian in the Catholic Church'). Berlin: Taschenbuch 2012.

Biallowons, Hubert and Imhof, Paul (eds), Egan, Harvey D. (trs). *Faith in a Wintry Season: Conversations and Interviews with Karl Rahner in the Last Years of His Life*. New York: Crossroad 1990. The original German version appeared four years earlier under the title *Glaube in winterlicher Zeit: Gespräche mit Karl Rahner aus d. Letzten Lebensjahre*. Düsseldorf: Patmos-Verl 1986.

Deckers, Daniel. *Der Kardinal: Karl Lehmann – eine Biographie*. Munich: Pattloch 2002.

Dostoyevsky, Fyodor. *The Brothers Karamazov*. Penguin Classics edition, trs David McDuff. London: Penguin 2003.

Drobinski, Matthias. *Oh Gott, die Kirche. Versuch über das katholische Deutschland* ('O God, the Church: An Investigation into Catholicism in Germany'). Düsseldorf: Patmos-Verl 2006.

Finocchiaro, Maurice (ed.) *The Galileo Affair: A Documentary History*. Berkeley: 1989. The text is available at http://web.archive.org/web/20070930013053/http://astro.wcupa.edu/mgagne/ess362/resources/finocchiaro.html#sentence (accessed on 18 March, 2013).

Hartmann, Gerhard. *Wählt die Bischöfe: Ein Vorschlag zur Güte* ('Elect the Bishops: A Conciliatory Proposal'). Regensburg: Topos Plus 2010.

Hessel, Stéphane. *Time for Outrage: Indignez-vous!* London: Quartet 2011.

Kuhn, Thomas S. *The Structure of Scientific Revolutions*. Chicago: University of Chicago Press 1962; 2nd edition 1970. The extensive German discussion of Kuhn's ideas began in 1976, when the Surkamp Verlag brought out in paperback form a revised and expanded translation of the 1970 revised English version.

I Millenari. *Via col vento in Vaticano* (*'Gone with the Wind in the Vatican'*). Rome: Kaos 2005.

Mitschke-Collande, Thomas von. *Kirche – was nun? Die Identitätskrise der katholischen Kirche in Deutschland* (*'What's Next for the Church? The Identity Crisis of the Catholic Church in Germany'*). 2010.

Nuzzi, Gianluigi. *Vaticano S.p.A.* (*'Vatican Ltd'*). Rome: Chiarelettere 2009.

Oschwald, Hanspeter. *Im Namen des Heiligen Vaters. Wie fundamentalistische Mächte den Vatikan steuern* (*'In the Name of the Holy Father: How Fundamentalist Powers Govern the Vatican'*). Munich: Heyne 2010.

Toulmin, Steven. *Human Understanding: The Collective Use and Evaluation of Concepts*. Princeton: Princeton University Press 1972.

Seewald, Peter and Ratzinger, Joseph. *Light of the World*. London: Catholic Truth Society 2010.

Ullman, Walter. *The Growth of Papal Government in the Middle Ages*. London: Methuen 1970.

Walf, Knut. 'The New Canon Law – The Same Old System: Preconciliar Spirit in Postconciliar Formulation', *The Church in Anguish – Has the Vatican Betrayed Vatican II?* Hans Küng, Norbert Greinacher and Leonard J. Swidler (eds). San Francisco: HarperSanFrancisco 1987.

Weigel, George. *Witness to Hope*. London: HarperCollins 2005.

Yallop, David A. *In God's Name: An Investigation into the Murder of Pope John Paul I*. London: Corgi 1987.